HORNSBY HIT ONE OVER MY HEAD

DAVID CATANEO

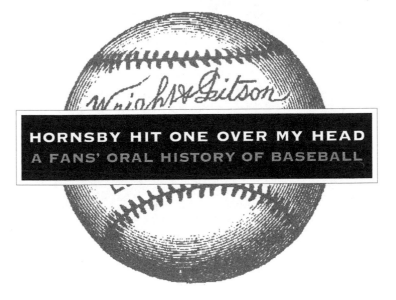

HORNSBY HIT ONE OVER MY HEAD
A FANS' ORAL HISTORY OF BASEBALL

A Harvest Original

HARCOURT BRACE & COMPANY

San Diego   New York   London

Library of Congress Cataloging-in-Publication Data
Cataneo, David.
Hornsby hit one over my head: a fans' oral history of baseball/
David Cataneo.—1st ed.
p.   cm.
"A Harvest original."
ISBN 0-15-600218-3
1. Baseball—United States—History.   2. Oral history.
3. Baseball fans—United States—History.   I. Title.
GV863.A1C38   1997
796.357'0973—dc21   96-39518

Text set in Adobe Caslon
Designed by Richard Hendel
Printed in the United States of America
A Harvest Original
First edition 1997
A   C   E   D   B

FOR MOM & DAD

CONTENTS

Anyone writing an oral history, like anyone performing oral surgery, relies on people to open their mouths. To the men and women whose baseball memoirs appear on these pages, thanks for talking.

I am also grateful to the following for their insights and memories: Eddie Kondayan, Paul Dietrich, Sister Mary Assumpta Zabas, Chick Veditz, Danny Wanner, Reverend Harry Gerdes, Howard Lenharth, Cathy Lenharth, Barry Mednick, Frank McCormack, Mary Willmes, Leo Ernstein, Rogert Woytych, and Clyde Partin.

Many thanks to those who helped in the nationwide search for baseball lovers. Among those pointing me in the right direction were Eddie Derba, Tom Sudow, Doug Roberts, Bob Browning, Nancy Purbeck, Rob Ruck, Jim Overmyer, Dottie Collins, Dick Johnson, Dick Clark, Steve Treder, Janet Bruce, Pepper Davis, Mark Alvarez, Robert J. Sales, Kevin Grace, Nat Rosenberg, Claude Page, Don Wardlow, Mary Hurley, Chris Pika, Dick Dobbins, Jeff Idelson, Lloyd Johnson, Deb Larson, Arthur Haley, Larry Hogan, Teddy Dibble, Bruce Ladd, Dutch Doyle, Bob Brown, Rick Vaughn, and Sister Frances Evans.

Betsy Warrior, Tom Clark, and Liz Pakula of the *Boston Herald* library were extra helpful. Steve DeMaggio was invaluable when the computer wouldn't work.

Morris Eckhouse, executive director of the Society for American Baseball Research in Cleveland, and Tim Wiles of the National Baseball Hall of Fame in Cooperstown, New York, deserve special thanks for helping me out of research dead ends.

I am forever grateful to Marie Morris, assistant sports

editor of the *Boston Herald,* whose encouragement and insight were vital from the earliest stages through the final draft.

My deepest thanks to Vicki Austin-Smith at Harcourt Brace, whose bright guidance and skilled editing improved every page. Also, my thanks to Harcourt's Sarah Longstaff.

None of this would have been possible without the love and devotion of Kathryn B. Cataneo. And I am especially grateful to Emily B. Cataneo, whose cooperation and patience were essential.

When we first got the farm
we made sure to get up every morning
at four o'clock. After a while we got up at
five o'clock, then six, then seven, then eight
and then Chico discovered that LaGrange was
near the Chicago ballpark. We didn't farm
anymore but we made sure to catch the
train to the ballpark.

GROUCHO MARX

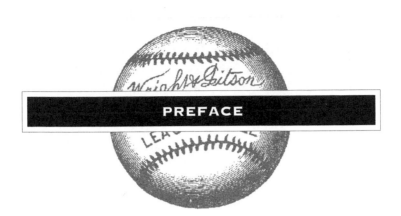

For most Americans for most of the twentieth century, base-ball has been the undisputed national pastime. Baseball was what we did when we weren't going to war or moving to the suburbs. It outlasted big cars, long-playing records, cowboy movies, smoking in public, and good manners. Baseball was around before jazz and the Home Shopping Network. It produced the most popular men's headgear of the century, the baseball cap. It produced the biggest celebrity of the century, Babe Ruth. The greatest engineering feat, after the airplane and the automobile, was the baseball card in bicycle spokes.

Baseball has been good for us. It's taught us loyalty: I still won't drink Rheingold because it was the beer of the Mets. It's taught us math: I learned at age fourteen how to calculate slugging averages, which unfortunately never showed up on the SAT. It's taught us multiculturalism: I put a Reginald Martinez Jackson poster on my bedroom wall and learned how to spell "Yastrzemski." Baseball has taught us a lot of stuff: when I was thirteen, two Yankee pitchers swapped wives, children, and dogs in spring training.

Baseball is still America's special game, despite players with dirigible-size egos and owners who run teams like Ralph

Kramden get-rich-quick schemes. Baseball stirs the kind of intense emotions you get after having whiskey for dinner. Baseball makes us warm and fluttery and dewy-eyed and forgetful that a ballpark frank costs seven dollars. Parents still get misty about playing catch with their children, even though the ball sometimes goes down the sewer. Baseball is different. Football fans play office pools; basketball fans buy lots of sneakers; baseball fans run out and make poignant PBS specials.

Baseball makes me run out and write books. I decided to document the long relationship between America and its pastime by turning to people who, when the baseball library swells with books by experts each spring, seldom get a word in edgewise. I decided to turn to baseball fans. I wanted to create an oral history with the premise that there's a lot of Bart Giamatti in the average fan, and I don't mean that he or she chain-smokes and reads a lot of Dante. I mean that the average baseball fan, just like the poets who get paid to be dreamy about the game, does heavy breathing upon walking into a ballpark and seeing green grass.

I wanted to inject populism into the baseball history business. You have not heard of any of the people interviewed for this book. But if you have ever clasped a baseball mitt over your face and inhaled because you liked the smell, you have something in common with all of them. To be eligible for inclusion in the following pages, a fan needed to:

1) be madly in love with baseball for at least part of his or her life;

2) never have emceed the Academy Awards, never had a short story published in the *New Yorker*, and never played touch football with the Kennedys.

Using those guidelines, I searched for fans all over the country. I wanted to get people from a wide variety of times and places. I wasn't trying to cover every team, so you Chicago

White Sox fans can save the postage and wait for the sequel. I searched for different baseball experiences. After finding them, it was simple. I asked people to tell me about their life and baseball. The result was a Zeliglike ride through the twentieth century, my greatest odyssey since the last time I took a cab from La Guardia to Manhattan.

They took me to the Huntington Avenue Grounds in Boston to see Cy Young and to Rockford, Illinois, to see the all-girl Peaches. I was in the North Atlantic during World War I, worrying about U-boats and thinking about the Red Sox, and I was in Vietnam in 1969, worrying about the Vietcong and thinking about the Cardinals. I played imaginary games by myself in a dark lot in Oakland and played for the Colorado Silver Bullets. I played corkball in St. Louis, catch on an aircraft carrier during World War II, stickball in New York, and Little League in California. I spent cool mornings in Washington, D.C., looking through the dewy grass for foul balls that had flown out of Griffith Stadium the night before. I stood under the magnolia tree at Ponce de León Park in Atlanta. I took the ferry to Oakland to see the Oaks on Sunday mornings. I rode in a rumble seat to watch the Reds and took a trolley to see the Cubs. I saw Babe Ruth hit three home runs in Pittsburgh and saw a midget pinch-hit in St. Louis. I played baseball at a concentration camp in Idaho and in a convent in Texas.

The ride was mostly fun and a little instructive, like a class trip to the zoo. For one thing, after a year and a half of hobnobbing with baseball fans, it's clear that Ken Burns wasn't imagining things. Baseball fans like to get romantic and talk about the game while someone plays a harmonica. I had a hard time tracking down some of the people in this book because they were out plowing the cornfield and waiting for Shoeless Joe Jackson. Mysticism is part of the fun. There are some baseball fans who like their sport straight up and without sugar, but there are also people who sit down for dinner at Tour d'Argent and say, "I'll have the lot of it; put the eggs on top."

For another thing, after a year and a half of listening to people sing love songs to baseball, it's clear that major league baseball owners and players are chuckleheads. Why don't they seem to like the game as much as we do? They inherited our national summer home, and they leave cigarette burns on the coffee table, stop up the toilets with empty beer cans, and ride motorcycles through the peonies. I'd like every major league owner and player to buy this book. It might make them listen up. If they had been paying attention to fans all these years, they would have never come up with fake grass, luxury boxes, midnight World Series games, the stupid wild-card system, and Albert Belle. Many of them would stop approaching the game as if it were torture and drudgery – in other words, the way the rest of us approach our jobs – and have a little more fun.

Then again, baseball players might read this book and feel extra smug. They can do anything they want. The baseball fans I spoke with grumbled and griped, but not too much – never the way women do about their ex-husbands (the exception was Brooklyn Dodgers fans, who still refuse to send support payments to Los Angeles). They griped the way women do about their current husbands: "For six years I've been waiting for something to be done about those mezzanine bathrooms. Would it kill them to talk to me a little before batting practice? And I'm sick and tired of finding three-million-dollar utility infielders lying all over the clubhouse." But when all is said and done, they love the big lug.

Baseball bounces back. Many of the interviews in this book were conducted in the teeth of the baseball strike (the one in 1994–95, not to be confused with the lockout in 1990 or the strike in 1985 or the strike in 1981 or the one in 1999). A few

· · · · ·

swore off big league baseball, and when I called back in the spring, they were on their way out the door to drive ninety miles to see the Class-A Backwater Warrior Fish play the Smallholler Liver Flukes. But they still loved baseball.

Baseball will survive. It's more resilient than Brooklyn cockroaches. I wore a baseball cap when I was eleven, and I'm wearing a baseball cap as I type this, although there's a lot less hair under it these days. Baseball has followed me around. Now I know there are at least forty-five other seamheads out there just like me, some of them old enough to remember Harry Hooper and some of them too young to remember Fred Lynn, but all of them just like me. And you. Baseball is a common ground, one of the few left in America. Put everybody in this book – from the cabdriver to the music teacher to the math professor to the cardiologist – around a great big dinner table and they'd have a lot more to talk about than who was going to pick up the check.

Baseball is still the best game, as simple as brushing your teeth and, at the same time, as complicated as falling in love with your ex-wife's sister. If I'm wrong and somehow it dies out – if the members of the younger generation fail to turn around their caps and trade those flannel shirts for flannel uniforms – we can at least remember baseball as twentieth-century America's favorite game. The following pages are evidence. And now I don't feel like thinking about it anymore. My six-year-old daughter has a plastic bat and wants to go down to the beach, where we will scratch out a diamond and play a little baseball.

David Cataneo
Goose Rocks, Maine
August 1995

HORNSBY HIT ONE OVER MY HEAD

MEN IN STRAW HATS

JOE DERBA, NINETY-FOUR,
WAS A RETIRED CABDRIVER AND LIVED IN
QUINCY, MASSACHUSETTS.
HE DIED IN 1995.

I remember Babe Ruth when he came along in 1914. He had a Stutz car and a big raccoon coat. I remember when he got married to a South Boston girl. His first wife. He had a face that you could love. Built like a bulldog. He used to wave to us. He loved kids. The kids, when they saw him, would jump on the running boards of his car, and Babe Ruth would take them right into Fenway Park. Free. They'd send them down the bleachers. Babe Ruth was a great man for kids.

. . . . .

I was raised in the West End of Boston. My cousin, Frank Mondello, worked at the Huntington Avenue Grounds from 1903. Frank had a stand there, where he used to sell peanuts, popcorn, cigars, cigarettes. He used to take me there and take me home on the open streetcars. I saw Cy Young pitch, around 1907 or 1908. It was an old park and I don't think they could have had more than fifteen thousand people there. I used to walk over there from the West End.

The population there was 85 percent Jewish. All the friends I used to chum with were Jewish boys. I'm of Italian descent, but there weren't many Italians in the West End. Italians came later, when the Jewish families moved out of the West End to go to Roxbury and Mattapan. They used to call me "Yussel." That means "Joe." We used to play from one neighborhood to the other, the boys from Poplar Street and the boys from Chambers Street. They couldn't speak English. They spoke Jewish. Italian. Polish. Very few could speak English. We used hand signals when we played. We used to play at Boston Common. And you know where Mass. General Hospital is? We used to play across the street from there. There was a playground there near the river.

I only went as far as grammar school. I liked to play center field. I don't know why. One time they sent me out to center field. They said, "Joe Derba, go out to center field." I'm out there and the ball is coming toward me. Then you know what happened. Hit me on the top of the head. What a lump I had. Across the street was Mass. General Hospital. They took me over there, because I had a lump on my head. Outpatient then cost fifty cents. I didn't have fifty cents.

I remember when they started building Fenway Park. I used to go over and get wood for the family. Me and another kid, we had a cart. We used to go over all the way from the West End to Fenway Park for firewood. People didn't have any furnaces then. My mother used to put irons on the stove and put them in bed with us at night to keep our feet warm. There was no Queensberry Street over there. There was no Audubon Road, Park Drive. There was no Jersey Street or Kilmarnock Street. It was all marsh. The only thing you could see from the stands at Fenway Park was Simmons College, and the Children's Hospital and the Deaconess Hospital. Fenway Park was beautiful.

When it opened up, I was only thirteen years old. I asked my cousin, "How about going to work at Fenway Park?" He said, "You'll have to see my boss, Joe Mancini." I started in 1912. I sold popcorn. Popcorn at that time was a nickel. It was that molasses popcorn, all stuck together. You sold one basket, you made fifty cents. I used to sell two baskets. You could hear me from the grandstand to the bleachers. My voice carried in them days. POP-corn! Kids I knew would be sitting in the bleachers and they could hear my voice. When you got all through selling your popcorn in the sixth inning, then you could sit down and watch the game.

You never forget 1912. What a team they had. I didn't go when the games started in April. I went when school closed, in June. When school closed, I was there every game. They had Jake Stahl, Duffy Lewis, Bill Carrigan – he was a great man. They had a catcher named Hick Cady. There were no automobiles in those days. It was all horses and carriages. When the games were called off on account of rain, when the players couldn't get a carriage, I used to go out to the street and get a carriage for them. I got one for Cady one day and he promised to give me a ball. Next day there was a foul ball and he caught it. I ran onto the field and said, "Do you remember me?" He said, "Yeah, you're the one who got me the carriage yesterday." He gave me the ball. At that time you could run out onto the field. I had a lot of baseballs. They used to try to get you to give them back. The usher would come up. People passed the ball along to one another. I remember people watching the game – men wearing derby hats and straw hats. I seen men put their hands right through their straw hats when the Red Sox went behind. They'd get mad and put their hands right through their straw hats.

Most all the players talked to you. Tris Speaker talked to you. He was a gentleman. He chummed with Joe Wood. Tris Speaker was tremendous. I seen him get guys running from first to second and get them at second base. I seen Harry Hooper in right field throw guys out at first base.

I worked there until I went in the service in 1917. I was a gunner on these merchant ships, against the U-boats. I volunteered for that. On one convoy, we lost ten ships. In front of my own eyes. Scared the hell out of you. Sailors from one ship would play baseball against the sailors from other ships. That was in England. I saw a game in New York. This was when I was in the navy. I saw the old Braves in New York play the Giants. Guess who I met there? Frank Mondello's brother, Nino. Hollering his head off. I said, "That sounds just like my cousin." I went up, it was Nino. There was about a dozen guys from Boston.

When I was in the service, I got an abscess in my lungs. I had to come home for thirty days, to get built up. I went to Mass. General. I told the doctor I was supposed to go to the Naval hospital in Charlestown, but I couldn't make that hill. He says, "You been here before?" I says, "Yeah. When I was a kid." They looked it up and found it. They say, "You know, you owe us fifty cents." From the day I got hit on the head with the ball.

I went to work driving a cab in 1923. I got my first cab in 1925. The cheapest players I ever had was the hockey players. They'd never tip you. I used to bring the ballplayers to the trains, to the Back Bay Station. They were good. I had my own stand at the corner of Berkeley and Newbury Street. I drove all the Kennedy family. I had Joe Kennedy in the World Series, 1946, at Fenway. He had my car for two days, twenty-five bucks a day. I'd drive him to the ballpark, pick him up, and take him back to the Ritz. You know what I did? I outsmarted him. I says, "Mr. Kennedy, when the game is

· · · · ·

over, where I'm leaving you now, be here. I don't know where I'm going to be parked." He said, "Good idea." I said, "When you get out of the ball game, don't move from that spot, where I'm leaving you off now. I'll never find you." He thought I was parked there at the ballpark all afternoon. I was out doing jobs. I had Mr. Yawkey in my cab many times. If you took the wrong streets, he'd make you go back and do it all over again. He didn't want to change the luck of the ball club.

I went to a lot of games. I took my sons to the first Sunday game. I took my oldest son there when he was six, seven years old. My wife and I went together. She was a bigger baseball fan than I was. My wife was Lithuanian. She came from the old country and first got interested in baseball when she was ironing. She listened to the game on the radio. She liked it. Then I took her to a game. She loved it. The Red Sox lost, she wouldn't talk to you.

I had season tickets for fifty years. When I had season tickets, I went to every night game. I'd drive during the day and go to the game at night. I gave them up. Gave them to my grandson. He has them now.

Baseball? It's just like your own religion. You can't wait till summer comes along. Baseball starts in three weeks, right? It's a feeling. I had that feeling when I was in the service. I was thinking about the Red Sox. I've loved baseball since I was six years old. It comes along regular, that feeling. Till you die.

GREEN FIELDS, SUNSHINE

BART GIBLIN, EIGHTY-THREE,
IS A RETIRED BANKER AND CONTRACT OFFICER
LIVING IN VERONA, NEW JERSEY.

My favorite team was the New York Giants. We used to always talk about the Giants. I remember many of their players: Dave Bancroft, Travis Jackson, Lefty O'Doul, and Bill Terry. My mother was a widow and she ran a boardinghouse for Irish immigrants. One of our boarders, a man named Martin McLaughlin, an Irishman, took me over to see a game and it was at the Polo Grounds. This was about 1920. I was ten or eleven. It was the Giants against the Boston Braves. I know the Giants lost that game. I felt bad about that. But it was so exciting to be in that great ballpark. To look at those guys who were big leaguers. We had hot dogs, peanuts. It was a wonderful experience.

· · · · ·

All we played in the summer was baseball. I grew up on North Willow Street in downtown Montclair. My street was all Irish kids, Italian kids. We had our own team: the Willow Giants. One block below us, on Greenwood Avenue, were black kids. We all played at the Grove Street School playground. We

6

played together, black kids and white kids, on the same team. We never thought anything different. It used to puzzle me why there weren't black players in the big leagues. That was over my head. I never understood it. As kids we all played together. Nobody seemed to be mad at anyone or anything. We bought our own bats and we stole our baseballs. We used to watch games at the Montclair Athletic Club, which was a fancy club. Their baseball team was generally made up of former Ivy League players. We'd go up there and get our supply of baseballs.

We didn't have uniforms. All we had was bats and balls and gloves. Now the best ballplayer on the street was a kid named Billy Johnson. Billy Johnson lived on the corner of Walnut and North Willow. Unfortunately, Billy's father liked to drink a little. In fact, drink a lot. I don't think he was ever sober. He worked for a moving van company. Billy never owned a glove. So we wouldn't let Billy play sometimes. So finally, there was a fellow who managed a grocery store, National Grocery across the street from the A&P, who was a real baseball fan. He was married, didn't have kids. One day he bought Billy a glove. When Billy came to our game, we couldn't believe it. What a great glove he had.

He became our third baseman. Billy was maybe twelve or thirteen. He wasn't the brightest kid in school. He finally quit school after seventh grade. He went on to play with the better semipro teams when he was sixteen or seventeen. And Bill Manning, the guy who bought him the glove, called the New York Yankees office and asked to talk to one of their scouts. He talked to a scout named Paul Krichell. And he told Paul Krichell that he'd been managing semipro teams in New Jersey for a long time and he had a real prospect infielder named Johnson. Krichell said sure, he'd come out. So they set a date about a week later and Bill arranged a game. Billy had a great game. He hit two home runs, handled every ball hit at him. I never saw a ball get past him. If he couldn't catch them, he knocked them down. So he got signed by the Yanks. They sent him to Butler, Pennsylvania. Then he went to Augusta, Georgia. And in about three years, he was up with the Yankees. He played with the Yankees for several years. The kid who didn't own a glove.

✦

My first exposure to baseball was maybe at six or seven. There was a fellow who used to come over to a baseball field across from our house. He was about thirteen or fourteen. I use to chase baseballs for him. I didn't realize at the time, but I was watching a great baseball player developing. His name was George Haas, later known as Mule Haas, center fielder of the Philadelphia Athletics.

By the time Haas was fifteen or sixteen, he was playing for a team called the Orange AA. They were about the best semipro team in the area. That team included Heinie Zimmerman, who had played third base for the New York Giants. That team was so good, they beat most of the other semipro teams in the area. But when the black teams came in, we never realized how good ballplayers could be.

We saw a lot of them. The Bacharachs from Atlantic City. The Philadelphia All-Stars. I think there was a team called the Lincoln Giants. The Pennsylvania Red Caps. They were supposedly employees of the Pennsylvania railroad. We used to see them over in Orange Playgrounds in Orange, New Jersey. We took the trolley over there for a nickel, and we'd hang around the gate until about the third inning, and they'd let kids in for free.

I'll never forget one ballplayer I saw there, a pitcher they called Cannonball Redding. That particular day he held the Orange AA to one hit. He struck out Haas three or four times, which we thought was unbelievable. I never saw

Satchel Paige, but the best pitcher I ever saw was this guy Cannonball Redding.

Two particular ballplayers I remember on one black team, I can't recall which. I think it was the Hilldales. One was a catcher named Biz Mackey. There was an older catcher on the team named Lou Santop. Santop was I think the best catcher I ever saw, anywhere. He'd put on an exhibition before the game. He would get in a squatting position like a catcher does, and they would have a workout, and he'd throw the ball from a squatting position. He never stood up. For fifteen or twenty minutes, he'd throw to first, he'd throw to third, he'd throw to second, he'd throw to short. The infielders never knew where he was going to throw the ball. He would throw that ball right on the base. And he never stood up. Mackey was later the manager of the Newark Eagles, a great black team.

Those teams, those black teams, only carried twelve or thirteen players. They played every night someplace. They traveled by bus. The pitchers played the outfield. They used to play doubleheaders on Saturdays and Sundays. During the week they played games in different small towns. They were tremendous teams. I don't know how these guys stood it. They must have loved baseball. I went to a game on July 4, 1947, and took a picture of Jackie Robinson. My recollection was he played first base in the game I saw. I went to Ebbets Field to see him play. I thought it was overdue. He was a fine ballplayer. I had seen black ballplayers in the past who were his equal, maybe better.

✦

Mule Haas was still our idol. Mule Haas, after he retired, had a bar in Montclair in partnership with his cousin, a fellow named Mulligan. I used to talk to Haasie about baseball a lot. He'd tell us some great stories. He told us a story about Babe

Ruth. He and the Babe were very good friends. He told us that one year the Athletics opened the season against the Yankees in Yankee Stadium the year Babe Ruth got an $85,000 contract. He said before the game he and the Babe exchanged a few comments. He said the Babe said, "Haasie, when the game's over, I want to see you outside the dressing room." So Haasie said, "Sure." So Babe came out and Babe said, "You know, they paid me all this money this year, eighty-five thousand dollars. When I signed a contract, Ruppert told me that he didn't want me running around to bars and nightclubs in New York every single night. He said, 'It's not good for the image of the Yankees and it's not good for you.'" So Babe said to Haasie, "What the hell did they pay me the big salary if they didn't want me to have any fun? I'd like to know if you know any places in Jersey where I might go after the ball game." This was in daylight baseball. Haasie said, "Yeah, I know a few places." So he went outside the stadium and Babe called a taxi, and the two of them got into the taxi, and they went to a place in Singac near what we used to call Two Bridges. Now that was about eighteen or twenty miles from the Bronx. Haasie brought him into a place called Donahue's. A bar. Haasie introduced him to the owner. They shook hands and Babe made that a regular spot from then on. Every afternoon after the game, he'd stop at Donahue's. It was a fabulous place. And when people heard that the Babe was going there, a lot of people would go up there to have a beer, hoping to see the Babe.

Another thing Haasie told me about Babe. Now, this is hard to believe. He said Babe used to do a lot of drinking at night and a lot of running around. And he said for breakfast the Babe could eat a dozen eggs and a half-pound of bacon with toast and a pot of coffee. That was some breakfast. He was a big man. I saw him play several times. By the time I saw him play, I was probably a teenager or in my early twenties.

. . . . .

There never has been a ballplayer as colorful and as exciting as the Babe. He did it so casually. He could hit balls out of the ballpark so easy. It was great just to watch him in practice. He kidded around with everybody, on both teams. That's one thing I see lacking in modern-day ballplayers. They aren't as colorful, for some reason.

◆

I worked in New York in my younger days. I often went to see games at the Yankee Stadium or the Polo Grounds. I enjoyed games at Ebbets Field. A wonderful ballpark. There was something about Brooklyn. There was always sort of a feud between the people in Brooklyn and the people in New York. The people from New York always thought they were superior to the people from Brooklyn. So when the Giants played in Brooklyn, it was really something. It was so easy to get into conversation with the people in the stands. In those days you could buy a hot dog for a dime, peanuts for a nickel. It was a real social afternoon to go to a ball game, particularly in Ebbets Field.

Everybody in the stands was an expert. No matter where you sat or who you sat with, they were all experts. They all knew the batting averages of all the players on both teams, whether it was the St. Louis Cardinals or the Yankees. You see, there were no other professional sports in those days. There was no National Football League. No National Basketball Association. As a result, ordinary people, their whole thing was baseball. You could so easily get into a conversation, with just buying a ticket and sitting down. Before you knew it, you were either in an agreement or disagreement. It was great.

I worked for Morgan Guaranty Trust Company from about 1929 to 1940. Then in 1940 I went to work for the Federal Reserve Bank in New York as a trade consultant. I was drafted into the army and went into the military police. The closest I ever came to the war was when I rode prisoner-of-war trains. After the war ... I think by that time my allegiance might have gone more to the Yankees. I don't think I ever saw a better ballplayer, except Babe Ruth, than Joe DiMaggio. With Joe DiMaggio, everything looked so easy.

I see a lot of baseball games. Last year I counted forty-three games – all high school, American Legion, or semipro. I like live baseball, played on a green field in the sunshine. That's what baseball means to me. I stop by and watch the Little League kids play sometimes. I like to just watch kids play on green grass on a sunny afternoon. I think it's just about as entertaining and relaxing a situation as you can find.

WE KNEW WHEN THEY
CHEERED THE PIRATES

FRANK BOLDEN, EIGHTY-ONE,

IS A RETIRED JOURNALIST LIVING IN

PITTSBURGH.

A million times I asked, Why were there no Pirates playing with them? Why don't the Homestead Grays play the Pirates? Segregation and discrimination were a way of life. And we were taught that someday white people will pay for this. Just be patient. So I lived to see Jackie Robinson come into the league by being patient. At the same time, I'll tell you, they should have been in a long time ago. But a lot of things should have happened a long time ago. Only God determines the time and place.

· · · · ·

When the teams played in smaller communities, where you played on a playground or in a field, the white and black population all mingled, watched the games, and they passed the hat. White and blacks would watch these teams play together, talk and all that, and when the game was over, you went your separate ways. That's the way I grew up. That's why I give baseball credit. It integrated the community when the community wasn't integrated. If you and I could watch the ball game together, then why couldn't we live in the same neighborhoods? I ask myself that question to this day.

I grew up in Washington, Pennsylvania. I played second base; I pitched. I was a pretty fair second baseman. My dad bought me a nice glove. And Joe Arena, the Italian boy across the street, his dad had bought him a bat. On Saturday mornings we'd go down to the Washington playground, nine o'clock in the morning. We didn't come home until dark. Play ball all day long.

I can remember Mrs. Gaston, who was German – if we played at night and it got dark, she just put us in bed with all the kids. Evergreen memories. They're valuable. I remember us all riding together and eating together, sleeping together and playing ball together, and beating the other team together, and rooting against the other team. In other words, we all supported the home team. Through ball, you met people you wouldn't have met otherwise. You picked up your skills from other people. For instance, we were terrific on the bases. We could run like hell. We had trouble fielding ground balls. We learned how to field ground balls from the German, Italian players. No one ever taught us you had to come in on a ground ball. They in turn learned how to hit from us. Very few black kids ever stepped out of the way of a curve ball. We were taught to step into a curve ball.

My dad took me to my first game, when the Homestead Grays played out in Washington, Pennsylvania. They played the Hazel-Atlas Glass factory. I was eight years old. I thought they were great players. I thought they were the greatest thing since sliced bread. The place was packed. I'd say the crowd was about three thousand. I remember when the black team played, most of the Negroes cheered for them. When the whites came to bat, the whites cheered for them. However, when the Washington Hazel-Atlas Glass factory team, which was white, played the Wheeling Stogies – that's where they made the tobacco, down in Wheeling – when they came to play, we blacks and whites all cheered for Washington.

We went to quite a few Pirate games. I saw my first game in 1920. I can hear the stands now when the Pirates were losing. Everybody would say, "Put in Yellow Horse!" He was an Indian pitcher the Pirates had. Chief Yellow Horse. We rode the streetcar over. Took us about an hour to get there. The hot dogs and peanuts and all that – oh, I had a good time. But I had trouble with the mustard. There was too much mustard and it ran all over.

I used to love to watch the people ride the streetcars. You remember those streetcars where you hung on the outside? As we were going to the park out to Forbes Field, you got a chance to see all that. And I had never seen crowds that big.

I remember the way people were dressed. A lot of the nationalities wore their own clothing. I recall the Germans from up in Germantown, they were kind of formal and stiff, and they wore dark clothes. Hungarians and Lithuanians, the women wore gingham; the men wore plaid shirts. Men in those days came to the ballpark with no tie, and they always had their sleeves rolled up. Why, I don't know. I couldn't understand what some of them were saying. They were speaking in a foreign tongue. I never heard that before. You haven't experienced anything until you as an American Negro sit and on each side of you, you've got an Italian, a German, a Hungarian speaking their foreign language. You didn't know what the hell they were saying. All we knew is when they cheered the Pirates.

My dad never took us until school was out. That was in June and then he never took us except on Fridays and Saturdays. Because of the blue laws, you couldn't play baseball on Sunday in Pennsylvania. It was like waiting for the circus. If the Pirates were going to play the Giants, with Frankie Frisch and them, if they were going to play say this coming Saturday, well, two days before, I started praying it wouldn't rain.

We had to get up around seven o'clock in the morning to catch a streetcar by nine o'clock, which would get us to Pittsburgh proper around 10:30. Then it took you almost a half hour to get from downtown Pittsburgh to Forbes Field on another streetcar. You went early, because the cars were packed. Everybody went to the ball game on Saturday. You could have robbed every bank in Pittsburgh. There wasn't anybody downtown. They were all at the ballpark. Even the police.

I saw Babe Ruth play. I saw him play his last game. When he hit the home runs, I was out there that day. He looked pitiful. He could hardly get around the bases. He was done. The Yanks had let him go. The people felt sorry for him. When he came to bat, the people applauded. He wasn't the Ruth of old. But he could hit that ball. I saw him in 1927 in the World Series. You only needed to see him once to appreciate him. He could hit that ball. No getting around that. You almost could tell it was a home run, just by the sound of the bat. It was one of those nice, thunderous smacks. He knew when it was going to be a home run, because he never took off right away. He would kind of pause and let you look at him. Then he would trot around the bases. He didn't run. He trotted. He would hit to all fields, right, left. He could hit a ball over the center-field fence like it was your front doorstep. Everybody stood up and applauded, and they stayed standing until he struck out or hit a home run. That's what we came to see. We came all the way from Washington, Pennsylvania, to see him hit a home run. Even if they lost, it didn't matter. I also saw the Senators here, in 1925. In the World Series. I saw Walter Johnson pitch. A big, strapping fellow. Healthy looking. Broad shouldered. He had hands like bear paws. He must have worn a size fifteen glove. He could bring that heat. You heard it, but you never saw it. It sounded like a pistol cracking.

We didn't go see the Grays as often. Oscar Jackson, Smokey Joe Williams, Josh Gibson. He was a combination of Babe Ruth and Frankie Frisch. He was short and stocky. He could hit that ball, too. Oscar Charleston, he was the first baseman. He was very good. My favorite was Martin Dihigo, a West Indian, who came to the Grays from the Cuban Giants. Because he could play all positions. See, in those days, the Grays would sometimes play three games a day. Play out in Washington in the morning, down in Beaver Falls in the afternoon, and come back in Forbes Field and play at four o'clock. Oscar Owens. What I liked about Oscar Owens was he used to give little exhibitions before the games. He could pitch four innings with his right hand and the other five innings with his left hand. I saw that many times. Whenever he pitched, we had to see him.

It's true the white sports world missed a lot of good players, and between you and me, they missed a hell of a lot of money. When Jackie got in, I remember people would come all the way from Detroit and Omaha, Nebraska, to see him play here in Pittsburgh. When the Dodgers played here, we had more people here from Detroit than we did from Pittsburgh. White America and black America missed seeing some great ball-players. Jackie was just one of them. And he wasn't the best of them.

You should have seen Oscar Hornes pitch the four innings with one hand and the five with the other. You should have seen Cool Papa Bell run the bases. You've heard the lies about how fast he was. Satchel Paige said Cool Papa Bell doubled down the right-field line and the ball hit him as he was going down to second base. I love that one. But he was fast. I seen him go from first base to home on a single. I used to eat sandwiches down the Grill with him, just sit around till three o'clock in the morning.

The Crawford Grill. That was the hangout, man. Satchel Paige and Oscar Charleston. Cool Papa Bell. When they all got in the league, Don Newcombe and them used to hang out there. Jackie Robinson, Hank Aaron. They used to kid each other and jostle each other. Hank was as big as your forefinger. He didn't weigh but 140-something pounds. He was a boy. Willie Mays was nothing but a child. He bought himself four electric trains with his first paycheck. We socialized there. Why would they socialize downtown? The white nightclubs didn't want them. We had a lot of fun.

Their stories that impressed me were about when the Crawfords and Grays used to travel in the South, when they couldn't get a drink of water and couldn't get a sandwich, after driving three or four hundred miles. Driving into a town at three o'clock in the morning, having to wait till six or seven to eat in a black home or wait till a black restaurant opened up. You wondered why they stuck to it. That's because they loved baseball. They had a lot of stories. No toilets. How they'd stop somewhere along the road, see a bucket over a well, use a cup and drink out of it, only to have the owners rush out there and break it up, crush it, or chop it up because blacks had used it.

I was a war correspondent during World War II. Following the scores and all that used to keep the troops occupied. Up on the Burma Road in the jungle and on the front lines in Germany, all those shells would be breaking around you. "Hey, Bill. What'd the Yankees do today? What did Milwaukee do? What did Stan Musial do today?" Baseball was quite the thing. I was in Europe, the Pacific, the Burma Road, Anzio. When white troops and black troops would meet up, how are you going to break the ice? Baseball was a great common denominator. I don't care if you were white or black if we were arguing about baseball. Both of us knew the Yankees, the Senators.

For instance, my jeep driver was from Alabama. He was white. His name was Beauregard Simmons. We became friends on the Burma Road. He kept insisting that I come see him in the summertime. I said, "What? And get lynched?" He said, "Oh, I'll take care of it. I'll tell the sheriff that you're coming." All up and down the Burma Road, that's all we talked about. Baseball. Today, men talk about sex all the time. Well, nobody talked a whole lot about sex in those days. Sports was the thing. Baseball.

A GIFT FROM AUNT MARY

HOWARD HILTON, EIGHTY-FIVE,

IS A RETIRED MATH PROFESSOR LIVING IN

CHICAGO.

In the stands one day, my aunt noticed a woman who had two very small children. The woman was having a very hard time looking after the both of them. One of them was still really a babe in arms. So Aunt Mary went over to this woman and asked if she could hold the little one while the woman dealt with the older one. The woman gratefully accepted. It turned out she was Mrs. Joe Judge. Joe Judge played first base and was one of the players who later helped them win pennants. As a result, my aunt became acquainted with quite a few of the Washington Senators. She did some baby-sitting for some of them.

. . . . .

I became a baseball fan in 1921. I had an aunt who spent the war years working in Washington, D.C. While she was in Washington, Aunt Mary had dated an army officer who was a baseball fan and took her to baseball games. She became a fan and continued to be a fan even after they broke up.

In 1921 Aunt Mary got laid off. On her way back home to Minnesota, she stopped in Galva, which is in western Illinois, to visit us. When she got to Galva and was staying with us, she wanted to talk baseball. I didn't know anything about it. I was twelve. This was the summer between my seventh and eighth grade. I got up early in the morning, before she got up, and read the paper, so I'd be able to talk baseball with her. And it took.

We hadn't lived in this town very long. The previous town where we had lived, boys my age played softball, which in those days meant sixteen-inch, indoor baseball. I'd never thrown a baseball, I don't think. But in the new town, we lived across the street from a park where the boys my age played baseball almost every day in the summer. So in order to keep with them, I played baseball. I never got to be any good at it, but I played enough to have a lot of fun.

Now the season's over. It's time for the World Series in 1921. On my way home from school, when I was in the eighth grade, I and many of the other boys that lived in my part of town walked home together and we went by this cigar store, which was the baseball headquarters for that town. They got the games on the ticker and posted the results in the window.

It was just a typical small-town, small storefront. There was an unbelievable amount of merchandise. This is where we boys bought our baseball gloves and bats. I can't remember the name of it, but there was a real foul-smelling stuff that came in a tube that we rubbed into our gloves to make them pliant.

The two brothers who ran the store were baseball fans, former semipro players. They were very well known and very well liked. They were Swedish. The older one was Elmer. He was seldom called anything except "Chum." About the time that I'm talking about, he was probably in his early forties.

He'd been a semipro baseball player when he was in his twenties. There were a lot of baseball fans and quite a few baseball players in Galva, and this place was their hangout.

Amongst other things, Chum got a few copies of the *Sporting News,* almost all of which were spoken for. The same fellows came in week after week to pick up their copy. After I found out about this place, I soon joined them. I got acquainted there. So I started buying the *Sporting News* every week. No question, I was a baseball fan. And I remained a baseball fan ever since.

The first big league game I saw was in 1924 in St. Louis. My father had a brother who lived in Alton, Illinois, which is down near St. Louis. He knew what a great baseball fan I was, so he took me down to see the Browns. The Sportsman's Park was really an old-fashioned park. In St. Louis at that time, the typical attendance was fifteen hundred. The team had been at its peak in 1922. That 1924 team, the team wasn't at its peak. But it had as fine an outfield that's ever played together.

They had Sisler and McManus. And Gerber and Severeid. These were all stars that played for the Browns at least ten years. Ken Williams, Jacobson, and Tobin – they were a fine hitting outfield. Jacobson was a fine outfielder. I saw Shocker the day I was there. He beat the Athletics, 4–1. But the Athletics in 1924 were just beginning to assemble the team that was the big team of the late '20s. Two fellows by the name of Joe Hauser and Al Simmons were kind of like Rice and Lynn of the Red Sox in the '70s. They were the big, young batter stars of the league. When those two fellows came up once in the early innings, with a possible rally under way, Shocker struck out both of them on six pitches, right across the letters over the inside corner. I remember a lot of things like that. To me, that was a great player rising to the occasion.

· · · · ·

I don't ever remember as a boy feeling anything but ecstasy when I was at a baseball game. If possible, I always got to the game an hour or so early. I wanted to see the batting practice and fielding practice. Up until the Second World War, I saw games occasionally in St. Louis. I saw an occasional game in Chicago, at each park. I saw some games that made quite an impression on me.

I'll never forget certain plays. One of the best fielding plays I ever saw by an infielder was by Vic Power. This was much more recent. He was with the Twins at the time. They were playing the White Sox at Comiskey. It was 2–2 in the last half of the ninth, White Sox at bat, Fox at third, two outs. The batter hit a dribble down the right side of the infield, just a little too fast for the pitcher to field. Power really went quite a ways to his right and quite a ways in to pick up the ball.

When he picked that ball up, he first looked at the plate. Fox was about two yards from the plate, so there was no play there. Then he looked at the fellow who had hit the ball. He was running down the first baseline and he was actually a little closer to first base than Power was. So now, where's the pitcher? The pitcher is running over to cover first, but his back is to Power. If Fox scores, the game is over. So Power lobbed that ball to first base, over the pitcher's head. It came down on the bag, just as the pitcher got there. And they got the base runner. I'll never forget that.

The only time in my life I was able to be a regular attendant at major league baseball was when I was in the navy and stationed in Washington in '43 to '47. I was in a branch of intelligence. As a matter of fact, we were working on the Japanese naval code. We worked shifts. A week at a time, I'd be working days, then I'd be working evenings, then I'd be working nights. Well, if I was working days, I could see the night games; if I was working nights, I could see the day games; and if I was working what we called the swing shift, I could see either one. Of course, the quality of baseball was not nearly standard major league quality until 1946.

I retired twenty years ago. While I was still working, I was able to go only to an occasional game, generally at the Cubs' park. We live on the North Side. Occasionally to the Sox's park. For a while, after I retired, I could go to the Cubs games a little more frequently. But then my eyes started going bad. The last time I attempted to go to a major league baseball game – I can't tell you the exact year, but do you remember the year Rod Carew, he must have been thirty-five, got forty-eight hits in the first ninety-eight times at bat? I went out to the Sox's park to see him. I thought this may be my last chance to see a .400 hitter. I was disappointed. They gave him the night off.

Something else I should tell you about the baseball games I saw: I kept score. That was one of the first things I learned to do. One of these two brothers who ran the cigar store taught me. Chum was the scorer for the Galva semipro team. I saw what he was doing and I wanted to do it myself. He taught me. Like any good scorekeeper, what he taught me was just the basics. Every competent scorekeeper devises his own system.

There's something else I have to tell you to make this story complete, about this aunt. She lives in Rochester, Minnesota. She's ninety-eight this fall. And she's still a baseball fan. The marvelous thing there is, little did she know, when she went back to Minnesota, that the Senators would follow her and change their name to the Twins. Of course, Puckett's her big hero now. My aunt Mary and I, we felt pretty good about it in 1987 and in 1991. So I figure next year will be the Twins' year again. I go up and visit her every two or three years. We had a very large family reunion on her ninety-fifth birthday. Two topics that we talk about: family history and baseball.

. . . . .

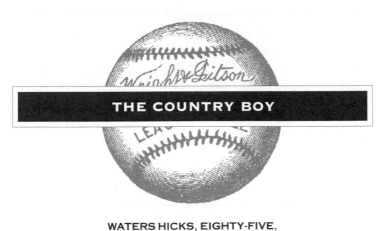

THE COUNTRY BOY

WATERS HICKS, EIGHTY-FIVE,

IS A RETIRED AUTOMOBILE SALESMAN LIVING IN

GREENWOOD, MISSISSIPPI.

My dad was not a baseball fan. No, sir. Not in the least. I never could get my dad to go but one time. I was in my early twenties. We had a family car that we shared. He wanted the car. I said, "Daddy, I got to go to the ball game." He said, "I'll pick you up." On our way to the ballpark, I said, "Daddy, come on. You ain't never been to a ball game. Please come on in." So he went in. After a few minutes, he was gone. So that night at the supper table, he says to my mother, "Ida Lou, can you believe I saw grown men stand up and shout?"

. . . . .

The name of the town I grew up in was McCarley, a little country town. I've been a baseball fan since I was eight years old. In those days everybody had a little semipro team. I followed them around. I think that's how I got started. They'd play in any kind of cow pasture. Really. No ballparks at all. If you had 150 fans, you were pretty good. Now, you get up to Boo Ferriss's bunch in Minter City, they'd have three or four hundred fans. They were real popular.

Anytime I was around baseball, I was a happy young man. I'm an old man and I'm still happy with it. Just the competition of the two teams. And the thrill of that base hit. The crack of the bat against the ball. I had polio when I was eighteen months old. I tried to play a little ball in high school. We had pickup teams and I was a crippled boy and I'd bat and somebody'd run for me. I'd participate in any way I could. One time I got in a real baseball game. A semipro game. Winona, Mississippi, versus Carrollton. I played for Carrollton. I was a couple of years out of high school. They were shorthanded. They put me at third base. The sun was in my eyes. A boy who played for the University of Alabama hit a line drive off of my glove. He hit my arm. I had a sore arm for two months. I run into some of my buddies now and they say, "Remember when you played ball out in Carroll County?"

Hugh Critz, who played for the Giants, was a Greenwood, Mississippi, boy. So I was a big Giants fan. I think it was '32 or '33 that the Giants and Cleveland came through here for an exhibition game. Walter Johnson was with the Indians. And, of course, Bill Terry was with the Giants. Through a friend of mine, I got to meet Mel Ott. The Giants were playing in Greenville this particular day. The next day they were going to be in Greenwood. This friend of mine, he said, "You be out tomorrow. I'll introduce you to Ott." That night I got a telegram from this guy. "Ott asked you to meet him at the ballpark." Well, I was a youngster then. I was a little bit scared. When I finally got nerve enough to meet him, he said, "I been looking for you, boy. Where you been?" He told me how to get the different autographs. He said, "Bill Terry. Don't bother him if he's talking to anybody." I think, somewhere, I still got that autographed baseball.

In this town, there was a doctor who was a big buddy of Hugh Critz's. Dr. Baskerville was his name. He went to the World Series. I'll never forget, we were all hanging around

· · · · ·

the hotel lobby to ask him about it when he came back. This one guy asked the doctor, "Who was the best ballplayer you saw up there?" He said, "Son, Hugh Critz is the best ballplayer in the world." Hugh Critz. We couldn't wait to see him come back after the season. We'd get him in a bull session. Anywhere in town where we could get ahold of him. The pool hall, in the hotel lobby. What kind of guy is McGraw? He'd tell us all about what kind of guy Bill Terry was.

I was working at a wholesale grocer. The games would start at four o'clock. I made a deal with my boss. If he'd let me get out an hour early to go to the games, that would be my vacation. I remember, they played sixty ball games. Half of them at home. So I'd get thirty hours off. That was my vacation. That's how much I loved baseball.

The first time I went to a major league ball game was in St. Louis. I was about thirty years old. They ran a special, a train with about six hundred people. I sold tickets, and I sold enough so I got a free ticket. This was my first time in St. Louis. We went out to the ballpark at about ten in the morning. Being a country boy, I'd never seen a stadium that big. I remember the first thing that impressed me about the big league ballplayers was how those outfielders could throw that ball.

I went to the World Series in '42. Five of us got a car and went up there. It was about 350 miles. We had four tickets. We had to find one ticket and we did. I had always wanted to listen to a ball game on the radio and watch one at the same time. Being a crippled fellow, I couldn't carry it in with me. One of my buddies, I told him, "I'll buy you dinner if you take my radio to the ball game." As soon as we got there, I turned the radio up. Some guys behind me says, "We've got to listen to that dadgum thing?" I turned it down. Three guys in front of me, great big guys, he says, "Turn that thing up." That's all I wanted – some support. I can still remember Dizzy Dean on the mound and hearing, "The pitcher is winding up" on the radio. I got a big kick out of that.

I'd watch any teams that'd come through, black, white, red, or yellow. I'm a churchgoing man. I had to leave a black baseball game one afternoon in the twelfth inning. It was 2–2. They had a left-handed catcher. Every pitch, he turned around to the crowd and shook the ball. I remember that. It was the twelfth inning, 2–2, and I had to leave to go to church. I didn't want to go.

Jackie Robinson? Well, Clay Hopper, who was the manager of Montreal after the war, he lived here. Clay Hopper said, "One thing about it. That black so-and-so will never play for me." That was before he went to spring training. About July I bought a baseball magazine. There was a picture of Clay and Jackie on the front steps hugging each other. Of course, that saved baseball. I don't know what we'd do if we didn't have blacks up there. Being from Mississippi, I probably resented it, to be truthful about it. But pretty soon it didn't make no difference to me what color a guy was in the major leagues. Monte Irvin. Willie Mays. I'm talking about the guys with the Giants, see? Now I'm pulling for all those blacks on the Braves just like they was my kinfolk. Color don't worry me no more. The good Lord made both of us, him and me, so I ain't going to fuss at them. If I'm pulling for the Braves and a base hit wins the World Series for them, I don't care what color the batter is.

My two biggest thrills. In 1951, when Bobby Thomson hit his home run. At that particular time, the Dodgers had a farm here in Greenwood. The business manager and I were good friends. He was in my office. Naturally, he was pulling for the Dodgers and I was pulling for the Giants. When Thomson hit his home run, I like to tear the office up. And this guy cried like a baby.

My next-biggest thrill is now. I live and die with the

· · · · ·

Atlanta Braves. My allegiance switched around when the Giants moved to the West Coast. That's too far out there. We started getting on TV the Braves all the time here. In '92, when this pinch-hitter in the ninth inning got a bloop single, Bream scored from second base. I can see him hobbling in there now. And Bonds made that bad throw. When that guy said safe at home plate, I like to tear up the house. I just loved those Braves. I still do.

SO FAR AWAY, ST. LOUIS WAS ANOTHER COUNTRY

BOB LEVIN, EIGHTY-FIVE,

IS A RETIRED LIFE INSURANCE SALESMAN

LIVING IN SAN FRANCISCO.

The Seals were very, very important to us. I would get a tennis ball and throw it against the step. The ball would come back pretty hard. I played a game. If I missed it, it was an error. If it went over my head and went so far, it was a double. If it went farther on, it was a triple or a home run. I actually kept score. I'd pretend the Seals were playing another team. I knew the players and I knew the pitchers. For some reason or another, the Seals always won. I guess I threw the ball a little harder.

. . . . .

I'm a native San Franciscan. We lived out in the Richmond District. In those days there weren't many automobiles. We played a lot of baseball on the street. We used a hardball; we used a softball. Because there were no houses on the other side, we didn't crack many windows.

My father and uncle were both very interested in baseball. My father grew up with it. When I was old enough, they started me out with a glove and a ball and a bat. I was a right-hander, but I got up to bat left-handed. That was the side where the houses were. So I learned to hit away from the houses. Believe it or not, all my life I hit straightaway or to left field. It must have been because of those houses. My uncle said I hit the ball and I slid into the telegraph pole where first base would be. That's my earliest recollection.

In my first grade of grammar school, to the chagrin of all my classmates, I was taken out of school for the opening of the Pacific Coast League season. The San Francisco Seals, which was a Triple-A minor league team, were playing. That's my first recollection of the importance of baseball, to be taken out of school. I remember taking the streetcar down to where my father had a store in the middle of the city. He picked me up at the store, and we went on another streetcar to Recreation Park.

Recreation Park was at 15th and Valencia Street. It was a typical old baseball park. It was all wood. The bleachers were just boards. The right field was shallow. But it had a very high wire fence. It took a high poke to get out of there. O'Doul could get it out nicely. Smead Jolley could get it out. There was what they called the Booze Cage underneath. They served beer there. Later, when I was maybe twelve or thirteen, I would sit in the Booze Cage. Not because of booze, but I could sit in the front row and talk to the players when they came down to get the bats. Also, the pitcher and catcher would warm up more or less in front of me. There was a screen there, of course. Sitting in the Booze Cage, I was a big shot, because they were all men around me. There were no ladies there. Although I think my mother came down a couple of times to investigate where I was.

At the same time, the Oakland Oaks were members of the Pacific Coast League. They played their home games in

Oakland, except Sunday afternoons and Thursday afternoons, they played their home games in San Francisco. The reciprocation was the Seals would play some of their home games in Oakland at the same time. In those days, of course, there were no bridges. So this same uncle – he had no children and I was like a son to him – he would take me to the Sunday games in Oakland.

My uncle used to get a box seat, and we would sit next to the telegraph operator, who was telegraphing the play-by-play. I guess to the newspapers. We would come back on the boat that the players came on. I remember they kept to themselves pretty much. As I recall, and this is hazy, they were dressed as I would be dressed. That would be with a coat and tie. There wasn't too much casual dress at that time. But it was a thrill to see players relatively close to you.

✦

The San Francisco Seals were a locally owned team. They sent a lot of players up to the majors. There wasn't hardly a year when one or two players didn't go up to the majors. Paul Waner. Smead Jolley. Earl Averill. Pretty good players. And Dutch Ruether. He was coming down. And Gomez. Lefty Gomez. Willie Kamm. The team for many, many years could have played major league ball, except they didn't have enough starting pitchers. I remember DiMaggio as being a very slick fielder. Sleek and slick. He didn't run, he glided. And he caught everything. He was special, of course. When they sold him, he had a bum leg, you know. They only got $25,000 for him, which was low, because he was damaged goods. These players didn't stay long in the Coast League. We felt bad when they were sold. But it was known as progress, with quotation marks. They sold Willie Kamm to the White Sox and got Eddie Mulligan in trade. Earl Averill went to Cleveland. Paul Waner went to Pittsburgh. I'd met Paul Waner when he was in my father's store. He was a very fresh-looking young man. When I say "fresh," I don't mean fresh in the sense of know-it-all. Not at all. I mean just being a clean-cut kid.

Walter "the Great" Mails. Does that name mean anything to you? He helped Cleveland win the World Series in 1920. He didn't pitch very long in the major leagues. He came down with the Seals. We had a lot of players who went up and a lot of players on their way down. He was very vocal. He had lots to say. His forte was picking people off first and second base. He was very clever at that. When he retired, he became a coach at first base. He never faced the field. He always faced the fans. He talked to the fans. Of course, we had Lefty O'Doul, too. He was revered in San Francisco as a manager. Very, very colorful. I remember Zee-Nut cards. There was a local candy maker who made Zee-Nuts, which were chocolate-coated, marshmallow nuts sold mostly in the ballpark. There was a baseball card in the package. They were Pacific Coast League baseball cards.

We were so far away. St. Louis was the nearest major league city, and that was another country. The major leagues hardly meant anything to us. But I will say Ty Cobb became my hero. I guess I was following the major leagues in the newspaper. I used to watch to see how the Tigers were doing. The greatest hitter of all time. Probably the greatest base stealer of his time. A great fielder. He won thirteen batting championships, nine in a row.

I saw him play. For several seasons they had what they called the Mid-Winter League in San Francisco. They played on weekends only. There were four teams. There was San Francisco, Oakland, and Los Angeles and Vernon. Vernon was a satellite of Los Angeles. They had four major league players as managers, playing managers. Ty Cobb was one. Babe Ruth was another. Rogers Hornsby was another. And

George Sisler was another. I saw them all play. I can remember one game when Ty Cobb got up to bat. He was a left-handed hitter, but he was a place hitter. I guess that's one of the reasons why I became a place hitter. He hit four balls over the shortstop's head. Texas Leaguers. Four doubles. You could almost put a handkerchief where the balls went.

I went to games quite a bit. The Seals were purchased by the Boston Red Sox for a farm club. Then it was a minor league club for the major league team, and the players were coming and going. It wasn't quite the same. Most of the teams became minor league teams. The players were changing, so you couldn't have a longtime feeling. It was different. It wasn't San Francisco. It was Boston.

Then, when the Giants came, they played two years at Seals Stadium. I saw my first major league game when the Giants moved out here in 1958. I guess I was forty-eight. I saw their first game here. I think it was with the Dodgers. It was like a new world. A major league team. We were a major league city. All the difference in the world.

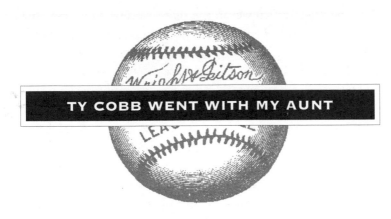

TY COBB WENT WITH MY AUNT

LOUIS LEMIEUX, SEVENTY-SEVEN,

IS A RETIRED CABDRIVER, BAR MANAGER, AND

STAND-UP COMEDIAN LIVING IN DETROIT.

The day they pat me in the face with a spade, I'll still love my Tigers. There wasn't any other game in Detroit. Nobody had any money. We didn't have any football fields. We didn't have any ice rinks. All we had was a lot of open fields. And every day those playgrounds were filled with baseball.

Baseball. That's all we knew. In my neighborhood, we had three or four playgrounds around there. As soon as school was over, everybody was out there with a ball and bat. We had neighborhood teams. We weren't organized. Somebody would say, "Hey, we're going to play them tonight from Sixth Street." And we'd all meet over there by one of the Houghton School playgrounds. We'd play ball.

. . . . .

I was born in Corktown, just three blocks away from the ballpark. I still live only four blocks from Tiger Stadium. I was four years old in Detroit the first time I went to a baseball game. My mother's cousin came down from Bay City, Michigan. He used to like to visit Navin Field. He always took me along. We used to sit over in the right-field pavilion. He used to call me Sonny. He'd say, "There's Ty Cobb. And that's Babe Ruth." From then on I fell in love with baseball.

Until I was seven, if my mother's cousin couldn't come down from Bay City to take me to the ball game, at that time you could stand out in front of Navin Field and when guys would go through alone, we'd go up to them and we'd say, "Double up, mister? Double up, mister?" Double up meant that I went in free as their son. At that time, a man paid one admission and he could bring his son in free.

When I was seven years old, Ty Cobb went with my aunt. My aunt lived right across the street from Navin Field on what was at that time National Avenue. Today it's Cochrane Street. There was a bunch of old houses there. And there was a space between these two houses, just enough for one car. Ty Cobb used to come over, and he'd park his car between those two houses. That's when he first asked my aunt, "Who's that?" And she said, "My nephew." At that time they let anybody run all over the field. When the game was over, everybody walked all over the field to the nearest exits. And Ty Cobb recognized me as being my aunt's nephew, and he used to sort of look for me. He'd call me over and say, "Hey, kid." Once in a while, he'd call me "Punk." He'd say, "Here," and he'd give me two bats. And he'd say, "Here. Carry them up to the car for me, kid." And he'd give me a half a dollar or a quarter. Can you imagine half a buck in 1924 for a seven-year-old kid? I mean, I almost felt like retiring to Florida at seven.

To me, he was always a fine man. He would come out after a ball game and he'd have a handful or a roll of quarters and he'd throw them up in the air. And he'd watch about 150, 200 kids scramble for those quarters. And believe you me, mister, some of the biggest riots in Watts was nothing compared to these kids scrambling for these quarters. To me, Ty Cobb

· · · · ·

loved children. He couldn't stand too many adults – except my aunt. When he was traded to Philadelphia, I felt a little sad about it.

When I went to Navin Field, I thought I was in heaven. I didn't have any money, so I had to figure a way to get in. The only way they would clean up the stadium was they'd get about a hundred kids after the game and they'd give each one of us an empty hundred-pound potato burlap bag. And we'd go up and down, picking up popcorn cartons, everything. And for that, we got a free pass for the next day. We all had to sit in the right-field pavilion. That was one of the ways you used to get into the stadium to watch a ball game.

You know how it's a no-no if you bump the umpire? I like to tell them about 1929. There used to be an umpire named Van Graflan. He was an umpire, and he was quite a drinker. Just because you're a umpire doesn't mean you're immune. Anyway, they were playing at Tiger Stadium one night. Joe Judge – he was a first baseman for the Washington Senators – was at bat. I forget who the pitcher was. The pitcher wound up and threw the ball. Van Graflan was so loaded – and, you know, at that time they had those great, big heavy rubber chest protectors – that he leaned over and fell on the catcher. The ball hit the catcher in the head. And the catcher got up and decked him. I was there. We all laughed like hell.

I was really captivated with baseball. It broke my heart when Dizzy Dean and his brother Daffy Dean beat the Tigers in the World Series in 1934. I was a messenger boy for Western Union. I listened to it on the radio. I read about it in the paper the next day. It broke my heart. In 1935 the Tigers won the pennant and also the World Series. They beat the Chicago Cubs. I was sitting in the car with my friend, and we were listening to the radio. We were only four blocks away. When Goose Goslin hit that single over second base and Mickey Cochrane scored from second and they won the

World Series, the town went crazy. We had streetcars then on Woodward Avenue. You couldn't get a streetcar. They were tied up for hours. People were sitting on the roofs. We just enjoyed the fact that we were the world's champions of 1935.

After a game, you could go out here and shake hands with Charlie Gehringer, Hank Greenberg, Rogell, Gerald Walker. Walker used to go to the same church I did on Sunday, with his brother Hubby. St. Boniface is only two blocks from Tiger Stadium. They used to sit about three or four rows in front of us. I was tickled pink. I was beginning to realize the importance of some of these ballplayers.

They were Detroit's team. These guys were human. They'd come out and walk amongst you and stop to talk to you and give you their autographs – free. Not no ten, fifteen dollars for an autograph. Charlie Gehringer used to stand out there under the left-field pavilion. I seen him stand out there an hour, an hour and a half, just signing autographs for all the kids. Hank Greenberg, the same way. They were the big show.

I saw Babe Ruth one time. In 1933 Prohibition was repealed. There were several bars opened up around Tiger Stadium. He was in a bar. I was standing outside. There'd be ten, twenty kids standing out on Michigan Avenue. Whenever a high foul ball would come over the roof, it landed on Michigan Avenue. Can you imagine, traffic going by, kids dodging the cars, to get that ball? Anyway, there was a bar down there, just about a block away. I was standing out there one day and he came out and I was standing out there waiting for a ball. And I went up and asked him for his autograph. And he gave me his autograph. He was going over to the bar to get himself a few swallows. I don't mean birds, either.

In 1941 I was in Pearl Harbor when the Japs hit us. I was on a destroyer, the USS *Dent*. I was on the *Pittsburgh* when it broke in half in a typhoon off Japan. But I was never really away from baseball as far as being a fan goes. The only thing was, during the war in the Pacific, we didn't have radios or anything. We were fighting a war. Anytime we would pull into port, which was very seldom, the first thing I'd do was to get ahold of a local newspaper and see how the Tigers did.

I was so glad to get out of the service. So I drifted along the West Coast for a little bit. I thought, "Well, I'm pretty talented. I'm a singer, a dancer, a magician. Maybe I can get a job in the movies." And I did. I got in a picture with Bob Hope. *The Paleface*. Bob Hope come into the saloon and he's looking for this guy and he says, "Where's that dirty coward?" I pointed and said, "There he is over there!" That was the extent of my movie career. I got fifty bucks and three meals.

I came back to Detroit. I was so happy to be back. You sort of get acclimated to the times and places of your old neighborhood. You see your old friends, you get together, you meet in a bar. "Hey, let's go to a ball game tonight. The Tigers are playing the White Sox."

Elmer Squires and I worked at the Cadillac distributor, and we went to ball games together all the time. Eddie Bellhorn used to operate the scoreboard in center field. We all grew up in Corktown. We all hung out in the same bars. In the summertime, real hot days, I used to go down to the concession stand and get a couple of beers. It was hotter than blazes up in that scoreboard. I'd walk up in the bleachers. The scoreboard was at the top of the bleachers. I'd holler in there and Eddie would poke his head out one of those holes. He'd pull a zero out of one of the scores and put his head out there. He'd throw the key down to me, and I'd bring him a couple of beers.

In '68 I was managing the Lucky Clover Club. That's only three blocks from Tiger Stadium on Michigan Avenue. When they won, it was mayhem. Everyone went crazy. The whole town. When your city wins the championship, everybody goes

· · · · ·

ape. I was here when they won in '84. That's when they tipped the police cars over and taxicabs and set fire to them. I felt bad, because the rest of the country, their papers played it up.

This must have been fifteen or twenty years ago. It was a night game. The Tigers were playing the Oakland A's. The Oakland A's had a big, fat first baseman. We had a Tiger pitcher named Lerrin LaGrow. He threw a pitch and knocked him down. And he got up and took off for Lerrin LaGrow. And they fought out there at the pitcher's mound. They had quite a ring-ding-doo. After the game, we were coming down a ramp. Bob Hope had been there that night. He was coming out; he had all police around him. Elmer Squires and I were walking fast down this runway. Elmer says, "Let's get the hell over to the bar." So I took a few fast steps and I tripped and I busted right through the cops and I knocked Bob Hope on his ass. I said, "How'd you like the Friday night fights, Bob?"

I haven't been to a Tiger game in about two years. I'm half blind and bedridden. I've got arthritis so bad, I'm lucky to be able to get up and get around. When you're seventy-seven, you don't get out and do a tap dance when they get a home run. But I'd love to be over there again. I can see at night games, them big lights, and, boy. They talk about tearing down Tiger Stadium. Rotten. If I was able to, I'd jump up and down in this bed and curse them. It just burns me up. It's been like a second home to me. I just feel good when I get in there.

• • • • •

TRUCK HANNAH'S LITTLE GIRL

HELEN HANNAH CAMPBELL, SEVENTY-NINE,

IS A RETIRED MARINE CORPS MASTER

GUNNERY SERGEANT LIVING IN

FOUNTAIN VALLEY, CALIFORNIA.

I'd come home and spend my winters with my folks in Whittier. The girls who lived in California got together every weekend and played pickup ball. They'd play in the little parks around. I got my dad to go with me one time. He said, "I don't know why I'm going over there to watch a bunch of girls play."

We got over there and one of them came up to me and said, "Would your dad umpire?" He had to stand behind the pitcher and call balls and strikes.

He came home talking to himself. He just didn't have any idea these girls were as good as they really were. He didn't think they could commit a double play. The biggest thing that impressed him that whole afternoon is he didn't think a girl could throw a curve ball. He just shook his head.

· · · · ·

My dad was on a road trip when I was born in Salt Lake City. He was playing for the Salt Lake Bees in the Pacific Coast League. In those days they traveled by train, and so when they made a road trip, they went to three towns and played a week in each one of them. I was three weeks old by the time he got home. One of the pitchers on the club, Dutch Ruether, he was left home with a sore arm. He was the first one to see me, so he became my godfather.

From there, my father went to the Yankees, just at the close of World War I. We were back there for three years. I don't remember much about that time, except the cockroaches in the apartment. When we'd come home, I used to run ahead to be the first one to turn on the lights and see them scamper across the floor. We came back out here to the Coast League when I was five or six years old.

We used to go to Wrigley Field in Los Angeles. It was on the south side of Los Angeles. My father was a catcher for the Angels. The Los Angeles Angels were a Triple-A, Pacific Coast League farm club for the Chicago Cubs. And all during my elementary school years, I went to a lot of ball games. My seat was right behind the dugout. Being there for so many years, you got to know everybody. You got to know all the hustlers, all the ushers, you knew all the ticket takers.

My dad caught many, many, many games in those fifteen years when he was with the Angels. His main forte was to tell a story to the batter. Just as the last pitch, he would tell him the punchline and usually he had these fellows swinging off of their back heels. He only chewed tobacco at the ballpark. It was an old plug of tobacco. If he was having trouble getting the attention of the batter, he would spit the tobacco juice at his shoes. I remember seeing him do that. Heavens, yes.

The clock on the tower said WRIGLEY FIELD. I can see that left-field fence. It had vines on it just like the Chicago Cubs' park had. It was brick. Watching a whole bunch of

· · · · ·

home runs going over it. I can remember Ted Williams and Joe DiMaggio and Lefty O'Doul and fellows like that. We looked at them as good ballplayers and smart ballplayers, and we knew eventually they would make their niche in the baseball world. This was a stepping-stone for them. At one time there was an effort to change the Pacific Coast League standing from a Triple-A class to a third major league. The boys who were here inevitably ended up in the major leagues someplace because they were that good. Many of them, after their tours were over in the major leagues, would float back down here.

I loved the games. I loved the people involved. Being in Hollywood, my dad had opportunity to meet many of the stars. A lot of the directors and producers and some of the stars were good baseball fans, and they spent a lot of time at Wrigley Field. Harry Ruby and Benny Rubin and Bert Kalmar and Joe Brown and Buster Keaton and Leo Carrillo and Richard Dix and Tom Mix. My father had the opportunity to play a lot of bit parts in baseball pictures that Joe Brown made.

Benny Rubin. He was a Jewish comedian. He and two or three of his buddies used to come out and take batting practice with the ball club. They would have rather played in a professional ball game than write a song hit or have a show on the stage. They were obsessed by baseball. I adored listening to them. Buster Keaton was a great guy. He was so funny. He was so spontaneous. So original. He ad-libbed a great deal. He could see humor in so many things. When he was with the ballplayers, he was even funnier.

One of the tricks that somebody played – I presume my dad was probably at the root of it – was while they were making a picture. And they had some dizzy blond Suzy, as my dad used to describe some of those ladies from Hollywood. She was rather an obnoxious young lady and thought of herself as quite a star. Anyway, they had a scene where for some reason her shoes were over at the side of the stage. High spike heels. So Daddy and a couple of the players went over to the carpenter's shop and got a hammer and a couple of nails, and they nailed her shoes to the floor. Then she went back over to them and stepped into them and tried to move. They thought that was a hysterical trick.

I played baseball in grammar school and high school. I went to such a small school, I had to play with the fellas most of the time. There weren't enough girls to play. And anyway, like my dad said, a lot of them would throw like girls. But he had played catch with me in the yard, showed me how to step when you released the ball. He'd hit to me. Gave me a fielder's glove so I could field. He never expressed regret about having a girl instead of a boy as offspring.

In high school I played a little bit. Our equipment was kind of crude. We had to make our own diamond. Whatever we could pick up, we'd use as a base. I used to get some old balls from my dad. Once in a while we'd get a broken bat and tape it up. I never became as good a ballplayer as I would have liked.

I went to high school with Dick Nixon. He was two years ahead of me. He was an avid baseball fan. He used to ride the streetcar from Whittier to Los Angeles, which was about fifteen or twenty miles, and go down to Wrigley Field and watch my dad play.

◆

The Cubs, instead of coming to Arizona, would come to California for spring training. Mr. Wrigley had a diamond at Catalina. He would bring the Cubs out there. There was one major hotel out there, called the St. Catherine. That was where the Cubs would be put up. He would take the Angels over there, and they would stay at the same hotel. They would train against each other. Those were the most interesting springs I can remember.

You've surely seen pictures of the big casino that's on the point on Avalon Bay. It was a home of all of the famous-name bands. The second deck was a huge, huge ballroom, just like the ballrooms that used to be around Chicago. I remember with much delight the times we'd go to the casino every night and just dance until our legs would fall off. My very favorite dancer of all times, besides my dad, was Jimmie Reese. He was with us, the Angels. I couldn't be bothered with the Cubs.

After Pearl Harbor, Mr. Wrigley was very, very concerned about the ballplayers being conscripted. He got the ball rolling as far as the organization of the girls' league around Chicago. The All-American Girls Professional Baseball League opened in 1943. I was on active duty in the Marine Corps by then. After peace had been declared, I stayed in another year. I was out here attending the winter meetings with my dad at the Biltmore Hotel in downtown Los Angeles and ran into Max Carey. He was a friend of my father's. He called me later and said, "I've got a job for you in Chicago. We're going to spring training in Havana, Cuba." It was a job in Michigan in a town called Muskegon. He said, "You'll be the chaperone and general business manager." The Muskegon Lassies. That was in 1947.

I was tickled to be around baseball again. The chaperone was like a surrogate mother for girls who are away from home for the first time. In Havana we drew more people than the Yankees did. Cuba was baseball crazy. Girls playing baseball the Cubans thought they had died and gone to heaven. We had a little trouble in the hotels with some of the girls. Some of the girls defied discipline. On May Day we couldn't let them out of their rooms because of the riots in the streets. They tied all their sheets together and made ropes out of them and dropped them out of the window. There were vendors going along selling fruit and tacos and tortillas. They'd drop money down and the vendors put stuff in the basket and they'd pull it back up.

The chaperones usually took the brunt of any of the old-timers' gags. They would put short sheets on your bed. And they would put those mechanical wiggly snakes on your pillows. They'd switch salt and sugar at the table. Crazy things like that.

When we came back out here after I got married, the Pacific Coast League was in existence, but it wasn't in as good a shape as it had been before. People in the East were making sounds like, "Now that we have jet planes, maybe we can play in California or Hawaii or Washington or Oregon." They decided the first ground should be broken out here. Anybody who had been in the Coast League as long as we were resented it a great deal. When Daddy was playing in the '20s and '30s and '40s around here, there was a camaraderie that has been lost and will never be attained again. The fast pace of life, the major leagues out here and them disrupting our Pacific Coast League – they've ruined it.

The Dodgers came out here, and Mr. O'Malley had great assistance from some of the city council people. Backyard payoffs and stuff like that to get the property. Uprooted a lot of innocent people. They had to play in the Coliseum and Wrigley Field. The California Angels had to play in there for a while until Mr. Autry got Anaheim to build a stadium. I went to games, because it was baseball. But it was a different attitude completely.

I've been an Angel booster for many years. I don't know whether "win me over" is the term or not. I still have visions of the Pacific Coast League. The ballparks are altogether different. They don't have Knothole Gangs for the kids, and they don't let them in for free to sit in the bleachers and eat

· · · · ·

peanuts. Wrigley Field is gone. It's been several years now. I knew they were going to destroy it. The neighborhood had changed so. They weren't using it for a baseball field anymore. The land was valuable. I've never been back there. I don't want to go out there. It brings back too many memories of things that are gone.

I HIT BABE RUTH WITH A PEANUT

SAM "LEADEN" BERNSTEIN, SEVENTY-NINE,

IS A RETIRED GARMENT WORKER

LIVING IN PHILADELPHIA.

I spent three and a half years in the States and over a year in Europe, in combat. I was with the 11th Armored. I was a rifleman. I started in France, then I went to Germany and Austria. The war was over in the spring. I had frozen feet and hands. I thought I'd never be able to play again. Then, before people started to go home, we began playing baseball. There's a certain word the Germans used called "verrückt." They'd say, "Americans are verrückt." That means they're crazy. Why do you think they said we were crazy? Wherever there was a field, we used to make a baseball diamond out of it.

. . . . .

I lived deep in South Philadelphia. I loved the game from the day I was born. They used to make a joke out of it: "Leaden must have been born with a baseball in his hand." I always had a glove in my hand. I used to practice, practice. I used to go to the outfield and have a man fungo to me, all by myself. I'd run and run. I loved it. I never thought I'd give it up. I

48

always say, "You know the Seven Wonders of the World? Well, there's eight. Baseball is the eighth one."

There was two fellows and myself. The three Jewish boys. They couldn't get over us. We used to play baseball even in the snow. It was a poor neighborhood. Where I lived, there was one street Jewish, and all around Irish. I can't lie. There was always that little friction there. The Jews and the Irish, they'd get into little fights here and there. But when we'd start playing ball, we were all the same. On this Jewish team, we had two Irish guys named Dugan. They changed their name to Duban when they played with us. You'd have a Jewish team, you'd have an Irish team – but as you got older, you found out this guy was better than that guy, so you all got together to have a better team. The nationalities didn't count anymore. As sandlotters, we were all one. White teams played black teams all the time.

My brother took me to the first game I ever saw. It was the A's playing the New York Yankees in 1927. Babe Ruth, Ty Cobb, Lou Gehrig, Lefty Grove, Herb Pennock, Mickey Cochrane, Zack Wheat, Tris Speaker – all these guys played that day. All Hall of Famers. Ty Cobb had four hits that day. He was forty-three years old and he had a stolen base. How can I forget that? Then my brother bought me a bag of peanuts. I saw Babe Ruth down below. I threw a couple of peanuts down there, and one of them hit him on the head. He looked up at me with a big smile on his face. I'll never forget that as long as I live. How many can say they saw Babe Ruth look at them and smile?

When we were kids, there were these books, Frank Merriwell books. All heroes. In reality, this was Al Simmons. He was, to me, a Frank Merriwell. It seems like he never got out. He just got the hits when it counted. He'd get a home run when they needed it. His average was .360 with the A's. He could throw; he could run – there was just something about him. He had moxie. He was my number one. I used to go down to the playground at Fourth and Shunk in South Philadelphia. When I was fourteen years old, this fellow, Joe Naccio, started teasing me about Al Simmons. He said he was no good. I really punched him out. Gave him a couple of black eyes.

I used to play for a team that was 90 percent Jewish. It was called the Jewish All-Stars. The games were at six o'clock at night. I worked in a factory, this guy worked in a factory, this guy worked in a factory. We used to have a truck pick us up where we worked. We'd get changed on the truck and go to the ball fields. We'd play anywhere. There's nothing like sandlot. Nothing. Lose or win, we'd have so much fun on that truck. We'd sing songs, we'd fight with each other. We were just so glad to be part of the game. I went to play a night game one time. I didn't have a glove. My luck, the center fielder was a left-hander like me. I said, "Will you lend me your glove?" OK. A guy hit a ball to deep right center. I made a running catch. You know, the next inning, the glove was not there. I had to use a right-handed glove the rest of the game.

I'd played for South Philadelphia High School for Boys. We won a championship. Then I started to play sandlot ball. In 1938 they had a Philadelphia paper that was called the *Record.* They had a contest that ran from '38 to the early part of '39. Every day there was a coupon you could send in to the *Record.* After about nine months, they added them up. They picked the six sandlot players who got the most votes. Three guys went to the Philadelphia Athletics and three guys went to the Philadelphia Phillies. The day they were going to say who won it, I was too chicken to hang around. So I went to the movies. I come out of the movie; I was way down on the end of Front Street. My mom was up at Second Street,

. . . . .

waiting for me. And when she saw me, she started screaming, "Sammy! You won! You won!"

I went to the Phillies. They took players for one month. I went to New Braunfels, Texas, where the Phillies trained that year. Chuck Klein was on the team. Pinky Whitney. Herschel Martin. Claude Passeau. They were a last-place team, but it was an experience. It was a kid's dream, and it came true. I got goose pimples when I saw Chuck Klein. I said, "What am I doing here?" Hans Lobert. He was the coach. He was the most lovable man in baseball. He treated me like a son. He showed me everything about baseball. All the trickeries. I got real friendly with Heinie Mueller. He used to be a mascot of the St. Louis Cardinals. I used to walk to church with him and wait outside until he was done. All we did was talk baseball. The whole team. I used to have a room with my buddy, called Johnny Nace. He and I were two winners of the *Record* contest. We used to listen to them outside of this hotel. And all they did was talk baseball. And they were last place. And I'll tell you, the spirit was there. It was so different then, from now.

It wasn't like we got a chance because we were great players. We won a contest. But after a while, they put us right in with them. They put us in the little games they had. We did the running with them. Go out to catch fly balls. Take infield. They treated us just like we was one of the guys out for the team. We had uniforms. I wish I had it today. We used to go barnstorming. They played against the St. Louis Browns about ten times before the season started. I didn't get into those games. But we'd sit in the dugout and we'd talk about every play. The manager would explain to us. The manager was Doc Prothro. He was a southern gentleman.

I got into one practice game. Intrasquad. I did all right. I didn't bat. But I made some nice plays in the field. I kept in the outfield. I didn't mix. I knew where I belonged. I tried to stay away from the guys when we were working out. They were out to make the team and I wasn't. You follow me? Then one day I hear somebody holler, "Bernstein! Sammy! Hey, Bernstein, Doc Prothro wants you."

So I go toward him at home plate. He said, "Get the bat." I get in there and bat. "Boy, oh boy," I said to myself. "This is great." I'd been around. I played a lot of sandlot ball. I wasn't going to swing at the first pitch. I wanted to see what the guy's got. It's only normal. I let the first pitch go by. Spud Davis was the catcher. You know what he said to me? "What's the matter, kid, didn't you see it?" I just looked at him. Gene Bearden, who later went up with the Indians and won a World Series game, he was pitching. He was only a kid. Then I did all right. I hit about six or seven shots and I laid a bunt down. That night, when I went back to the hotel, Doc Prothro was waiting for me. He put his arm around me. He said, "Kid, you're good. You remind me of Goody Rosen." Because I was Jewish. It's like a dream, when I think of it now. A kid's dream came true. I went to the big leagues for one month.

When I got in the army in 1941, I was twenty-five years old. That's when I started playing good baseball. They sent me to Fort Totten, Long Island, New York, the headquarters of the 79th Artillery. They had a baseball team there. Ex–big leaguers, college players. We had a terrific season. We beat the Philadelphia Athletics. We beat Bushwick. We beat West Point. I played in Yankee Stadium. When I went to Yankee Stadium, I went to center field. They had a gully there. It was like a slope. I said, "I can't believe this. Joe DiMaggio played this? Boy, he's better than ever. If he could play with this here hazard."

I played in the Polo Grounds. At eleven o'clock at night, we went out and played against this other army team. I batted against Marius Russo from the Yankees. Al Schacht came over to our dugout and said, "I need a guy to help me with my gimmick." They said, "Go ahead, Bernstein. You're the clown here." He had a guy named Sam Byrd with him. Sam Byrd who used to play with the Yankees. Here's how they used me. Schacht said, "You get in back of me, and I'll be on the pitcher's mound." They had a big glove and a crazy hat. He winds up and the other guy's got a big bat. He throws the first pitch and this guy Byrd swings and Schacht says, "Oh, no. This guy's a good hitter. Go back. Go back." You know where I ended up? The top seat at the Polo Grounds. Imagine, a little punk like me, thirty-five thousand people are watching me.

I'm in Fort Totten, and we're playing the Philadelphia Athletics at three o'clock in the afternoon. At ten o'clock in the morning, I figured I'd go to the library. I got a book and I'm walking around and there's a civilian walking toward me. It was Joe Naccio. He was barnstorming with the A's. He was a pretty good ballplayer. He says, "Leaden! What are you doing here?" I said, "I'm playing against the A's." He said, "Remember that day?" I said, "Do I remember it? I'm sorry, Joe." He said, "I've got to tell Al Simmons about you." He went back and told him all about me and all about the fight. So when I went out there to the field, I heard my name. "Hey, Sammy, how are you doing?" It was Al Simmons. I was a shy kid, so I just more or less waved to him. In the late innings, he pinch-hit. He hit a humpback line drive over the shortstop and I'm running, running, running, and I'm saying to myself, "I'm trying to get it, but I hope I don't." I didn't want to catch it. I wanted him to get a hit. Thank God, I couldn't get it.

After it was all over, we had a banquet. Al Simmons went over to our captain and said, "Do you mind if I sit with the soldiers? I want to sit next to Sammy." And we sat and sat and talked. He got a ball out and he wrote, "To my friend, Sammy Bernstein, 1944, Fort Totten." I sent it to my brother

· · · · ·

when I went overseas and he lost it. When I got overseas, I said, "Well, I got my dream to come true. I guess I'll never make it home." But I got home to live to tell about it.

When I come out, I got married. I used to go to the playground and try to play baseball. I'd bring my bat and glove. I used to love to run after fly balls. I'd see nobody around. So I started shooting the basketball. After the war, baseball wasn't the same. All my buddies were gone. They got older. But I still wanted to play.

I worked forty years. Went to games whenever I could. I started to favor the Phillies. The Athletics weren't that good. No more Al Simmons. In 1950 my buddy, he was my best friend, he and I listened on the radio. The Phillies beat the Dodgers. All the neighbors came out and started hollering. We went out on the street. We were screaming, hollering. We were going crazy. My buddy. His name was Al Luboff. He lived next door. He was ten years younger than me. The best friend I ever had. We never went to a game without each other. Every baseball game, we went together. He used to pick me up and take me, and we'd go out before the game and after the game. He passed away about twenty years ago. Every time I watch a ball game, I think of him. How can I forget 1980? I loved that team. There's nobody like Pete Rose. Nobody. He gave too much to baseball. I don't care what he did in the outside world. He knew how to win. When they won, I jumped all over the place. Like a kid. Baseball? Like a kid.

I FELL FOR THEM RIGHT AWAY

ED OISETH, SEVENTY-FOUR,

IS A RETIRED POLICE DISPATCHER LIVING IN

MAGALIA, CALIFORNIA.

In the summer of 1951, we were expecting a baby, and my wife had a girl's name all picked out. It turned out to be a boy, so she told me to name him. I said, "Well, Musial's hitting about .380. Let's call him Stan Musial." She says, "OK."

Then I come back to the hospital the next day and they asked me, "You got to get a name for the baby." I says, "We've already got a name." My mother-in-law and my sisters-in-law had come in there and changed my wife's mind. So we had to rename him. I got the name Stanley on him, yet. But they picked a different middle name. Goddarnit.

· · · · ·

My father. I guess that's the case with a lot of us. I grew up in North Dakota. My father homesteaded up there, north of Minot, in 1901. He came to this country from Norway. He followed baseball. I can remember in 1929, when the stock market fell and everybody in town lost everything they had and they were all crying and all that, I can remember him saying, "I feel more sorry for Connie Mack. He's got to sell his ballplayers to keep his team." Well, I thought baseball must really be something.

He was a Connie Mack fan. In the World Series of 1931, the Athletics were playing the Cardinals. He came over to the school one day, and he asked the teacher, "You know, this ought to be a national holiday. How come you got school today? The World Series is on the radio." He said, "I'd like my son to come home." I went home with him. But I had to pay attention as he explained things to me. So I became a fan of Jimmie Foxx of the Athletics. As time went on, Foxx was my favorite, my number one.

When I was a kid, about thirteen years old, Joe Hauser was playing for the Minneapolis Millers in the American Association. That summer he hit sixty-nine home runs. That was a Triple-A team. That was good baseball. Up there in that little town, we had a baseball team. I'd hang around a lot, and they'd talk about it all the time. "Joe hit another one. Joe hit two today." My dad was interested. It was the first thing he looked at in the sports section, to see what Joe Hauser did. I thought, "Gee, that Joe Hauser, he must be one of the greatest in the whole world."

My father died in 1934, but I kept following the game. I moved away in the dust bowl days of 1936 to Sacramento. We didn't live too far from the Coast League ballpark. It was known as Cardinal Field in those days. It was a wooden structure. I had a buddy in school. He was a pretty fair pitcher, so he pitched batting practice down there for the Sacramento Solons. When he got through with his batting practice pitching, why, he'd walk over to the fence and he'd holler, "Eddie, are you there?" I'd say, "I sure am." He'd flip me a ball. That way I could walk around and turn the ball in and get a nice seat. That's the way they operated in those days. If you got a ball, you brought it back and got a good seat. You saw some good ballplayers. I saw Ted Williams in 1937. He was with the Padres. He was a tall, skinny kid. The Angels had a player by the name of Jigger Statz. He was an outstanding outfielder and outstanding hitter. He was up for the bigs for a while, but he just couldn't cut it. When Dominic DiMaggio come into town, I remember we had a guy on third base. The batter hit a long ball out to center field. DiMaggio got the guy out. Nobody ran on DiMaggio's arm after that.

One interesting time, the Seals were in town, with Lefty O'Doul. In the late part of the game, his starting pitcher was having trouble getting the ball over the plate. So he took him out and put in another one. And that guy was worse than the first guy. He kept on going and used about three or four pitchers in the inning. He got real mad and walked out to the mound. He had a left-hander out there. He went up and ripped the glove off his hand and said, "Let me have that glove." He took about two warm-up tosses. And he got the side out. I saw that.

I went back to North Dakota and started at the University of North Dakota. I lived in a fraternity house and worked for my board and room. They had a team in the Northern League at that time, Grand Forks did. That was with Winnipeg and Duluth, Superior, Fargo, Wausau, and Eau Claire. Had some good ballplayers in that Northern League. That was a Class D league. I went to all of those games. The manager was Johnny Mostil. Johnny was the center fielder for the White Sox years before. He was one of the fastest outfielders in the league. Supposedly he was the only center fielder who ever caught a foul ball.

Every team had a rickety old bus. I used to ride with them once in a while. I think it was a 1922 model. It didn't sound too good. They'd play an exhibition game in some little town forty miles out. Johnny'd let me sit up front with him. He was always smoking a cigar. We'd talk baseball, and I think he enjoyed having me up there with him. We had one bus driver who was a character. He was a utility player; he could pinch-hit a little, and he'd play in the field now and then. By golly, one day he went out and stole all our baseballs and bats he could get his hands on and left town in a hurry. You even had thieves in those days.

Baseball has been an easy game for me to follow. I tried all the time. In World War II, in the days of wine and roses, I drank a lot. I was in the brig one time for being drunk. I had a marine who knew I was a fan and he was, too. So he'd come back every inning and give me a play-by-play. "They had two men on with two out and so-and-so flied out." Do you remember that movie *One Flew over the Cuckoo's Nest*? The guy in the nuthouse was broadcasting the World Series game? That's the way this marine was to me. It was a World Series game. Of all things, it was a game in 1944 between the St. Louis Browns and St. Louis Cardinals.

When World War II ended in Europe, I'd been flying down in the Caribbean, South America – we were doing air-sea rescue. Three of us took a JIF, an amphibian plane, up to Lakehurst, New Jersey. One wanted to go to Atlantic City to see a girlfriend, another wanted to go home to Brooklyn. I said, "The Phillies are playing the Giants tomorrow in a doubleheader. I'm going over there." I hadn't seen a baseball game in over three years. We all sat there and drank all that night. I wound up in Philadelphia, all right. I was sleeping in somebody's car, in the backseat, in the parking garage below a hotel. So I got out of there and I wound up on the street. It was Sunday and the bars in Philly were all closed that day. I run into a guy, though, who took me up to the Eagles and bought me a couple of drinks, and he gave me a pint of whiskey. Everybody was good to guys in uniform in those days. I went out to the ballpark. Beautiful day and nice crowd. Of course, by now, I'm half loaded again. I doze off and I wake up and everybody's gone. I'm the only one in the park. Goddamn. It was a doubleheader. The sun was setting. So I hitchhike back to Lakehurst. The next morning a guy says, "So how'd the ball game come out?" I said, "You know what? I've got to get a paper to find out." And I saw where Jimmie Foxx come in as a relief pitcher for the Phillies that day. I missed it. I slept through it. Goddamn. It really turned me off, you know?

I had to go with the Giants. I adopted them as soon as they moved out to California. It was a big deal for me. They played in Seals Stadium for two years. They came out there with a wonderful team. Willie Mays and Orlando Cepeda – he was a rookie. I fell for them right away. In the summer of 1962, I kept a scrapbook. Every day I'd put a page in my notebook of the box score and highlights of the game. All the guys I worked with, they'd say, "Oh, the Giants don't have a chance. The Dodgers have too good a team. They got Drysdale; they got Koufax." All summer long the Dodgers were in the lead. They wound up the season in a dead heat. They both won 101 games.

In those days they had a three-game play-off. I had this damn job as a police dispatcher. In San Jose. That building we were in was supposed to be a bomb-proof building. The walls were very thick, and you couldn't receive anything in there to listen on the radio. I had a couple of good friends I worked with who were good fans, too. So what I'd do, I'd call my house and have my wife put the phone next to the radio. We'd all listen in, see? When you were on the phone working the radio at the same time, everybody thought you were doing police work. The captain would walk through, and he wouldn't interfere with you. He thought you were too busy to talk.

The first game, the Giants won. The second game was played in L.A. The Dodgers won that game, 8–7. Then the

· · · · ·

third game, the Dodgers got a lead of 4–2 in the ninth inning. The Giants scored four runs in the top of the ninth. That was wild. You're hollering; you're jumping around. And we had a couple of Mexican janitors in, and they were fans of Orlando Cepeda and Juan Marichal. They were jumping around with us. So we missed a few calls, maybe. But it was all worth it.

Game seven of the World Series that year, I was working. The Yankees scored a run on a double play, sometime in the middle of the game. In the ninth, the score now is 1–0. Matty Alou is at third and Willie Mays is at second. Now you've got Willie McCovey coming up. The first ball McCovey hit was a real shot, but it went foul. The next one, you could hear the shot it was, but it went right into Bobby Richardson's glove. There was a cartoon that came out by Charlie Schulz, the guy who does *Peanuts,* that about says it all. He's sitting on the curb with his buddy. He doesn't say anything for a while. Then he jumps up and says, "Why couldn't McCovey's drive have been two feet higher?"

THE DAY MOTHER BOOED

C. ALLYN RUSSELL, SEVENTY-TWO,

IS PROFESSOR EMERITUS OF RELIGION

AT BOSTON UNIVERSITY. HE LIVES

IN CONCORD, MASSACHUSETTS.

My greatest baseball thrill was Ted Williams hitting a home run in his last time ever at bat, on September 28, 1960. I knew it was his last game. It was talked up in the papers. This was one game I wanted to go to.

We were living in Rhode Island. It was a rainy day, a soggy day, a cold day, a weekday afternoon. The crowd was different. An overcoated crowd. He hit a towering home run against Jack Fisher. I never heard a crowd of ten thousand people make such a noise. When I got home that night, my wife asked me what I had done when Ted Williams hit his home run. I said, "Betty, I was jumping up and down and yelling and throwing my raincoat in the air." She asked me if I felt silly doing that. I said, "Not at all, because 10,453 people were doing the same thing."

· · · · ·

I grew up in upstate New York in the area of the Catskill Mountains. I sat by the hour watching the Delhi Aggies and the Oneonta Merchants. I also listened by radio to major league games from such distant places as New York City and Chicago and Philadelphia. It was probably a Philco. I had it in my room, and I'd press my ear against it. I read box scores and remembered batting averages and pitchers' records. In my younger days, baseball was the major sport in upstate New York. It did not have competition as it does today from soccer, hockey, from basketball, and even professional football.

The centerpiece of baseball, of course, was the World Series. Scores were posted half-inning by half-inning in store windows. As you walked down the street, you could pick up half-inning scores along the way. Bill Hallahan of the St. Louis Cardinals, Wild Bill Hallahan, was born in Binghamton, New York, just sixty-two miles away. The *Binghamton Press* newspaper came through Oneonta with its evening edition, and we became very much fans of Bill Hallahan. One year, probably 1931, my father took me down to Binghamton during World Series time, and we watched from a park across the street a huge electronic scoreboard which had been placed on the side of a business building. They had a little white baseball that went from home plate to first base to second base to third base, back to home. It was a telegraph report coming in from where the World Series was being played. There were thousands watching from across the street. When Hallahan snuffed out a rally in the ninth inning of the seventh game to win for the Cardinals, the crowd in Binghamton went wild.

✦

I played high school baseball my sophomore year. I was injured the beginning of my junior year. That put an end to my baseball career. We played sandlot games. We played in a little alleyway between my father's store and the next building. First base was usually a mark on the wall, second base was a pillow we'd put in the middle of the alley. Third base was a mark on the wall of my father's store. When my parents were working, I went down to the end of the street and watched the Delhi Aggies play by the hour. My parents both worked in the store. They were comfortable; they knew where I was – on a side bank watching the Delhi Aggies play.

My first big league game was in 1933, when my dad and I traveled to New York City to watch the Philadelphia Phillies and the old New York Giants at the Polo Grounds. The score that day was 2–0. Both runs were home runs by the Phillies first baseman, big Don Hurst. Carl Hubbell was pitching for the Giants. I remember Carl Hubbell, skinny, thin, looking tall. Since that day, I've attended major league games in twenty-three different stadia in some twenty different cities. I also have memories of fifteen to twenty minor league parks.

I went to the World Series in 1936. I went with a city judge and his son from Oneonta. It was a subway series between the Yankees and the Giants. I was impressed by the number of dignitaries there. Gentleman Jim Farley, the postmaster of his day. And ex-president Herbert Hoover was there. When he left after about the seventh or eight inning, most of the seventy thousand people there booed. I was close enough to see him flush a crimson red.

Before the start of the game, a fight broke out at one end of the Yankee dugout. The ushers and police rushed over to take control. With all the brashness of a wide-eyed sixteen-year-old, I rushed to the other end of the dugout, unlatched the low gate to the field, and walked onto the hallowed field at Yankee Stadium.

I had my box camera with me and a little autograph book. I joined the media taking interviews of the players before the game. I took several photographs. The one I cherish the most is of a young rookie just completing his first year. His name was Joe DiMaggio. Others were Bill Dickey, Monte Pearson, Frankie Crosetti. Someone took a photograph of Tony Lazzeri and myself, and the next day that picture appeared in the *New York Daily Mirror*. My parents purchased all available copies in Oneonta.

July 26, 1937, in Gloversville, New York, was the day the Pittsburgh Pirates played an exhibition game with their farm team. I hitchhiked there that day. When the players disembarked from the bus in civilian clothes, I walked boldly into the middle of their group and proceeded with them into the clubhouse and eventually their dugout. No one flagged me down.

The Yankees played an exhibition game against the Binghamton Triplets on May 27, 1938. Cutting my classes at Oneonta High School, I managed to get into the Yankee dugout and onto the field before the game. I took photographs of Lou Gehrig, Joe DiMaggio, Joe Gordon, Bump Hadley, Red Ruffing, and Babe Dahlgren. Gehrig was the big attraction. I remember sitting in the dugout next to him. I did not carry on a conversation. The Yankees were a lively group. Lou Gehrig had just made a film, a cops-and-robbers film, and they were teasing him about it. They were imitating cops-and-robbers scenes, giving him the needle. The game was halted after seven innings when fans rushed onto the field and encircled Lou Gehrig and Joe DiMaggio. I was not among them. I had my fun before the game.

June 12, 1939, was the first Hall of Fame game at Cooperstown, New York, the dedication of the Hall of Fame and Museum, nineteen miles from my hometown. I saw up close the first class of living inductees to the hall. This was the first time they met as a group. That afternoon I was on the field at the end of the dugout with the all-stars on the third-base side. I saw Rogers Hornsby motion to his pitcher to groove one to

· · · · ·

Babe Ruth so the Babe could hit one last long ball. The out-of-shape, overweight Babe took a mighty swing and popped up in foul territory. It was the only time in history he visited Cooperstown.

I have two other memories of the Babe. My mother was a baseball widow, as you can imagine. My father and I decided we would go to New York City for a doubleheader between the Tigers and the Yankees. Mother wanted to go and see Babe Ruth hit a home run. Mother did not usually go to games with us. She waited outside or stayed home. She wasn't as interested in baseball as we were. Best as I can remember, the Babe played the doubleheader and came to bat eight times. The Tigers walked him eight times; seventy thousand fans booed the Tigers, and none booed more vociferously than my mother. Never saw my mother boo before.

The other story about Babe Ruth took place at Hawkins Stadium in Albany. An overflow crowd was permitted on the field, just outside the foul line. A foul ball went into the crowd down the right-field foul line. This big kid took the ball away from a little kid. The stands were high enough so that this could be viewed from the grandstand. Babe Ruth heard the response and looked over into the crowd and saw what was going on. He tore into the crowd, knocked down the bully, picked up the ball, lifted the kid up in the crook of his left arm so everyone could see, took the ball in his right hand, drew the two together, and nine thousand people roared.

In the mid-1940s, my first seven dates with the person who would become my lifetime partner were at old Shibe Park in Philadelphia. We were both students in the Eastern Baptist Theological Seminary in Philadelphia at the time, she in the music department, I in the theological division. I liked her in part because she learned quickly and accurately to keep the scorecard. I felt comfortable at the park. I felt comfortable with her. It was a good place to be.

· · · · ·

In the 1970s a painful and poignant memory is of the one-game play-off between the Red Sox and Yankees. I had a single, scalped box seat down the right-field line near the foul pole. I was at BU then. I will hastily add, I have never cut a class to attend a baseball game. I may have cut fifteen minutes early one seminar one afternoon, but I never cut a class.

October 25, 1986. I watched on television. Twice the Red Sox were one strike away from winning the World Championship. I had a committee meeting at the university the next day. I was surprised how many of my colleagues in the academic world said they did not sleep very well the night before. Utterly incredible. I was riding in the elevator this last week at Emerson Hospital. We were speaking about Reggie Lewis with a cardiologist. I said, "Basketball season is winding down. It's regretful about Reggie Lewis. I guess we'll have to turn our attention to the Red Sox now." He said, "Not after eighty-six. I had all the bottles opened."

This season I shall be standing for my share of games behind section thirteen at Fenway Park, hoping for the World Championship. The Red Sox had better win it soon, for if time is not running out for them, it's running out for me. If I don't live to see a World Championship banner flying over Boston, I won't feel cheated. The national pastime has provided me and many others with a dugout full of memories, and a stadium full of hope.

IN CHICAGO, IT WAS THE CUBS

BERNIE ROSENBERG, SEVENTY-THREE,

IS A RETIRED CANDY SALESMAN LIVING IN

WOODRIDGE, ILLINOIS.

I played second base. Hornsby was my idol. My first baseball glove was a Rogers Hornsby model. Everybody in my neighborhood called me Hornsby.

Later on in life, I was working. A friend of mine had a big manufacturing plant. I happened to be near there and I thought, "I'll stop. Maybe we can have lunch together." So I come in and I said, "Is Byron in?" She said, "Who's calling? Is this business or personal?" I said, "It's personal." She said, "What's your name?" I said, "Bernard Rosenberg." I see her on the phone, I see her shaking her head. She's looking at me funny. She said, "Well, wait a minute. He'll be out in a minute." He walks up and says, "Hornsby! How the hell do I know who Bernard Rosenberg is?"

. . . . .

I originally grew up on the west side of Chicago. It was an Irish Catholic area. There were a handful of Jewish families. I played on three baseball teams. There was an empty lot near us, which was full of cans, glass, and everything else. One of the kids in our neighborhood said to us one day, "My uncle's a scout for the St. Louis Cardinals. And he wants to see us play. He may be able to push us up into the majors. But we got to clean the lot up." Well, we get about twenty kids, and we clean that place up so it's spic-and-span. We lay out a diamond. It shows how naive we were. It was just the owner of the lot wanted us to clean it up.

My father took me to my first ball game in 1928 to see the Cubs. He took us to the game, we fell in love with baseball, been a Cub fan ever since. My father and I would go see the Cubs or White Sox every Saturday. And on Sunday there was a semipro team called the Mills.

This was at 42nd and Kilpatrick. I saw some of the great Negro players, because the Chicago American Giants played there. I saw Rube Foster pitch. My father thought he was the greatest pitcher that ever lived. I was there another time. There was a railroad that ran in back of Mills Stadium. A train was coming by when Josh Gibson was batting. He hit one over the left-field wall. The ball fell into the train, into a hopper, and it's an old joke – what's the longest home run? We'd say six hundred miles and they'd look and say, "What do you mean?" We'd say, "Well, Gibson hit the ball into the train, and the train didn't stop for six hundred miles."

My father played semipro ball for the Bantam Shirt Company. He played against Buck Leonard. They became good friends. You know where the Union depot is in Chicago? Before that was built, that was an empty lot. On Sunday they used to play baseball there. The fans would stand up above on the bridges on the streets. And after the game, of course, they would pass the hat. They became good friends. When my son, Nat, and I went to the Hall of Fame, when Buck Leonard went in, I met him and we talked together for about an hour. He told me my father was a good ballplayer.

I went to Senn High School, which was farther north from the Cub ballpark, and we would take the Clark Street streetcar home. And as we came past Wrigley Field, we would see the scoreboard. They would let you in free after the seventh inning. So we'd look up at the scoreboard, and if the score was close, we'd jump off the streetcar, run into Wrigley Field hoping we'd get an extra-inning game.

The 1929 World Series, my mother let me stay home from school to listen to it on the radio. That was the day Ehmke pitched and struck out the thirteen Cubs. Of course, we were heartbroken. We thought we were going to kill them. We couldn't believe it. We were crying. We were winners all the time. We never could believe the Cubs could do anything wrong.

This is hard to believe, but I used to go to a baseball book on Saturday and bet on the Cubs. You could bet on anybody. Also, you could take three ballplayers and if they got six hits, you would win. That was the bet. The betting in the bleachers at Wrigley Field was rampant, too. This is in the '30s. They were betting on every pitch. "A dime he goes. A dime he doesn't. A dime he strikes out. A quarter he doesn't." There was a bookie sitting about two rows down in front of us. There was a guy sitting about eight rows in back of us. The guy yells, "What's it on a home run?" The bookie yelled "Twenty-five to one." The guy says, "I'll take it for ten." The bookie turned around and said, "Send it down." When he turns around, the guy hits a homer. The ball's coming right at him. I think the bookie turned white.

In every city where there's two teams, there's always one that drew well and one that didn't. In Boston it was the Red Sox. The Braves didn't do much. In Philadelphia it was the

Phillies. The Athletics didn't do much. In Chicago it was the Cubs. The White Sox never really did much. In the neighborhood I grew up in, I remember two of my friends were big Sox fans; everybody else was a Cub fan. We used to have the biggest arguments on the merits of Appling of the Sox and Jurges of the Cubs.

We went to see Joe DiMaggio. I think he was the most graceful ballplayer I'd ever seen. I don't know if you know the old Sox ballpark, but it ran about 450 feet to center field. A ball was hit to deep center. DiMaggio put his back to the batter and started to go. He'd turn around, there was the ball, and he caught it. He was so wonderful.

I met a lot of players as I got older. A lot of them lived in my neighborhood because I didn't live far from the ballpark. My father and I would walk over to Grace and Broadway to get the papers on Sunday morning. In those days all the drugstores had lunch counters. There would be Wilson, Flint Rhem, all these guys sobering up from the night before.

I was shooting craps behind the signboards one night at the Marine Drive and Irving Park, not far from the Cub ballpark. There are a lot of high-rises there, and a guy stuck his head out and said, "Hey, you kids. Knock off the noise." We said, 'Yeah? Come on down here and make us." So the guy comes down and it's Billy Herman. He was second baseman for the Cubs. He gets into the game with us and we all became friends.

These are just little things. Frank Demaree had come over from the Giants, was playing right field for the Cubs. He was living in the Shoreham Hotel, which was our hangout. And every morning we'd go over there, during the summer when we weren't in school, and his wife – who was a beautiful lady – would come down and she'd say, "Who wants to go to the ball game?" And we'd say, "We do." So she would take us to the ball game.

. . . . .

This is something that I don't think will ever happen again. We used to play at Waveland, which was a baseball field. On Saturday mornings – this would be in the '30s – a lot of the Cub ballplayers, Augie Galan, Stan Hack, Tuck Stainback, would come over and show us how to play. Honestly. And I can't imagine anything like that happening today.

We talked about sports every night at dinner. My mother, my father, my sister, and I. All the games were played in the daytime. My dad would come home from work with the final paper. Hence we had all the box scores and we would go through them. We ate it, we talked it, we lived it. We bought gloves and we'd play catch every day. As I got a little older, he started to pitch to me. Out on the sidewalk. Out on the street. There were no cars. On the street I lived on, only two men owned cars.

I mean, it's like a storybook. My father took me to the games. I have a daughter besides Nat. I took them to the games. They're dyed-in-the-wool Cubs fans. Nat and I have always been extremely close. We went to Sears and we bought two Ted Williams model gloves. We each had one. We played catch. He said, "Throw me a curve, Dad." I couldn't throw a curve. He said, "Gee, that's a great curve, Dad."

We joke around a lot about it. I'm seventy-three. I say, "Boy, if I can live long enough to see the Cubs win a World Series, I'm going to live to be well over a hundred." We want it so badly we can taste it. Every year we say this is it. We're going to be led to the promised land. And it doesn't happen. We want it badly.

If the Cubs ever moved out of Wrigley Field, I think we'd die. For one thing, it's a perfect field. It's 335 down the line, it's 400 to deep center. It's the most wonderful place in the world to go a ball game. It's part of us. We grew up with it. We hope it will always be there.

I still go. I go to about twenty games a year. See the White

. . . . .

Sox play five or six times. If you really want to get down to philosophies of life, I think everybody has to have something to live for. You're a young man, you have a family, you're probably very busy. It takes up your time and your thoughts. As you get older, your children grow up, they go out on their own. You still have to have something to fall back on. When my wife was ill and we were going through some bad times, I sometimes think if it wasn't for baseball, I would have gone out of my mind. Anytime we could go, we would go. For a while I was able to take her. Then it got worse, and I would get a sitter and Nat and I would go to a game. For the three or four hours I was away, it was like I was back in my youth. Back in a different world, without worries.

OPENING DAY FOR CHRISTMAS

BOB LITTLEJOHN, SEVENTY-TWO,

IS A RETIRED ACCOUNTANT LIVING IN

CINCINNATI.

My dad would hit fly balls to me in the yard. Sometime after supper, in the evenings. We would just toss in the driveway. Between Dad and me, we had two or three gloves. The first glove was a Jake Daubert model first baseman's mitt. He played with the Reds in 1919 when they won the World Series. His name was stamped on the glove. That was a dandy. Dad picked up, somewhere, a fielder's glove signed by Lew Fonseca. I think he won the batting championship with the White Sox one year. Then we had a catcher's glove. Still got them in the basement.

· · · · ·

Opening Day here in town was always something special. The first opening game I saw was in 1932. Somebody gave my dad a couple of seats. We ended up sitting on the cold steel chairs. I can remember how chilly it was. Dad picked me up at school at noontime and it was a driving snow coming down, and I can remember in the afternoon editions of the papers, they both had a picture of Crosley Field – it was

Redland Field then – and they showed the snow coming down. But they got the game in. I can remember they were playing with the Cubs, and I looked out there, they had a whole bag of balls, and one of the Cub players was throwing the balls out to the bleachers.

If everyone who was excused from school went to Opening Day, there'd have been about fifty thousand people there. You'd get on the bus going to school, all the girls were writing excuses to go to opening game for all the kids. The school got wise to them, so they sent postcards out. So the kids had to hurry home to waylay the postcard. Then they found out that was being abused, so they started school at 7:30 on Opening Day so everybody got out at one o'clock. It was always a festive time. Everybody was excited to see the season get started. There were all kinds of parties around town.

In 1936 I went all by myself. I was in the eighth grade. I got the ticket for Christmas. I couldn't wait for Opening Day. This one little biddy eighth-grade teacher, she couldn't wait to get ahold of my mother. "Did you know he went to the ball game on Opening Day?" I went to school in the morning and then hopped on the streetcar and went to the ball game. My mother said, "Is that so? That was his Christmas present."

In 1934 Larry MacPhail came in here, and they started the Knothole Club. I was in sixth grade, I guess, and everybody in school got a Knothole card and you got to see the games 100 percent free. We were getting the equivalent of eight-and-a-half-dollar seats now. It got to the point where you could go any days except Ladies' Days, night games, which were seven games a year at that point, and Sundays. So we could go down as many as four or five times a week.

We'd get a streetcar and go down by ourselves, show our card, and go in, and we felt we were late if we didn't get there an hour before game time to watch everything that was going on. Then after the game was over, we'd get out autograph

· · · · ·

books and wait for the players to change clothes. They didn't have these buses that were inside the park. Players would come out the gate to get taxicabs, and you had plenty of opportunity to get autographs. I got all kinds of autographs and never paid a dime for them.

The Reds had a clubhouse over the main entrance. They were up on the third floor of this building. They had to walk all the way up the steps. So one time I was standing down below, standing all by myself, I'm looking up the window, I see some commotion, and here's Babe Herman leaning out the window. He dropped the ball down at my feet. All I had to do was pick it up. It wasn't a brand-new ball. It was kind of scuffed up, so I just used that to play with.

I saw the first night game. Sat in the bleachers. It wasn't a sellout. This was in '35. We got in there and the lights weren't on. President Roosevelt in Washington was supposed to press the switch and turn the lights on. They made a big to-do about that. Not anyone doubted that he was really turning the lights on. The Reds won, 2–1. I had to be in on it. It was history. At that time, the night games didn't start until 8:30. But they didn't last more than two hours. You could set your watch by it.

When I got to high school, in the paper they said they were putting on ushers at the park. I ushered down there during some of the best years for the Reds. I started ushering there in '37 and ushered through '38, '39, and '40.

Thirty-eight was the year Vandy pitched his two no-hitters, and I saw the first one. Thirty-eight was a tremendous year. The next year they came back and won the pennant. They clinched the pennant on the 26th of September, beating the Cardinals, who were in second place. That was a tremendous game. That was one of the best games I've ever seen, because everything went on in that game. Derringer was pitching, and I think later on he said he didn't have his best stuff. They beat the Cardinals 8–6, or something like that. One of the Cardinals doubled, and Ernie Lombardi picked him off second base. The Cardinals were a fast running team. Somebody hits a line ball out to Ival Goodman in right field and got a double. He goes to try to stretch it to a triple, and Goodman threw him out.

The following year was the only time in Reds history when they won the last game of the World Series at home. Derringer won that game, 2–1, beating Buck Newsom. The Reds came from behind. It was 1–0, and they came from behind with two doubles and an outfield fly. The whole town celebrated that. That was tremendous. Our whole family was there. My folks, they were tickled to death to get seats in the bleachers.

I was working the game. We met after the game and we went out to eat. I said to Dad, "Let's all go downtown." He said, "Oh, there won't be that much going on downtown." But everybody went downtown. They rerouted all the buses and streetcars away from the heart of town, what they call Fountain Square. There was no violence. Just celebration. Everybody was just milling around. The club had a celebration at the Netherland Plaza, the biggest hotel in town. I ran with some other fellow, to see what we could see. We were inside the hotel, but they closed the hotel unless you had good reason to be in there. It wasn't open to the public anymore because there were so many people in there. It went on and on, well past midnight.

I've seen all the home World Series games in Cincinnati except 1919, and that's before my time. I've seen fifty-eight opening games. All of them from 1936 to date, with the exception of two years I was overseas in the service. I've got tickets for the next Opening Day already. I've got tickets upstairs.

. . . . .

I WAS ROOTING FOR THE BROWNS

ERWIN FISCHER, SIXTY-NINE,
IS A RETIRED INSURANCE EXECUTIVE
LIVING IN ST. LOUIS.

Ballplayers were different at that time. I wrote a letter to Billy Southworth, who was the manager of the Cardinals, and told him we were a communication unit with the navy attached with the marines and we called ourself the Cardinal outfit, and would there be any chance he could send up some Cardinal caps? Much to my surprise one day, there came a package. A bunch of Cardinal caps for us. We wore them everywhere. When we went to Japan, one day we were asked to go over to a big ship that was out in the harbor. We went over wearing our Cardinal caps. We were loading the stuff from the ship and somebody yelled, "Attention!" One of the brass wanted to know who the hell we were, dressed the way we were. We wore those caps all the time.

· · · · ·

I grew up in South St. Louis. Predominantly German and Dutch. All the kids were baseball fans. We all played baseball. Corkball was a great thing. Corkball was a little bitty ball, about one-sixth the size of a baseball. You used a very thin stick or bat. You'd have just a pitcher and a catcher. You'd have one strike – if you missed and the catcher caught it, you were out. We were famous for that. We had these corkball things at various taverns. It was a cage and you'd play and you'd drink beer. I remember when I went into the service, most of the people didn't know about it. But usually guys from this area, we'd have some corkballs and we'd get a broomstick and play. I remember playing corkball at Pearl Harbor. We played corkball when we were in the occupation forces in Kagoshima, Japan.

My dad first started taking me out to the ball games in 1933. In 1934 I was able to join the Knothole Gang. You got a free pass to go to the ball games and you got to sit out in the left-field bleachers. The Browns also had a Boys Brigade and Girls Brigade.

We'd go three, four, or five times a week. All the games started at three o'clock. Even while school was in session, we'd get down there around the second or third inning. With the Cardinals, it was great. We were down the left-field line all the time with Joe Medwick. Of course, Joe Medwick was a popular player. They called him "Ducky-Wucky." He would interact with the kids. During batting practice, they'd throw balls to us.

In '34 was the Gashouse Gang, and they were just a bunch of characters. That was Dizzy and Paul Dean. Dizzy won thirty games and Paul won nineteen. They were a ball club that would scrap and fight, get their uniforms dirty. Pepper Martin would race little midget auto racing cars during the season. The thing was their spirit and their dirty uniforms. Just the way they played.

· · · · ·

I'd got a Christmas present of a little radio. That was my whole Christmas present. During the season, most of the time, the games at home would be broadcast. The games on the road would be re-created by ticker. I'd listen all the time. I'd get home from school and turn on the radio. I became a great Cardinal and Browns fan. It was unusual in that you were usually either a Browns fan or a Cardinal fan. I just got hooked on baseball. One of the reasons I wanted to see the Browns was to get to see the other ballplayers. I loved to see Joe DiMaggio and those kind of players. I'd occupy my summers going to the ball games every day. I'd stay out of trouble. For twenty cents a day, you couldn't beat that.

The thing that was most exciting was, when the ball game was over, we'd stand out on Dodier and Spring, which was where the ballplayers came out, and we'd wait and get autographs. The ballplayers would park their cars across the street, which were actually private residences. They'd use their yards. I remember walking across the street and following Dizzy Dean to get his autograph. Walking halfway down the block with Enos Slaughter to get his autograph. They were all part of the city. Most of them were around all the time. There was a closeness.

In September 1941 the Cardinals brought up Stan Musial. I got to see Stan Musial play his first game here in St. Louis. It was against the Boston Braves and pitcher Johnny Tobin. It was a Sunday doubleheader and I was sitting in the bleachers. In the second game, he played right field. The thing that was so surprising to everybody was his unique batting stance. That corkscrew? We had never seen that before.

In '42 it was one of the greatest pennant races of all time, between the Dodgers and the Cardinals. The thing I remember is they brought up Stan Musial, Whitey Kurowski, and Johnny Beazley. Almost the entire ball club was from the Cardinal organization. Branch Rickey had built a great farm system. I think they won forty-three out of their last fifty-one games to clinch the pennant. I remember the way they had taken hold of the crowd. They were known as the St. Louis Swifties. They would run the bases. Not so much stealing, but they would go from first to third on a single. Big Mort Cooper was one of the pitchers. He normally wore uniform number thirteen. What he did that year was every time he'd win a game, he'd switch numbers.

Three of my buddies and I, we wanted to go to the World Series. We went over the night before, I guess about four o'clock in the afternoon. You had to establish your place in line. There was a YMCA across the street from Sportsman's Park. You wouldn't do this unless you were a kid: We got a room and at about nine o'clock, two of us went over and slept. About midnight, one went over and got those two and came back. We switched back and forth like that until it was time to let us into the ballpark. I think the greatest thing about that was the camaraderie. There was a guy who attended all the World Series. He was usually number one. He slept in one of these refrigerator crates. I remember he was there. I think we were ninth, tenth, eleventh, and twelfth in line. By the next morning, that line wrapped all the way around the ballpark. Much to the surprise of everybody, they opened the gates at nine o'clock. The game didn't start until one o'clock. So we sat there.

In the first game, the Cardinals – no one gave them much chance against the Yankees – were losing by something like 7–0. They didn't even have a hit until the eighth inning. Anyhow, they did rally for four runs in the bottom of the ninth. One of the unusual things was Musial batted twice in that inning and made two outs.

Anyhow, after the Cardinals had lost, we decided, heck, we wanted to see the second game. We called home and my mother said, "What about school?" I said we'd just tell the

. . . . .

teacher we were going to see the second game. We went back and we rented the room at the YMCA. We showered and ate and stood in line again for the second game, with much happier results. Beazley beat the Yankees. And the Cardinals went on to New York and won three straight. I'll never forget the last game. We got out of high school and we walked across the street to a drugstore. Everybody had the radio on. We got there in time to hear Whitey Kurowski hit a two-run homer. And then they won the ball game. We were tickled to death. I think we all ordered a Coke or something.

The Cardinals played in a World Series in '43 and '44, and I was in the service. We were over in the South Pacific listening to the Armed Forces Radio, three or four o'clock in the morning, listening to the World Series. In 1944 the Cardinals played the Browns. You're a Cardinal and Browns fans, and for the one time in your life that there's a World Series in St. Louis, you didn't get to see it. I was rooting for the Browns. I think all of St. Louis was. Sentimentally, you've got to remember, the Browns never won anything.

I was discharged in late April '46, and as a coming-home present, my folks gave me season tickets to the Cardinal games. It was a great thing for me. I got tickets to the very first play-off game. The Cardinals and Dodgers finished in a tie. Howie Pollet beat the Dodgers. Then there was the World Series with the Boston Red Sox. Everybody was looking forward to the World series with Stan Musial and Ted Williams. And neither one did anything.

Thank God I was there for the seventh game, when I saw Slaughter's mad dash for home. Slaughter was on first base. I was sitting between home and first base. Harry Walker hit a ball out between right and right center field. I remember Slaughter rounding second and going to third. I was watching the retrieve of the ball. The next thing I know, I saw the ball come in to Pesky. Pesky had his back turned to the infield. I saw Slaughter heading home and sliding. I remember the third-base coach, Mike Gonzalez, was trying to hold him up.

I was a Browns fan right up until they left. I was there August 19, 1951, when the midget batted. It was a double-header against the Detroit Tigers. In between games, they brought out a big wagon with one of these papier-mâché birthday cakes. Everyone expected a beautiful young gal to jump out of that cake. And this little midget jumped out of the cake and he ran into the dugout. They had some more entertainment. They had Satchel Paige and a couple of guys play a string ensemble, or something like that. The second game started and you didn't think nothing of it. When the bottom of the first inning came up, we saw this little midget coming out of the dugout swinging a couple of bats. The next thing we saw was the umpire go over and talk to Zack Taylor, the manager. We didn't know what the hell was going on. We were astonished. He wore uniform number one-eighth. The pitcher, Bob Cain, was befuddled. He threw four pitches, and they weren't even close. That little midget – I can still see it – as Delsing came to first base, he patted Delsing on the behind and he ran into the dugout. The fans just buzzed. They just couldn't believe it.

The last game at Sportsman's Park was in May 1966. I'm very nostalgic. They brought a helicopter in, and they picked up home plate and flew it out to take over to the new stadium. We were playing the San Francisco Giants. I remember Willie Mays hit the last home run in Sportsman's Park. Now that neighborhood is totally decimated. It's in the heart of the city. I think that's one of the things, too, that everybody became a little concerned about the last couple of years at old Sportsman's Park. The neighborhood, I put it as bad as when the Kansas City A's first moved to Kansas City at the corner of 22nd and Brooklyn. You took your life in your hands when you walked those two or three blocks to the ballpark. I was

· · · · ·

there for the last game there and the first game at Busch Stadium. Busch Stadium is a beautiful ballpark and they keep it up. It's with the times.

Up until a few years ago, I used to play. We'd get a bunch of guys together and buy a couple of cases of beer and play corkball. It was still fun. I still run into one or two of the guys I waited with overnight for World Series tickets. We still talk about it. And our wives still say that we were crazy.

THERE WERE
BALLPLAYERS EVERYWHERE

WILLIAM KOLB, SEVENTY,

IS A RETIRED STEEL RULE DIE WORKER IN

SANTA CLARA, CALIFORNIA.

We followed Cincinnati because that's only ninety-five miles from Louisville. The only games I ever saw when I was growing up was twice one of my uncles went to Cincinnati and I got to go along to see the Reds play. I had to ride in the rumble seat of my uncle's car. It was pretty windy, but it didn't make any difference. We got to go, that was good enough.

Crosley Field had a section in right field that went uphill. They called it the porch or something. It was quite unique, I thought. I think everybody else who ever saw Crosley Field thought that, too. It kind of took my breath away, I guess. Just the fact that the grass was so green. It looked so much bigger than Parkway Field. The fact that it was big league baseball. Cincinnati was going to play the Chicago Cubs. Wow. I'm not quite sure how to explain it, but it's a thrill, the kind you get only once or twice in your whole life.

· · · · ·

I had visions like everybody else. "One of these days, I'll play in the big leagues. I'll play pro ball." I harbored those dreams for a number of years and kept thinking it would happen, but it never did. I played semipro ball and I crossed paths with a considerable number of major league ballplayers, pretty good ballplayers, but I was always on the fringe of it all.

I grew up in Louisville, Kentucky. We lived on the edge of town, not really country, but there were vacant lots. A few people kept cows in the pasture, and a few people gardened in some of the vacant lots. We as kids would find somebody that would let us, and we'd clear one or a couple of them and build our own baseball diamond. So we'd play and we'd play. We'd just pick up the kids in the neighborhood. If we had enough to have a game, we'd challenge other districts or neighborhoods.

If we didn't have enough, we played a game called peggie. There was the pitcher and the catcher and the outfielders, and you got to keep batting until somebody caught a fly ball. You caught a fly, you got to go in and bat and give the batter your glove. During the Depression I didn't have a glove, so if I caught it, they'd hate it, because they didn't get a glove. Actually, most of us didn't have gloves. We played with our bare hands. We made do. Eventually I got a glove. A friend of ours next door who was quite a bit older got a new glove, and he gave me his old one. I was nine or ten. It was made by Rawlings. I know that it was torn and pretty flimsy, but I played with it for years.

Louisville at the time was a hotbed of semipro ball and church leagues, amateur baseball of all types. A couple of the outlying towns, St. Helen's, Shively, had town teams. There were a number of parks, but one particular park, Shawnee Park – all the parks in the area were named after Indian tribes – had, I think, nineteen baseball fields. They were kind of in a square, so the outfields were all interchangeable. If somebody hit a ball really good, why, it would often run into

· · · · ·
There Were Ballplayers Everywhere   85

the other outfield and they'd have to hold up play. Many times in the summer, on the weekends especially, all of the fields would be in action at the same time. There were ballplayers everywhere.

It was kind of far from our house. When I was younger, I had to rely on one of my uncles, my dad, or somebody to get to the games. Then I became a batboy for National Distillers semipro team. I'd go over to the offices of National Distillers and somebody there'd give me a ride. I'd take care of the bats, the balls, catcher's equipment, chase down balls. I enjoyed it a lot. I got to meet and play catch with some of the ballplayers. Very often they were people hoping to go up to pro ball or had played and were on their way down. I can remember one pitcher who pitched for the Louisville Colonels, Al Lecompte. He pitched a doubleheader one day, a no-hitter in the first game and a one-hitter in the second game for National Distillers against Kentucky Dairies. What an arm. They were my heroes. There were the Cunningham brothers, Orville and Wes. Wes was a pitcher; Orville was a shortstop. Of course, Pee Wee Reese was playing in '35 and '36. He played for the New Covenant Presbyterian Church in a church league and for one of these Industrial League teams. Then he went to the Colonels.

All the schools in the area were given passes to the Knothole Gang at Parkway Field, where the Colonels played. If you signed up to belong to the Knothole Gang, you got a little pin that said you were a member, and you could get into the Colonels games for a dime. We all had to sit out in the right field, as far out as they could put us. But we got in for a dime. That was a big thing. Every Saturday home game was a Knothole game. If they were home on a Saturday, why, most everybody in our neighborhood would go to a game. If they could scrape up a dime.

We'd walk. It was quite a ways. Parkway Field was at least

three-and-a-half or four miles from our house. It was an old-fashioned ballpark. I'm sure it didn't hold more than ten thousand. I can remember seeing a couple of guys hit home runs over the left field wall – that's how we got baseballs sometimes. Instead of going to the game, we'd stay out and hope somebody would hit a home run and we could chase down the ball. After watching some of the semipro teams and some of the sandlot games, these future major leaguers, these pro ballplayers, were really something.

✦

Teams from the Negro Leagues would play at Parkway Field. There wasn't a team in Louisville, but they came through on their barnstorming trips. They'd play against some of the major league teams during exhibition season. I went once. It was the Homestead Grays and the New York Yankees. This was in 1936. A couple of times, probably when I was about thirteen, we played a team from Colored Town. We didn't call it that. We used the regular euphemism that came from the South.

They had a team, and they were six blocks away from us in the colored district. We challenged them, and they came over and played on our diamond. They beat us. So we went back and played on a field that they had. We beat them. We derided the colored people. I had a complete change of heart later on. But as kids we challenged them, or they challenged us, and we said, "Oh, come on. We can beat you, no problem." They came to our field and beat us, we went to their field and beat them, so we felt we better not push it anymore. It surprised me that they could play.

After Jackie Robinson first came up, I went home for a visit. I went to watch the Colonels play. They were playing St. Paul. St. Paul had Roy Campanella catching for them. Campanella was about to go up the next year. Robinson had already broken the color line. I can remember a lot of people in the stands yelling at Campanella. "Get that ink spot out of here." They were still being derisive. They didn't want him in there. I can't think that I was necessarily thrilled about Robinson going up, but it didn't bother me. I can remember thinking when I was watching that game against the Colonels and St. Paul, "Hey man, this guy can catch. He can play." I looked at it as "What can you do?" And he could do it. I'm not necessarily typical of all the guys in the neighborhood, because a lot of them never changed their attitude. For some reason, I did.

◆

I followed the Reds and at that time they were my favorite team. After Pee Wee Reese went up to Brooklyn, everybody in the neighborhood all followed Brooklyn. Brooklyn became our favorite team. We looked in the sports pages or followed by word of mouth: "Pee Wee did this; Pee Wee got four hits," or "He didn't do anything yesterday." In '41 I had gone into the navy. I was seventeen and starry-eyed. For the '41 World Series, I was in boot camp, in Great Lakes. When Brooklyn had it all wrapped up and dropped that third strike, we just about died. I was out on the drill field. I got reports about it later. There were a couple of guys from Kentucky that'd gone into the navy the same time I did and we were in boot camp together. All of us were rooting for Brooklyn and were dyed-in-the-wool Brooklyn fans.

After the war broke out, the following spring they sent us overseas. I went to Pearl Harbor, the Ford Island Naval Air Station. It was still a mess. The *California*, the *Pennsylvania*, the *Oklahoma*, the *West Virginia*, and the *Arizona* and the *Utah* were all still sunk. They were working on raising the others. We just went to work there. There were softball games; there were baseball games. I went out for the team and

I made the team. I was third-string third baseman. This was Ford Island Naval Air Station team. We played against the army from Hickam Field; we played different teams. The Aiea naval barracks had their sub base, Kaneohe naval station, Barbers Point navy station – they all had baseball teams. We had three major leaguers on our team. Everybody started getting a few of them. A pitcher from the Washington Senators, Tom Ferrick, pitched for us. Joe Grace, who had been with the St. Louis Browns, was kind of our manager/center fielder. They kept me on, but I was really just there to fill in for practice games. As long as it got me out of a little bit of work, it didn't bother me. We got to rub shoulders with these guys. I can remember Joe Grace was always telling Tom Ferrick that he could throw a better knuckleball than Tom could. He'd throw that thing and I'd try to catch it and, boy, it was a humdinger.

In the army and navy and marines, when they went to some of the islands, they'd get a game. In my particular case, there was always an athletic department. There was no lack of baseball. I had my own glove that I kept with me and a couple of balls to play catch with. Most of my time was spent in Hawaii. I spent six months on Midway. I tried to get transferred into the fleet. I wanted to get on a carrier and go to war. I got transferred to the USS *Franklin,* which had been hit by a bomb and was on its way back for repairs. You could throw the ball in the hangar deck. If we didn't have planes in there, at night we had nothing to do, as long as our duties were done. We played catch a couple of times. The kid with me, Milton Venter, was from Ottumwa, Iowa. He was a lefty, a great ballplayer. He and I would play catch at the drop of a hat. Anytime, we were apt to play catch. So we did a couple of times on the *Franklin* on the way back to the States.

When we got back, they transferred me to Alameda Naval Air Station, where I finished out the war, met my wife, got married. Alameda at the time had a lot of major leaguers. Cookie Lavagetto was playing there. Billy Rigney was shortstop. Milton and I went out for the team. We couldn't even make that team. We watched Alameda play, then we started going to see the Oaks and the Seals. I went to see the Oaks play in the old Emeryville ballpark. I got married in 1945 and my wife's family liked baseball, so we all went to see the Oaks. We couldn't always afford to go, but we saw eight or nine games a year. We'd listen to them on the radio. Casey Stengel was there.

I played semipro ball after I got out of the service. Alameda had a big ballpark. A lot of major league and Pacific Coast League ballplayers played there in the wintertime. Les Scarsella, who had been up to the major leagues and was the first baseman for the Oakland Oaks, owned Babe's Play Haven, a bar, and sponsored this team and played for them. I played for them for three years. My path crossed over a couple of times with Billy Martin. He was still in high school in '46. He was a hotshot. He played for a team called the Base Hit Cafe. We played against each other and practiced with him in Berkeley a couple of times. Cocky. He knew he had it. And everybody else knew he had it. When he went to Oakland right after high school, there was no doubt.

I hung on until I was about twenty-six or twenty-seven years old, playing semipro ball. I had four children and another one on the way. I had to start working two jobs. I didn't have time to play ball anymore. I wanted to keep playing, but I couldn't. I had a desire and an ache to go back and play. Even years later I'd go and watch the high school teams around here. In the summer I'd go watch the American Legion teams. Baseball, it doesn't make any difference if it's major league or Pony League. We go to watch the San Jose Giants quite often. The price is right and everybody has a box seat.

. . . . .

When the Giants moved out here, we went to a number of games the first year at Seals Stadium. I've been a dyed-in-the-wool Giants fan since. My allegiance at the time was still tied up between Brooklyn and the Giants, but eventually the Giants kind of won out. And now I don't know why I ever rooted for Brooklyn. I don't root for the Dodgers.

We had nine girls and one boy. The company I worked for, we'd have picnics and we'd have pickup softball games. I'd get out and pitch for both sides. If there's a ball game, I'll still go play. I'll play with my son-in-laws, I'll play with my kids, I'll play with my grandkids. Do I still have my own mitt? I have my glove upstairs. Absolutely.

NEXT THING YOU KNOW,
WE WERE PLAYING BASEBALL

SHIRO KASHINO, SEVENTY-THREE,
IS A SEMIRETIRED MANAGER OF AN
AUTOMOBILE DEALERSHIP IN
SEATTLE.

It was kind of a spontaneous thing. It was between barracks. We'd hit the ball and pitch. It made us forget a lot of problems. We were at Puyallup Fairgrounds. They had barbed-wire fence around it. They had guard towers with machine guns at the top. I guess it's just like combat. To explain combat to an individual, it's hard unless you've been in it. Being put in a concentration camp, overnight now, after losing all your belongings. Getting on a bus and they dump you off in a concentration camp. It's kind of hard to explain the hardship. It was hard to believe they would do it. Baseball helped us forget.

· · · · ·

I was born in the Depression, and the only entertainment we had was sports. Even before entering grammar school, the neighbor kids played baseball in the vacant lots. We had a lot behind a couple of the people's houses which we made into a baseball diamond, and we used to play there all the time.

The competition, the go-for-broke feeling of playing hard. I think it was quite a factor in my life. It made me very competitive.

I played softball as a catcher for Leschi Grade School, which is in Seattle. It was a nice neighborhood near Lake Washington. My family was one of the few nonwhites attending that school. One of our neighbors went to Garfield High School and he was a terrific player. His name was Jeff Heath. We used to go watch him play up at the high school. A lot of people used to watch high school baseball in those days. I remember they would rope the playfield off. I'd say there would be five thousand people watching.

When we were young kids, we would go to the Civic Auditorium, where the Seattle Rainiers used to play in the Pacific Coast League. We'd climb the fence and sneak into the game. There were a bunch of brothers who played for San Francisco. The DiMaggio boys. Jeez, what a bunch of ballplayers. Dominic and Joe and Vince. We'd always talk about them.

I can name some of the Rainiers. Kewpie Barrett, Hal Turpin, Mike Hunt. They had some real good baseball players. Emil Sick was a brew man who bought the Rainiers and built a new stadium out on Rainier Avenue called Sick's Stadium. A fellow named Fred Hutchinson played for the Rainiers. What a ballplayer. We used to watch him play at Sick's Stadium. A lot of times we didn't have money to go, so we used to go on top of a hill behind the stadium and look down and watch. Money in those days was tough.

In 1936 I entered Garfield High School. I went out for baseball and made the varsity squad my freshman year, playing third base. At that time, since my family lived away from the Japanese communities, I didn't have many Japanese friends. But during practice we played against some Japanese teams. I was later invited to join them.

·····

The Courier League in Seattle was started in 1928 by the editor/publisher – a gentleman named James Sakamoto – of the Japanese American *Courier,* an English newspaper for the Japanese community. The Courier League sponsored baseball, basketball, and football for Japanese Americans. It was composed of teams from Seattle and the surrounding small towns. In 1940 there were some twenty-three teams playing for baseball alone. There were over five hundred players.

Each small town had a baseball team in the league. All the players were Japanese Americans. They were mostly farmers in that area. I got to play with them and I really enjoyed it. We used to have bazaars and dances, and from those proceeds we would buy uniforms, bats, and stuff. We went to Oregon and played in tournaments. We went to Idaho. We kind of traveled around. My team was called the Cadets. We used to play on Rainier Playfield on Rainier Avenue. Every Fourth of July we used to have a baseball tournament among the Japanese Americans. There were teams from eastern Washington, Oregon. I'll tell you, you can't believe the spectators, the people who would come and watch. I would say four thousand people. It was really good for the community.

In 1942 we were first interned in a fairground in Puyallup, Washington. It was a fairground where they used to have the animal shows. Our housing was in animal stalls with dirt floors and hastily thrown-together wooden barracks. It was spring; we had a lot of time on our hands. The guys would bring their baseball mitts and bats out. Next thing you know, we were playing baseball.

From Puyallup we moved to our permanent relocation center in Hunt, Idaho, in August of 1942. Baseball continued to be a major pastime. Hunt was a desert, with sagebrush and sand. They put up barbed-wire fences and guard towers. All the people got together, and they cleared the place and made roads and made it more comfortable to live. And then we made a baseball field.

Because there were internees from the Seattle area as well as Oregon, we were able to get some real good baseball players together. Therefore we were able to participate in competition with the semipro teams around the surrounding towns in Idaho. I was one of the lucky ones to go outside to play baseball. We qualified for the state semipro tournament in Blackfoot, Idaho. We played at the state tournament there, which was quite a thrill. There were some navy and army teams that competed with us. There was no problem at all. We had a lot of harassment from the fans, but that's normal. The fans have a right to boo or yell at you. That's part of baseball, right? But the players themselves, we had no fights. I think it helped a lot. Those people, I don't think they saw so many Japanese in their life. I think they had a good feeling, and we had a good feeling meeting them.

It helped in the camp, because the old folks could watch something that they really enjoyed. It brought smiles to their faces to watch baseball, instead of being so morbid about the living conditions. Baseball made them smile. They all came to watch and they forgot their problems. Baseball in camp brought a little happiness to a bunch of people.

When they interned us, we were classified 4-C, enemy aliens. On February 1, 1943, President Roosevelt made a decision to organize a regimental combat team of Americans of Japanese descent. From our concentration camp, many young men volunteered. A large number were the athletes from our camp, including myself. That unit was called the 442nd Regimental Combat team.

When we went overseas, we did play. In Italy. We had a little spare time. Next thing we know, we hustled some mitts and baseballs. We played baseball. We played the day before we went up to combat. I remember that, because they had a good pitcher from Hawaii. I caught for him, and I remember we had a real good time. His name was Fred Kameda. The next day, our first day in action, Fred was killed.

. . . . .

THE NIGHT MEL OTT DIED

EVERETT PARKER, SIXTY-FIVE,
IS A RETIRED DEPUTY INSPECTOR WITH THE NEW
YORK CITY POLICE DEPARTMENT. HE LIVES IN
QUEENS, NEW YORK.

In the summer of '36, my dad was going to get a vacation. He said to me, "Pick out a game, because I'll be on vacation, the Giants will be home at the Polo Grounds, and we'll go up and see the Giants." Until this time I had only seen the Bushwicks.

So up we went on a summer day to the Polo Grounds. We watched the Giants play the Cincinnati Reds. The Giants won. I remember two things about that game. I saw Kiki Cuyler, center fielder for the Reds, make a diving, tumbling catch, the likes of which I had never seen before. I saw Dick Bartell make a play in the hole, I saw him make a play behind second base, I saw him hit a ball on the left-field chalk line. The chalk, I can still see flying. And I saw him hit a ball almost on the right-field chalk line. And my father said, "Now that's bat control."

That was the high point of my entire summer of 1936. The smell and the sounds. And the fact that these guys below me, these fellows

were big league baseball players. It was like I had reached a bench-
mark in my life.

. . . . .

I don't go to games anymore. What's to see at Shea Stadium, really? The game I grew up with is gone. I understand that. But it's still played on that diamond. There's something about it that has me turn on a Seattle or a Los Angeles or an Anaheim game. I'll watch a ball game, even if it's a high school game as I'm going by.

I had a dad and three older brothers who were all Giant fans. And a mom who understood that the household was happiest when the Giants won. I grew up in Ridgewood, in Queens. Then we moved to Glendale, where we were neighbors of Phil Rizzuto and Mama and Papa Rizzuto. I never told Rizzuto this, but we were Dick Bartell fans. We rooted for Rizzuto, but we were Giant fans. As early as those years, I heard of Bill Terry and Mel Ott and Carl Hubbell before I ever saw them. My dad in the Depression was trying to make a living for four sons driving a cab. He was a McGraw fan. An old East Side New Yorker. I remember him talking about Frankie Frisch, the Fordham Flash.

He used to take me from Queens to nearby Dexter Park. Dexter Park was the home of the famous, in those days, all-white club, the Bushwicks. Being Giant fans, we used to root for the underdog every Sunday. We'd root for whoever it was – the Glendale Farmers, the Cedarhurst club, what have you. But once or twice a summer, Max Rosner – old, feisty, owned the Bushwicks – would book a traveling team from the Negro National League.

My father used to say to me, even at five or six years old, "Today, you're going to see some real baseball." I remember seeing teams like the Homestead Grays. The Baltimore Elite

Giants. The Kansas City Monarchs. I remember him pointing out to me Josh Gibson. One particular Sunday he hit two home runs – the first I'd ever seen hit at any distance like that – onto a hill at Dexter Park. Behind the ball field sat houses. One-family homes. I saw Gibson hit two up there and I couldn't believe it. One Sunday I remember seeing Satchel Paige.

The Bushwicks were mechanical. They played with a dull precision. They wore black socks and black hats. They beat all the white semipro clubs in the metropolitan area. But when these Negro National League teams came in, I remember Satchel Paige looked like he was toying with them. Another thing I noticed – they didn't play like the Bushwicks. They played with flair, with exuberance. They actually played like they enjoyed baseball. I remember one day on the old Stony Hill trolley car – because what the hell do you know when you're six or seven years old? – I said to my dad, "Are any of these Negro players, are any of them good enough to play in the big leagues?" My father said to me, "Are they good enough? Some of them are better than the big leaguers that you've seen already." The next natural question – and I'll never forget asking him – was, "Then why aren't they in the big leagues?" Then he gave me a lesson, that day, on that trolley, that I never got in school. He tried to explain discrimination, without using the word. He told me, "They're not allowed. There's a color line. They're not allowed in. It's not right, but that's the way it is." And that's the way it was.

When Jackie Robinson came along in '47, I wanted very badly to see him make it. But I very soon came to hate him. Not because of his color. But because he was a Brooklyn Dodger. When Willie Mays came along and Monte Irvin before him, I loved it. I always thought of those days at Dexter Park and how good those guys played. And as I got older, I thought how that must have ached for these guys to live and die a dream, not because of ability, but because of color.

✦

We lived in a six-family cold-water flat. In those days every block had a team. I lived on Catalpa Avenue, and the Catalpa Avenue boys played the Madison Street boys, or they played the Seneca Avenue boys. And what did you play? You played stickball in the gutter. And how could you do that? There weren't that many cars around. You'd chalk first base in the gutter, third base in the gutter, second was a sewer. And if a man had a car and he parked on first base, you'd tell him, "Hey, mister. Will you get your car off first base?" That's the way we played. I remember a guy in the police department who turned into a chief, a fellow named Jim McGowan. He lived on my block. He was the only guy I ever saw who consistently struck out in stickball. Later, when I was a captain, I ran into Jimmy McGowan and we talked about old times, and I said, "You know, how could you miss the ball?" He said, "I don't know. But when I hit it, I hit it three sewers."

We had a farm system in those days. If you played good enough, there were the ballparks and school yards nearby. Somebody would say to you, "Hey, kid. You're old enough to leave your block now." You were twelve, or thirteen or fourteen. They had the Glendale Boys' Club, the Ridgewood Warriors, clubs like that. I ended up playing school-yard ball. In the school yards, it was baseball. Everybody played on rock piles in sneakers. There were no bases – you'd put flat rocks out. The next step up in the farm system was when I went to Grover Cleveland High School. It had to be 1944, '45. The war was on. I was a third baseman. My brothers, who were in the service, had told me before, "When they ask you what you play, tell them you're a catcher. Because everybody needs catchers." So when I went to Grover Cleveland and the coach sorted out the kids, I said, "I'm a catcher." And he was interested. I got my first sliding pads and my first sunglasses. That was big league. The first time I ever wore sliding pads, I didn't get on base. So having this jinx in my mind, I never wore sliding pads again.

My last game at Grover Cleveland was in '48. We played Bryant High School, also from northern Queens. Billy Loes, he was a flake with the Dodgers and he was a flake back in Astoria. In an earlier game that season, I hit a line drive off Billy Loes's left shoulder and it caromed out into the outfield. Loes did not forget. The last game we played was at home in a place called Farmer's Oval. He walked me in the game four times. He had scouts there watching him. He didn't want to walk me. He wanted to hit me. I was ducking and diving all afternoon. He never did hit me.

My career batting average at Grover Cleveland was .321. I got one offer – no money was ever discussed – that I didn't answer from the Brooklyn Dodgers. And I never went after it. My brothers were as mad as hell at me after the war. I didn't have enough confidence. I didn't think I was good enough.

The day Bobby Thomson hit his home run in 1951, I was home in Glendale. My mother had a black-and-white Magnavox television. I took those three days off. I was working at a bank, the Bank of America, in New York. The first of three play-off days, I went to Ebbets Field and couldn't get into the damn ballpark. I couldn't get near it. That's the day Jim Hearn beat the Dodgers. The second game, I went up to the Polo Grounds, and there were plenty of seats. The only problem was, I jinxed them. The Giants got beat ten to nothing. There was a man sitting next me, a guy about eighty. He kept a newspaper in front of his face every time a pitch was made. I finally said to him, "Do you mind missing the pitch?" He said, "No, no. I just can't look." He just couldn't look. He was a Giant fan.

The third day I was sitting in the basement of my mom's house. By the ninth inning I was disconsolate. It was 4–1. It was over. And my mother was very quiet. Alvin Dark got a hit. Don Mueller got a hit. Whitey Lockman got a hit. And now I was off the chair. But I figured Newcombe was throwing aspirins. It was going to be a good run and nothing more. With the score 4–2 with runners on second and third, Bobby Thomson – who I never liked; I never had much confidence in him – was up against Ralph Branca. When he hit that ball, I went down on my knees in front of this Magnavox. I'm saying, "Thank God. Thank God." I immediately left my house in Glendale, running to get down to Myrtle Avenue because a fella named Copy the cab guy used to park down there and he was a Brooklyn Dodger fan. When Copy saw me in his rearview approaching him at full speed, he took off in his cab.

Thinking of it now, seeing the Giants and Dodgers leave New York was as remote in my mind as Franklin Delano Roosevelt playing out his contract and signing on as prime minister of Canada. But we had plenty of advance notice. They left in September of '57. The attendance was dwindling. The Giants' fortunes were sinking. You knew it was coming. But it was an awful ache.

In the spring of 1958, I was walking a beat in Brooklyn. I worked out of the 88th Precinct. It was like something empty. Come April it was an empty feeling. And everywhere I went, people cursed O'Malley and Horace Stoneham. To this day some of them do. I could not root for the Yankees. I used to root for the seven clubs who played the Yankees. San Francisco Giant games would come in on TV. But it was like foreign. They were too far away to latch on to.

I was in Brooklyn in '58 on foot patrol. It was a chilly

· · · · ·

November night. I was doing the four-to-twelve. I'm making my last walk west on Myrtle Avenue. Across the street from Cumberland Hospital was Sal's all-night fruit stand. Sal was a disgruntled Dodger fan. He knew I was a Giant fan because whenever I had the post, we'd talk baseball. It's getting near midnight and Sal said to me, "Did you hear the news?" I looked at him and said, "What news, Sal?" He said, "Mel Ott got killed." I looked at him. He said he just heard it on the radio. Mel Ott was in a car with his wife and they got hit by another car. The last thing I ever thought I'd hear was the news he gave me, on a Brooklyn street corner. Here was an old Dodger fan and he felt bad, because he knew I was a Giant fan. Going home that night, I felt like I lost a family friend. I'll never forget that.

There was a night when I worked up in Harlem in 1960. I was driving a crusty old sergeant, George McClancy. Nobody liked him. George McClancy was going to be a long eight hours, driving him in a radio car. He directed me to park up on Coogan's Bluff. He had to do some writing and that was a quiet spot in the Three-two Precinct. When we were up there, I was looking down at the abandoned horseshoe, the Polo Grounds. I told him, "Geez, I don't know how many times I went through these gates." Turned out George McClancy was human: he was a Giant fan. He said, "Forget 'em. They're gone forever." But I never forgot them.

A CHILDHOOD DREAM

JED WEISMAN, SIXTY-ONE,
IS AN ATTORNEY IN CLEVELAND.

Frequently the ballplayers were in our home. In the '40s most games were played during the day. It was not unusual at all for my dad to call home at three in the afternoon when the game was over and say, "Hey, Sally, Joe Gordon and Hegan are coming over." It became my life. When these guys would come to the house, there'd always be a beer or a drink. We had a piano in our house, and there'd usually be someone who could mess around on the piano. Jim Hegan was one. He had a great voice. Joe Gordon, my dad, Kenny Keltner – they'd sit around and sing songs. The Irish ballad-type things. The next-door neighbor kids would say, "Who's going to be over tonight?" There was a different affinity for ballplayers in those days than there is today. For lack of a better term, it was a family affair.

· · · · ·

My father and mother were raised in the Boston area. My dad was selling newspapers, which was a way of making a living in those days, on the corner of Boylston and Massachusetts. Fenway Park is in that area. My dad and Tris Speaker struck up an acquaintance which became rather close. My dad, of

Jewish descent, would sing Irish ballads. He was a tenor. And Speaker used to just love it. The story goes that it used to soothe him. My dad used to deliver papers to Speaker daily at an apartment where he lived near the ballpark. When Speaker got traded to the Indians in 1919, the breakup between the two of them was a sad situation. Speaker told my dad, "If I ever become manager in Cleveland, I'm going to bring you there." Sure enough, Speaker did become manager in 1920. And in 1921 he brings my dad to Cleveland to be the trainer. That's how he got to Cleveland.

Being born into a baseball family, the game was there from day one. I have a vague, almost dreamlike memory of being around the clubhouse with the ballplayers. For instance, Earl Averill. Earl was a cutup. He used to scare the hell out of me, as a matter of fact. A very gruff guy. A sweetheart, but a gruff, tough guy. When I was a kid, I couldn't have been four, five, six years old, I would be in the clubhouse over in the old League Park. And Averill would grab me and stick me up on the training table, and he'd take a pair of scissors and tell me, "I'm going to cut your ears off."

The clubhouse in those days was rather small. Wooden floors. As a little guy around there, you had to sort of stay out of the way. Players were playing cards. Chewing tobacco and spitting on the wooden floor. They'd have spittoons on the floor, but these guys would miss them all the time.

Steve O'Neill was a catcher with the Indians, who also caught for the Tigers, who ended up managing the Indians and the Tigers. Steve and his family lived about three blocks away from us. He and my dad, particularly in the off-season, managed to frequent the corner bar. My dad wasn't much of a drinker, but Steve O'Neill was. He could put it away. He'd take my dad along, and my dad would come back half in the bag all the time.

As I got a little older, I would work out on a regular basis down at the stadium or at League Park, particularly during the summer when school was out. One of the coaches in the '40s was George Susce. He was one of Lou Boudreau's coaches, and he had five boys. We were all roughly in the same age group. We'd get down there very early and work out at the ballpark. Some of the ballplayers who would come in for early batting practice would give you some instruction. Most of the time we'd be out shagging fly balls for these guys. My friends and neighbors idolized the fact that I could go down there and do that.

You were used to going out on a little sandlot diamond, so to go out at Cleveland Municipal Stadium, it was like being in this big, empty cavern. I mean, you had this place that could seat eighty thousand people. And there was nobody there. One time, I must have been twelve or thirteen years old and we were getting an opportunity to do some hitting. I remember going up and hitting a ball that I thought I just really smashed. And it didn't even make it out of the infield. I remember that like yesterday. I knew I'd made good contact, and the ball went nowhere.

The years between when I was probably ten to fifteen, I would make one road trip a year with my dad. I'd make a western swing. At that time the western swing would be Detroit, Chicago, St. Louis. The first train trip I made had to be in the spring of '41. I was in second or third grade. My dad decided he was going to take me down to spring training. We took a train from Cleveland to Clearwater, Florida, which is where the Indians trained. It was two nights, three days on the train. The players were good-time kinds of guys. They were playing cards, having a few drinks, smoking cigarettes. Giving hotfoots. I can picture Al Milnar, who was a pitcher, giving Jim Bagby, who was another pitcher, a hotfoot. It was fun. At this point of my life, I look back and it was like a dream. Here I am doing this thing, and I'm supposed to be in

· · · · ·

my bed, at home. Instead you're going along on this train with a bunch of ballplayers.

In '48, I recall very vividly, this was the thrill of a lifetime. We were in St. Louis playing the Browns. While infield practice was going on, fungoes were being hit. I would act like a cutoff man and get the throw from the outfielder and throw it to whoever was catching for the fungo hitter. They had taken like one round of infield practice, and Boudreau comes over and says, "Hey, Jed, come on over here and take short-stop." And I went over and took infield practice. I was scared out of my wits. They wouldn't let me take the throws from the catcher, Hegan, when he made them down to second because they were afraid I might get hurt. Here I am out there with Joe Gordon at second and Keltner at third and Boudreau and Robinson over there on first. It was terrific.

✦

Baseball was a big, big thing here in Cleveland. We grew up in Cleveland Heights. We would play in the streets. With the hardball. We'd be out there tearing the cover off the ball in the streets. At that time there were a number of corner lots. Not everything was filled with houses. We'd use those as ball fields. In the school district where we lived, they would have a baseball clinic. One of the coaches from the high school would come up with a canvas bag that had some bats and catcher's equipment and some balls, and he oversaw and organized a game every day of the summer. You'd start at nine in the morning and you'd go to noon and then back from one till four. You made sure you got there early so you'd get chosen in. I had a cousin in Chicago who would come to Cleveland three or four weeks in the summer just so he could play ball. These were the days before Little League. It was the thing to do. There were two things to do in the summer: you played baseball and you went swimming.

Everybody was wrapped up in it. Everybody was wrapped up in the Cleveland Indians. By the time '48 came around, this city went bananas. In '48 we managed to knock off the Red Sox in the play-off game. That particular play-off game was the Jewish holiday of Rosh Hashanah. I was playing high school football at the time. The Jewish kids on the team didn't go to school that day. And our parents said we couldn't practice. Most of us went up to the high school anyhow to just sort of listen to the coaches and watch. That day, we got up there and the coaches kept everybody in the locker room listening to the play-off. You're talking about the old concrete locker room, and we're sitting there and everybody is going nuts. When they won, everybody went nuts. Everybody was hugging each other. It was like you were the team that had won. Every once in a while they'll show a film of that game, and at the end of it, I can catch a glimpse of my dad – you see him for about two seconds – and he was crying. There was a big parade. The schools actually were closed, they just closed the schools, so the kids could go down to the parade.

At that time the Negro Leagues team in Cleveland was the Cleveland Buckeyes. They used to play at League Park. I saw a number of their games, mainly because I would go down and sell Coke in the stands. I was ten, twelve. In those days you'd sell Coke by the bottle. You carry one or two cases at a time. They'd play doubleheaders down there on Sundays when the Indians weren't in town. They had pretty good crowds. League Park sat approximately twenty-seven thousand. They'd have crowds in the neighborhood of ten thousand. Mostly black. The thing I remember most was watching the game and it was no different from watching the Indians, in terms of quality of play. It never crossed my mind to wonder why they weren't playing in the big leagues. Robinson came up in '47. At the time I realized, "God, this is the first black guy in the big leagues." Larry Doby came along that same year. It's funny. I guess I knew that there was a black and white difference. But I didn't recognize it.

I can recall when Doby first came up, I can remember him being booed. And I remember in my mind, I couldn't understand it. You cheer on your team. I didn't understand the booing. Some people tried to explain it to me – because he was black. But that didn't register with me. Why would you boo a guy because he was black? The way we were brought up, there was no color difference. Just like there was no religion difference. We're of the Jewish faith. You could have counted the number of Jewish players in those days on one hand. So maybe that was part of it.

My dad passed away in '49, after the season was over, when I was fifteen. Baseball has always remained a very big part of my life. I played ball all the way through college. I played hardball or softball all the way until I was fifty. I follow the Indians very closely. People laugh at me as being the optimist. Every other year I would go out to Tucson for spring training. I'd come back every year saying, "They look good, they had this going, they had that going." Then they'd fall flat on their faces. But I've never given up on Cleveland. Disappointed? Yes. But I was always optimistic. Wait till next year.

MY LOVE WAS THE
BIRMINGHAM BARONS

BILL LUMPKIN, SIXTY-SIX,
IS RETIRED SPORTS EDITOR OF THE
BIRMINGHAM POST-HERALD.

When I came out of the Korean War, I went to work in Augusta, Georgia, as a police reporter. Augusta was one of those towns where blacks and whites didn't play together. I remember when they got the first black player. Me and the wife, we'd go out and see him.

The ballpark was located right next to a little textile mill. They had these mill houses. You've seen them – three- or four-room shotgun houses. They were right there by the ballpark. At night all these dang guys would pile out of them dang houses and go to the ballpark. Only a handful of blacks that would come.

But when they brought the black player in there, for the first game, they had to rope off the stands. They divided the stands fifty-fifty. On one side was all black; the other side was all white. The black player, I forget his name, had a good game. Goddang, the whites were cheering him. When he did something, all the stands just stood up and cheered.

. . . . .

I grew up in Ensley, Alabama, which is the steel mill community of Birmingham. Most everybody who lived in the Ensley area worked in the mills. When I was growing up, the steel mills had their own baseball league. Probably some of the players in the Industrial League would be major leaguers today. And some of them were then. Harry Walker played in the old Industrial League. Ben Chapman, who played for the Yankees and led the American League in stolen bases several times, played in the Industrial League. It was a hard-working citizen who lived in Ensley. The team that they followed was the Birmingham Barons.

It was back when Labor Day was a big baseball day. Not just in Birmingham, but just about every southern city. The politicians would come out. There'd be an early-afternoon and a late-afternoon doubleheader. In between they'd cook barbecue and the politicians would speak. That's the way it was, too, on the Fourth of July. It was a big, big baseball day in the South.

We lived about three-quarters of a mile from Rickwood Field, where the Barons played. I was probably ten, eleven, twelve years old the first time I can remember going. They had the Knothole Gang. For a dollar or two dollars, you got a season pass. All the kids sat together in the left-field bleachers. I started throwing the old *Birmingham Post* when I was eleven. They were always giving carriers tickets to the baseball games. But not too many of my buddies threw papers. So when we went to the baseball game, they'd all slip in. I wouldn't dare go through the gate with a pass. I had to slip in with them. They had this chain-link fence. We'd stand across the street from the stadium and when it looked like there weren't too many people, we'd all run over and hit the fence at the same time, then go over it and scatter in different directions. If they got after us, they could only catch one of us.

. . . . .

My Love Was the Birmingham Barons   III

Rickwood was a very important part of my life. Rickwood was painted kind of a dark green. It's a beautiful ballpark. The crowds were vocal, but I don't remember them as being vulgar. People really worked on the umpire. We had an old fellow that sat down on the third-base side. Every game, the umpires would start walking out and he'd holler, "Here come the blind mice." You remember the guys coming through the stands selling hot dogs and peanuts. In Birmingham you could not sell beer in the stands. They had a little beer garden out back.

My love was really the Birmingham Barons. I remember one of my favorite players was a guy named Jodie Beeler. Jodie Beeler was a third baseman. I think he got a cup of coffee at Cincinnati. The Barons worked with the Cincinnati Reds. We had some pretty good ballplayers come through here. Hank Sauer came through in about '41 or '42. Hank Sauer was one of my first heroes. He hit a home run that cleared the scoreboard. The scoreboard was four-hundred-and-something feet from home plate and it was thirty-four feet high and it was back up against a brick wall. The ball left the ballpark.

Cincinnati had the first deaf-mute player. Well, that first deaf-mute player was an outfielder named Dick Sipek, who played in Birmingham. Then we had Joe Nuxhall. He was real young. We're talking about during the war. Atlanta had a great favorite called Country Brown. Finally, we got Country Brown. We followed old Country Brown when he played with the Atlanta Crackers. We didn't like him, until he came to Birmingham.

It was big news when you'd pick up a paper and see "Lou Limmer's coming to Birmingham." I remember Lou. He played first base for the New York Yankees. I don't care if he didn't play but one game. It was about 1950 and the Yankees sent Joe Collins down. Gosh, that was big to us. I remember

· · · · ·

Collins hitting a home run in the ninth inning. We had a right-field grandstand. On top of the grandstand, probably forty feet, they had a little fence. It was a wooden fence. I remember it was in the bottom of the ninth inning, it was 1–1, and Joe Collins hit a home run that hit that wooden fence and bounced back into the park.

I'll never forget. There was guy who ran the Shell station up by Rickwood on the main drag on Third Avenue West. His name was Frank Little. The players, after the game was over, would stand around the Shell station and talk to Frank. Then they'd go next door and get a beer. His wife was a good friend of my mother's. She comes out to see us one day and brings one of the Birmingham Barons. His name was Gene Bradley. I don't know whatever happen to Gene Bradley. I think his career might have started and stopped in Birmingham. Anyway, Gene gets out in the street and plays baseball with us. Goddang – Gene Bradley. To us, he was a great player. He was out there, throwing the ball with us in the street, hitting with us. It was just a great treat.

Things that you remember. I remember Pete Gray. The other day we were talking about baseball and somebody brought up the one-armed outfielder that Bill Veeck brought up to the St. Louis Browns. Pete Gray played left field for the Memphis Chicks, right in front of the Knothole Gang. We were just all eyes. All of us crowded up against the fence to watch. They'd hit him a fly ball and he caught it one-handed, and then he'd throw the ball up in the air. And he'd take the glove and put it under his nub, and then he'd catch the ball and he'd throw it. God, we'd go crazy.

We had great, great amateur teams. The railroads would have teams in these little mining towns. They'd get a flatcar and the players would get on the flatcar and all the fans would get on the flatcar and then the train would take them to the next little old mining town, where they would play the game.

· · · · ·

They'd get off and play in an old field with no fences, no bleachers or anything. Just a dirt field. And when the game was over, they'd get back on the flatcar and they'd take them back to the mining towns where they came from.

✦

It was an all-white game. For the Barons, we had a right-field grandstand. Next to it were some bleachers. Your black fans sat in the right-field grandstand. It was a good following. The Birmingham Black Barons played at Rickwood on Sunday. When the Black Barons played, the white fans sat in the right-field grandstand. I remember doing that. The Black Barons' game was a lot livelier than the white Barons' game. The Black Barons, the Negro American League, played a lot more entertaining kind of baseball. They had a lot more characters in the league. They were serious. But not like the white Barons' game. The Black Barons would have one guy come out and play every position.

It was about 1961. The Barons had been playing for sixty years. They had an ordinance on the books in Birmingham that blacks and whites could not play together. Except in the neighborhood, we'd play together. Most of the neighborhoods in Birmingham, blacks lived across the street or behind you or right down the street. We'd get out there and we'd play together.

It came to a head where they were going to have to put black players in the Southern Association. The guy that owned the ball club was named Albert Belcher. He was a big multimillionaire. A lumberman. He didn't feel like he could fight city hall. Which he couldn't, because Bull Connor was the police commissioner. So he folded the baseball club. And when he did, they folded the Southern Association. The whole league folded. There were other cities that had the same ordinance. The summers were dead. All of a sudden there's no baseball. I'm working on the morning paper. Well, a lot of times, if I got off at nine o'clock or ten o'clock, I'd swing by Rickwood and just sit in the stands, drink a beer, and watch the game. This was kind of a ritual with me. Now, all of a sudden, you're talking about going from April to September without baseball. It was a bad feeling. I still think about it.

I think a majority of the people were embarrassed by blacks being denied rights that we all had. Around 1964 Sam Smith, who was the president of the South Atlantic League, the old Sally League, he decided to revive the Southern Association under the banner of the Southern League. Sam brought Birmingham back into baseball. Albert Belcher still owned the Barons. We were still having some bad times in Birmingham. I never will forget. National writers all came in. What kind of problems are we going to have? Are they going to blow up the stadium? Are there going to be shootings and things? About four nights before they played the opener, somebody knocked on Albert Belcher's back door. It was the Imperial Wizard of the Ku Klux Klan. He said, "Mr. Belcher, I'd like you to come out into the yard. I'd like to talk to you." So Albert Belcher walked out in the yard. He said, "Mr. Belcher, the Klan will not interfere with the start of baseball in Birmingham." Albert told me this.

Baseball came back with a pretty big bang. Rickwood was in a black neighborhood. At the seventh inning, they opened the gates. All these old black guys, most of them probably retired, they'd come over and they all sat in the grandstand behind the box seats behind home plate. There'd be about thirty of them. Most of the time when I'd get off, I'd go in and I'd sit right there because I liked to sit in a place where I could watch the pitcher. It was quite an experience. These guys were great baseball fans. They knew what the guy was throwing and they knew what he was supposed to throw and they knew what the manager was supposed to do.

The Barons left Rickwood. They no longer play there. They built a new park out in Hoover, which is where the flight of the white fans has gone. Now the baseball park is forty miles from my home. That right there ended my love affair with the Barons. No more just going by and sitting in the stands and watching a few innings.

A SWEET SPOT IN TIME

MARTY ADLER, FIFTY-SEVEN,

LIVES IN WANTAGH, NEW YORK, ON LONG ISLAND.

HE RETIRED AS PRINCIPAL OF BROOKLYN'S

JACKIE ROBINSON JUNIOR HIGH SCHOOL

IN 1992.

My neighborhood was split in half, Italian-Jewish, like any other neighborhood. Your day was defined by what the Dodgers did. There was rumored to be a non-Dodger fan a few blocks away, but we couldn't believe it. If they won, everyone was happy. If they lost, there were long faces. You could walk in any neighborhood, walk up and down the street, and you'd pass someone with a radio and holler out, "How are the Bums doing?" and instantly you had a companion. You had a person you could relate to. It didn't matter if you never saw them before.

· · · · ·

You'll never see anything like it again. It will never happen again. Never. The sun, the moon, and the planets must have been aligned or something.

A number of things made it happen. Brooklyn was made up of immigrants. It's not like we were here four thousand years. There was a feeling you're the underdog, which the Dodgers were all the time. Then there was Ebbets Field: small, intimate, cozy. A little dilapidated. You got a rivalry – the Giants. The Yankees – the Wall Street enemy. All the Dodgers lived in Brooklyn. This is not like nowadays, where Joe Schmuck lives up in Scarsdale and comes in by helicopter. The guys lived here; their children went to the schools here with us. They lived here in the off-season. The same players stayed. The same players were on the team year after year after year. They all were there. There was no changeover. This says something. And they were good. If we had won seventeen more games between '46 and '57, seventeen more games, we would have won the pennant every year.

I grew up in an area called Borough Park, which is adjacent to Bensonhurst and Bay Ridge. My father was a Giants fan. He grew up in tenements in the city. John McGraw was the hero then, because the Dodgers weren't really anything. My first game was a Yankee game, in '46, when I was ten years old. We saw the Red Sox beat the Yankees at the stadium. Ted Williams hit a couple of home runs. Then we started going to the Dodger games.

The first time I went to Ebbets Field was in '47. I was awed by it. The Dodger uniforms – the blue and the white. The grass was greener than any grass I'd ever seen. Directly across the street from the subway, which everyone got out of, there was a Bond's Bread factory. And the smell. As soon as you smelled the baking bread, that was the first sign that Ebbets Field was around the block. If you ever come across that smell, the memories, the flood of memories, would come back. It would be overwhelming. The cigar smoke and the beer. Tears come to your eyes when you think about it.

We'd get autographs. Not like today, where you get them on the sweet spot of the ball. We'd get them on programs, which you'd get for three cents, and then we'd lose them. We didn't save them. The players weren't as obliging as people like to think they were. The players would sometimes brush by you. I remember Mantle, for years, he would spit at you, curse you, or kick you. Mantle was miserable. Bob Cerv was another – whoa. You didn't go over to him. If he'd kick you in the knee, you were out for a week. He would laugh doing it.

The day rose and fell on the Dodgers. And at night the newspapers came out at 10:30. So at night you'd go up to the candy store – there was a candy store on every block – and you'd get the *News* and the *Mirror*, three cents, four cents. You'd buy an egg cream, two pretzels for a dime, and you'd read the day's results in the paper.

All the games that you grew up playing – stoopball, punchball, stickball, salugi, running bases – these were all games that developed your skills toward baseball. Everybody played. It was part of the culture. You had to. You played on the street and in the school yards. You didn't have the amount of traffic then. And the school yards were open. If they weren't open, you just hopped the fence.

Stickball is played with a broom handle for a bat. You'd take an old tennis ball, take a match to it, and burn the hair off. Or you'd use a Spaldeen. It was a high-bouncing rubber ball. Sometimes someone would pitch the ball in to you. Or you would hit it yourself. After that, after you hit the ball, it was regular baseball rules.

Everybody emulated their favorite players. When Jackie was up, everybody walked pigeon-toed. Hodges, everyone was quiet, one foot went into the bucket – before he changed in '52. Campanella, you were short and squat. Pee Wee was Pee Wee. And if you liked Duke Snider, all of a sudden everybody was learning how to bat left handed.

Most of us had to work some portion of the week. If it wasn't after school, it was at night. You had to run errands for the grocer or wash cars. In our family, it was a gas station. A couple of my uncles owned it. So I had to fix flats for a couple hours a day. Wash cars on weekends. You played when it was slow at the gas station. You'd have a catch at the station. A radio would be blasting. Guys would come in, "Five gallons of gas, please. Hey, what's the score?" It was a wonderful time to grow up. It was a time when the air and the water was clean and sex was dirty.

We'd listen to games on the radio, as soon as we got a radio, in '45, '46. One radio to a family – we were still immigrants. Everybody would sit around and listen to it. Marty Glickman came on with replays at seven o'clock every day. Marty Glickman, Art Rust, Jr., and the lady tennis player Gussie Moran. They did the replays of that day's game. My mother was cleaning up, and we would listen to the game.

I was coming home from school when Bobby Thomson hit his home run. I just cried. We heard it on the radio. The streets were blaring with it. When the Dodgers won the World Series in '55, the closest thing that I can compare it to is 1945, V-J Day, when the war was over. A million cars, three million people, blowing horns. Screaming, dancing. It's like nothing you will see again, ever, ever. I was driving home from college that day. I went to Brooklyn College. We just stopped the car. And we just looked at each other. We just had to stop the car and take it all in. I hate to keep saying it will never be the same again. But it will never be the same again.

When the Dodgers left, the last game in '57, I don't think four or five thousand people attended. People were angry. They were just angry. Not disappointed. None of that bullshit. Just angry. Then the Mets came along, four or five years later. They brought a couple of Dodgers with them to build up the gate. But the realization set in that baseball is a business.

It was terrible. I'll tell you, we were wishing and praying

. . . . .

that the Dodgers would do poorly in L.A. And the first year they did. They were seventh or something. And we were happy. Those people had to learn to suffer a little bit. That was our first feeling.

I was an assistant principal at a junior high directly across the street from where Ebbets Field used to be. I'd reminisce every time I'd look out the window. I started playing a lot of basketball. Jogging. I could watch baseball. But baseball can be boring. The Dodgers were different. Where else are you going to see a Jackie Robinson? The best ballplayer – not the best, but the most exciting. Or the Duke coming up to take those swishes.

I've gone to a few games. I'm not angry or bitter or anything like that. I just don't take to baseball. I just stopped. I don't enjoy it. Not because they're not good. The players now are certainly better physically. Over the years there have been some great pennant runs. I was aware of them. But the intensity is gone. The same verve and feeling will never be there again. When the Dodgers left, it left. Brooklyn changed. When they left, the *Brooklyn Eagle* stopped publishing. The Brooklyn Navy Yard shut down. Everything stopped.

IN THE SHADOW OF THE WALL

RONALD CROCKETT, SIXTY,

IS A DATA PROCESSING DIRECTOR AT HOWARD

UNIVERSITY IN WASHINGTON, D.C.

There was an alley behind the right-field wall and then there were houses. You had to climb over a fence to get the balls. Not a very easy thing to do – some of the people had dogs. My thing was to get foul balls over the left-field stands, especially in night games. They would disappear in the bushes. The grounds were adjacent to the Howard University Medical School. They had a lot of bushes there. Early in the morning, I would climb over this fence behind the medical school and run down there and search for balls. They would show up very nicely in the early morning light.

. . . . .

I grew up right behind Griffith Stadium in a section called Ledroit Park. I remember a lot of cars driving through the neighborhood, trying to find parking spaces. We used to always hear crowd noise. Fifth Street was right behind the bleacher wall. There was a gate that used to let cars and trucks and stuff in. They would open up that gate to let people out. Of course, we would run in and they would let us stay. We were always in the ballpark for one thing or the other. The thing that struck me was just the beautiful grounds. The grass was such a beautiful green color. I was always so amazed. It was more grass than I had ever seen before.

Getting out to the ballpark was always a treat for me. Sometimes we would get in early and hide. A lot of guys in the neighborhood worked there, and they would tell you where to hide. We'd get in real early before they closed the gates and watch the team practice. We'd go somewhere in the far reaches of the outfield behind some seats and just stay there until people started coming in. Then you were OK. Griffith Stadium was a nice place to watch a ball game. The stands were close in to the field and it was kind of personal.

The players I remember, one was a first baseman named Joe Kuhel. He was the fanciest first baseman I had ever seen. I wanted to be a first baseman. They had a way of straddling the bag and reaching out in whichever direction the ball would come and reach back for the bag at the same time. I liked to watch that. I remember Buddy Lewis, a center fielder named Stan Spence, and in left field there was a guy named George Case. He was our speedster. He led the team in stolen bases. I remember they traded him to Cleveland and he came back. We had a replacement, a guy named Gil Coan. And they had the Great Race, a challenge race. I was in the bleachers at the time. They drew a line from left field to right field behind second base, on a diagonal. They came out before the game and got down in the starter's position and raced across the outfield. Of course, George Case won that race.

Opening Day was the most exciting thing. The place was packed. The president was always there to throw out the first ball. You could see them in the box behind first base. They had bands. We'd get out of school around three o'clock and cars would be all over the place. We'd get home and listen to the games on the radio. You could hear the crowd noise and at the same time you were listening on the radio.

As I grew older, we began to watch just various players. We were always trying to copy their batting styles. You remember some of the visiting players. I remember Ted Williams. You wanted to get out there early to see the big hitters. I don't remember Joe DiMaggio so much. But I sure do remember Ted Williams putting them up against that right-field wall. The right-field wall was a solid tin-metal wall with a lot of ads on it. Biggs Meat Products. Fussell's Ice Cream. Lifebuoy. Ted Williams used to put them over the right-field wall on a regular basis during batting practice.

One of the exciting things was the first night games. I think that was during the war. It was all lit up. I thought that was the most fascinating thing. The lights were visible through my back window. I was going to bed and I could see the lights. In the neighborhood, there were a couple of rackets. One was parking cars and the other was watching cars. "Want me to watch your car, mister?" I guess it was one of the early protection rackets. The night games kind of ruined that. You had to be around when the guy came back. "I watched your car and kept the little kids off." The night games ended so late, you were usually in bed by that time.

There were a lot of kids. Everybody knew everybody. I was one of eight children. I was the second oldest. We were always playing baseball. We played softball until we were in junior high school. Then we started playing hardball. That's when the guys learned to throw overhand and learned to throw a curve, learned to throw other pitches. We played at the playground. The Howard Playground. It is now a parking lot for the university. We were there from sunup to sundown. We just played baseball all day long.

We'd play with a tennis ball. We'd play where a guy would stay in front of the bleacher wall and we'd throw the tennis ball at a target on the wall. It was a form of stickball. It was just pitching and hitting. We'd play baseball in the alleys. That was with bats and a softball. Then we started breaking windows and we had to move that off and go on up to the playground. The big kids were at the playground and we'd have to play somewhere else. Then we got to be the big kids and we were there all the time. We played baseball. That was all I played.

They had a playground director. They would bring in teams from the other playgrounds and we'd play each other. We were J. O. Williams's boys. J. O. Williams was a big father figure to a lot of guys. He was a recreation department employee and a Boy Scout leader. He was just a wonderful guy. I don't think they make them like that anymore. We'd get out early in the morning, get enough of us together, we'd have a nice game. If we didn't have enough to put everybody on the field, we'd rotate and play a lot of different positions. I still wanted to be a first baseman. Then I got run out of my job by, of all people, Walter Fauntroy, who became a representative from Washington, D.C. He was in the House for a long time. He was a left-hander and a real good baseball player. I had to go find another position. I tried third base for a while. I ended up being a catcher. I caught in junior high school, high school, and into college. I played three years at Howard.

◆

When the Senators were away, the Homestead Grays played their home games there. I didn't realize it then, but they had started up around Pittsburgh, in Homestead, Pennsylvania. But they were playing their home games in Washington, D.C. I remember Josh Gibson. Cool Papa Bell was the center fielder. He was a very, very fast guy in his younger days. One of the things I remember is, people used to like to dress up to go to the ball game, especially Sunday games. They would come directly from church. The men wore suits and the ladies had their nice print dresses. That was a big day. And they oftentimes played doubleheaders on Sunday. Sometimes they would have four different teams play. They'd have a nice crowd, mostly seated in the lower stands.

The place would always be packed when Satchel Paige would come in with his Kansas City team. The Monarchs. Indianapolis, they had the Clowns. Goose Tatum played on that team. He was a first baseman for a while. He did some crazy stuff. That was always enjoyable. They were colorful, and they played good baseball. The Philadelphia team had a guy named Sam West. I thought Joe Kuhel was a fancy first baseman. But this guy, West, he could catch the ball behind his back, between his legs.

I remember seeing Jackie Robinson play. You'd hear the old folks talking about the players. "Yeah, they got this young boy. He's really good." I think they were talking more about the chances of these players making it in the big leagues. Of course, the conversation was always, "How would these guys do if they were playing in the major leagues?" We wouldn't find that out until later on. That was something that was just accepted. That's the way things were. There were a lot of things that you just accepted. I don't remember feeling angry about it. Of course, when we were little kids, we used to ask questions. Why can't you do this and why can't you do that? Washington, D.C., was an interesting town. You could ride buses and streetcars. There wasn't any sitting in the back or anything like that. But when you got downtown, there were just certain things you couldn't do. And you grow up just accepting that. It wasn't until later on that we started to question these things.

In '47, when Jackie Robinson started with the Dodgers,

. . . . .

that put me at thirteen years old. That was big, big excitement. Just the thought of those guys being able to play, to finally get the chance to see what they were going to do. I remember reading everything about him and listening to people talk about him. Of course, he endured a lot of hardship. They sure picked the right man. I can't imagine anybody else being able to go through that and doing well. You wouldn't find that many blacks at the games normally. But, man, they started coming out to the ballpark. Let me tell you, they started packing the ballpark in droves. I remember when some of the other teams started getting more black players in. That place would be packed when the visiting teams came. Larry Doby, I remember particularly, hit a ball to dead center field that hit the loudspeakers. That was quite a distance. Satchel Paige was a big crowd favorite. A lot of the older guys remembered him. That was big news. They got him in his later years, when his better years were behind him, but he could still throw the ball.

I wanted to see the black players, and I wanted to see them do well. It was such a novelty. I remember the St. Louis team. They had black players. I remember seeing a situation where this guy came up with the bases loaded in a very clutch situation and you could just feel the tension. He got a single. And people were so relieved. I don't think they really cared whether Washington won the game or not. They wanted to see the black players do well. Of course, it was the death knell for the Negro baseball leagues.

I just stopped going to Senators games. When they made the move to RFK, that just didn't seem right. It just didn't seem the same. At RFK, if you were sitting in the outfield, you need opyglaoooo. Griffith Stadium was so much a part of my life. It was such a beautiful field. Then you started seeing weeds growing there. That was kind of sad. I went out there a couple of times. You just shook your head. It was like an old friend that had died. They tore it down eventually. The Howard University Hospital is there right now. When I visited somebody there once, I said, "You know, your room is juuust about in dead center field." I had to laugh. I was still relating to how things used to be.

HEAVEN AT 3:36

JIM SLOPEY, SIXTY,

IS AN INSURANCE SALESMAN IN PITTSBURGH.

I remember sitting in the stands. I can still smell the cigar smoke. I would get those little programs. I can still see old Honus Wagner – he was a coach at the time – sitting in the Pirate dugout. Forbes Field was just a homey ballpark. I can almost remember the first time I walked into that thing and took a look at it. All the green grass. The dirt. I remember looking out at this spacious thing. Beyond the wall – it was brick and ivy and beautiful – beyond the wall was Schenley Park, which was a green mass. And in the fall, the leaves would change. Forbes Field just meant so much to me.

· · · · ·

I grew up in a small mining community. The name of the town was New Millport, up in the central part of the state. It was a very small town. Two churches and a post office and a couple little general stores. My dad had this love for baseball. My dad actually had been a semipro baseball player. He was a catcher. We used to live in this little ramshackle house. We didn't have indoor plumbing, nor did we have electricity. But my dad used to take me in back of this old coal house and he would get down in his catching position and he'd have me fire the ball in there. We played catch many, many a time.

The towns in that area all had little sandlot baseball teams. My dad had played for the town team at one time. He was in his forties when I was born and he had given up baseball. But he and I would chase around to watch the games in the little town we lived in and the other little towns. I would always hear the stories. "Boy, you should have seen your dad play."

They were tough games. They were the coal miners and they were the farmers, and they just lived for baseball. They didn't have anything else going on there. We would go to those games, and they usually started at six o'clock a couple times a week. Long summer evenings. The games would be over and there'd still be some light; we'd go to the local gas station and replay every inning. Guys who had played were still walking around in their uniforms. As a matter of fact, I can remember when I finally made that team, a bunch of us after the games, we would stand around and talk about the game. And then we would go to the old swimming hole, take off our uniforms, with a cake of Ivory soap, and go skinny-dipping. That's how we'd clean up, because we didn't have any running water in the house.

When there weren't enough guys around for a game, I remember a lot of times just a couple of us would go over to an old cow pasture where there was a fence, and we would toss the ball up and try to hit it out of that pasture. The others would try to flag it down and catch it at the wall, at the edge of the fence. Even when we were by ourselves, we'd play. I'll tell you what, I had a life-size statue of Ralph Kiner, with a bat on his shoulder, that was put out by a milk company, the Sealtest Milk Company. When there was nobody else to play ball, I'd go out under the old apple tree, get a bunch of apples, and see how many times I could find the strike zone past old Ralph. He never took the bat off his shoulder.

. . . . .

We would find ways to come to Pittsburgh, which was about 120 miles, and watch the Pirates at old Forbes Field. It was a long drive. It took about two-and-a-half hours. But there was always a Sunday doubleheader. In those days there was a caravan of people who would come down. Two or three carloads of us. We would stop in a little town called Indiana, Pennsylvania, which is the hometown of Jimmy Stewart. And that's where we would always have our breakfast on the way down and our dinner on the way home. In those days they had a curfew where you couldn't start an inning after seven o'clock at night on Sunday. So sometimes we didn't even see a full game. Hank Greenberg, who had played for the Tigers, was a Bucco. So we would come and see Hank Greenberg. They shortened the fence and put the bullpen out there. "Greenberg Gardens." About that time Ralph Kiner was hitting home runs. Home-run-hitting Ralph. It was worth hanging around to the end to see if he would hit one out.

I listened to every one of those games on radio. I listened to a guy named Rosey Rowswell, who re-created those games. He never traveled with the Pirates. He would always re-create the games from ticker tape. You'd hear this ticker in the background, and he'd be there describing this game as if he were there. It was years and years and years before I realized he had never been there.

When I was going to college, I can remember in 1956 – which is the year I got out of Penn State – Dale Long set a record for consecutive home runs. I can remember in the spring of that year, I would still listen to those old ball games. By that time Bob Prince was our guy behind the microphone. I'd listen to those games and lived them. After college I went into the service. I was on a battleship, sailing all over the Mediterranean, and my parents would still send me box scores. I was far enough away, I couldn't hear anything, but I would still keep up with what was going on.

· · · · ·

I got married in 1958, and my wife and I settled in Washington, D.C., where I took a job as a personnel assistant. In those times you could pick up KDKA, and many, many a night I would listen to those ball games while I was prancing the floor with our newborn baby. I can remember the whole season of 1960. As a matter of fact, I still have a program from that year and a schedule in that program where I had written the score of every game. Kept track of it and lived with the Pirates.

Tickets for the 1960 World Series were on a lottery basis. Both my dad and I sent in for tickets. My dad didn't get them. I got two bleacher seats. I got them for Game One. I can remember driving from Washington, D.C., to central Pennsylvania, picking him up, bringing him down to the ball game, watching the Pirates win that game, taking him back to central Pennsylvania, then back to Washington so I could go to work. It was a lot of driving. It was all worth it.

I can remember very well the final game, Game Seven. I was working. My fellow workers were American Leaguers. We were all listening to that game and of course it sounded like the Pirates were out of it. But I was betting lunches like they were going out of style. We were all huddled around a radio. These guys were all razzing me, that the Pirates were down the tubes. Then Hal Smith hit a home run. I was in gravy. I won all kinds of lunches. It looked like all the Buccos had to do was get through the ninth. But in the ninth, the Yankees came back. Again, everybody was on me. In the last of the ninth, with the game tied, we were still huddled around that radio. Still betting lunches. At 3:36 Maz hit the second pitch out. My wife still tells the story. She was in the apartment in Alexandria, Virginia. Our son was born in July of 1959, so he was just more than a year old. She was holding him and watching the game on our old black-and-white

. . . . .

television. When that ball went over the fence, it's strange my son survived. She was tossing him up in the air.

We moved back to Pittsburgh, and I went to as many games as I could. Clemente has got to be the best ballplayer I've ever seen. I can picture him catching that ball in deep right field and throwing that thing on a rope to third base. I can picture him running the bases. I can picture him coming up to bat – he always had a kink in his neck. He was always flipping his neck around. I was at Three Rivers Stadium on the night he got his three thousandth hit. His last hit. He was an extra-special ballplayer. My wife and I were on vacation in Florida. My wife woke me up on New Year's morning and gave me the word that Clemente was dead. I couldn't believe it. It was like a member of the family was gone.

We have two sons. The one who was getting his cranium bashed when he was getting thrown around by his mother in Washington is now thirty-five years old. Of course, the thing to do was to introduce him to baseball. So I managed a Little League team that he played on. And I would do the same things that I could remember doing with my dad. Just playing a lot of catch with him and going out on empty ball fields and hitting him grounders and hitting him fly balls. Then we have another son. He's a Down's syndrome boy. He has also gotten a love for the game. He and I and my wife, we go to spring training from time to time. Our second son was born three days before the last game at Forbes Field. My parents were in town for the birth of this younger fellow and took my older son to the game. Everybody left the ballpark with something. He left with one of those menu things from the wall and a Forbes Field seat. I still have it.

They tore down Forbes Field, but they left a wall. I have a very close friend. He's probably my best friend. He's a minister at a Presbyterian church here. I went to a Bible study of his one time and I don't even know how the conversation came up, but we mentioned our love for baseball. And I said, "It's probably crazy. But I still take my son down to the wall at Forbes Field. We get a hot dog at the original hot dog stand, because hot dogs always taste better at a ballpark. And we have a hot dog and have a little picnic and play catch." He says, "You know, I do the same thing." So we started doing that together. We started doing it on the Sunday before the season started. Then a few years ago we decided that maybe the time to go down there was on the anniversary of Maz's home run. We go down there every October 13, we listen to the replay of the game on a cassette, play some catch. I take my Forbes Field seat with me. Try to coincide so that at 3:36, Maz's home run goes out, and everybody goes nuts like they never heard it before.

I have three mitts. I have my original mitt that my dad got me when I was about twelve years old. It's a lousy, falling-apart thing. I have another that I had gotten when I was in college. Then I have a new one. I have a duffel full of baseballs that I keep in my car. And a baseball bat. This friend of mine and I, we go out and hit fly balls to each other. And if one of us isn't available, I go to a ball field, I'll throw the ball up and hit that whole duffel bag full of balls. And I'll go and pick them up, go back and hit them again. I just love to hear the crack of the bat. And I'm sixty. My son and I still throw the ball to one another. He bought a farm up near those little towns where I grew up. He's starting to hear the same thing I used to hear. "You should have seen your dad play."

SEALS AND OAKS AND ALL
THOSE GOOD THINGS

DICK BEVERAGE, FIFTY-EIGHT,

IS A FINANCIAL CONSULTANT LIVING IN

PLACENTIA, CALIFORNIA.

When I got out of school, I lived in New York for a year. That was the last year the Giants and Dodgers were there. I just lived at those ballparks. I'd almost always go on Friday night. And I'd go on Sunday. That summer I'd guess I saw about fifty games. Occasionally I took a date. I remember one time I had a girlfriend of mine who I had known in high school. I took her to the Polo Grounds for a doubleheader. They were playing the Cardinals. As we walked in – we got there a little bit late – Stan Musial was up. And as soon as we walked in, he hit a home run. She just about collapsed, because Stan Musial was a big deal to us. It was a good date. Haven't seen her since.

· · · · ·

It's part and parcel of my whole existence. It's just like Christmas, New Year's, the seasons of the year. I follow it. I go to games. Periodically I say, "This is it. I'm not going to any games." I get perturbed for one reason or another, because of the management, because of the emphasis on nonplaying things. This lasts for a couple of weeks, maybe. Ten days.

I was born in Omaha, Nebraska. My very best friend's father went to the 1944 World Series, the Browns and the Cardinals. And he came back and told my friend about that. And my friend told me about it. The next year, when the season started, we got into it again, and I naturally expected the Browns to win the pennant again and be in the World Series. They weren't. But the Cubs were.

My uncle, who was a returning war veteran – he got shot up fairly badly at D-Day – he came back through Chicago, and somehow or another he got some tickets to go to the World Series between the Cubs and the Tigers. And he brought the scorecard back. I thought, "Gee, this is neat. All these pictures of the players." And I thought, "Well, of course they're going to be in it again." I was about nine. I think there's a window there, when you're eight, nine, and ten, and you latch on to things and they just sort of stay with you.

The next year we came to California. We came out here as a look-see, you might say. My uncle lived in Alameda and we stayed with him and I discovered the Pacific Coast League. That's where I saw my first game. And I fell in love with that. The Oakland Oaks. Casey Stengel was the third-base coach. He was the manager and he was also the third-base coach. What I remember is, when we were standing outside getting ready to go in, I heard the public address announcer and he's giving this lineup. We walked in and they sort of had a ramp you walked up. And you looked down on the field. We weren't very high, but I'm ten. It seemed like quite a distance. You saw all these guys and the lights were peering down on them and some were wearing white. The Hollywood Stars were the other team. We walked out there and we took our seats. They started the game and there it was. It was like a big play. It was like going to the theater.

Then about three days later, why, we went again. That

. . . . .

time the Seals were in town. They were very good that year and the Oaks were very good that year. Larry Jansen pitched against Gene Bearden. We sat about the same place, down the right-field line. Larry Jansen was a thirty-game winner in the Coast League that year. It was 1–1 and I think it was about the eighth, and Gene Bearden – who was a pretty good hitter – hit this little pop fly and it was a home run. I can still see that in my mind's eye.

Baseball grabbed me. I subscribed to the *Sporting News*. It was fifteen cents a copy. I read all these box scores from all these different leagues and all these different places. One thing about baseball is it gave you a sense of geography. You said, "Well, where is Syracuse? What's it like in Syracuse?" Newark. The Newark Bears. Well, that's right outside New York City. These were all just names in the *Sporting News*, but pretty soon you got acquainted with them. I devised this card game and I put these leagues into play. One time I was running all three of the Triple-A leagues. I had another game that I ran the major leagues on. I had five leagues going. This was in 1947 or '48. I kept the averages and kept the boxes. Funny thing about it, nothing really related to reality. I had guys who were Punch-and-Judy hitters hitting thirty-five home runs. And vice versa.

We went back to Nebraska. We got a team in Omaha in the Western League. Quite a few good players came through there, too. The Omaha Cardinals. Nice park. It was fairly new. The dimensions were fairly large, so you didn't see a lot of home runs. The lights were very good. The uniforms were very white. You could go down and lean over and talk to the players. I got friendly with quite a few.

In Omaha they had a kind of a passageway that the players would walk out of to go to the buses. You could stand out there and get autographs, and they were all very friendly and willing to do that. Well, the first time I went to Wrigley Field,

I did the same thing. I vividly recall Alvin Dark pushing me out of the way. That was my first encounter with a major league player. My uncle lived with us. He worked for the railroad and he used to get these passes, so we were able to go to Chicago on the railroad. It was a seven-hour train ride. We would go back there and take in Cubs games. Sal Maglie pitched the first game I saw there.

I grew up with Harry Caray. He's my very favorite announcer. He was my father's very favorite announcer. My father was a Cubs fan, and in those days Harry was a Cardinal announcer. My father used to get so exasperated. He'd say, "I really like this guy, but why doesn't he do the Cubs games?" Of course, he does the Cubs today. My father is deceased. So many times I've thought, "God, if my dad had lived."

I played a lot, but I wasn't any good. We played almost every day in the summer. We didn't have any umpires or anything. We made up the rules. We did everything they did in the major leagues. We played every day, for two or three hours. Surprising we didn't get any better.

When I graduated from high school, I went east to college. I went to Colgate. I got down to New York a few times. First time I saw the Polo Grounds, that was just unforgettable. I got off the subway at the wrong stop and I had to wander around. I ended up on top of Coogan's Bluff looking down at the Polo Grounds. It was for a night game. That was spectacular. I really remember that. Another time, we went to Yankee Stadium. The Yankees were playing Cleveland. The Indians were ahead. This was in the last of the eighth. The Yankees rallied to tie it. Two on, two out, and they brought in a pinch hitter. It was Johnny Mize. And the first pitch was in the right-field bleachers. I can still see that ball. That was a thrill. All of these things, I just got moved by them.

I saw the last Brooklyn Dodger–New York Giant game at the Polo Grounds. I didn't believe it. No one believed it.

• • • • •

"They're not going. This isn't going to happen." There's no way it was going to happen. That's the way I felt about it. I always had a soft spot in my heart for the New York Giants. But as soon as they moved to San Francisco, I thought, "No way. The team in San Francisco is the Seals. It is not the Giants. The Giants are in New York." I still feel very strongly about that. I was at Berkeley then. Everybody would ask, "How did the Giants do?" I said, "Wait a minute. These aren't the Giants. These should be the Seals." I was a reactionary, to say the least. I went up to Sacramento. Sacramento still had a team in the Coast League. The Solons. When the Cubs came to town, I went to Cubs games.

I was in southern California in '69, on the verge of committing suicide because of the Cubs. I knew we wouldn't win it. We couldn't. I just knew we weren't going to win. Even when we had the big lead. I worked for a company whose headquarters was in Illinois. You could call there in the middle of the afternoon and somebody always had the game on the radio there, so you could find out what was happening. That was pleasant. Then the Cubs started to lose. I just felt they weren't going to do it about Labor Day. On Labor Day I thought we were going to be OK, then we lost a game. Then I thought, "We're not going to do it." And we didn't.

We just sort of moped around. Then we got angry that they weren't winning. Then we got angry that the Mets were winning. There should be no Mets, as far as I'm concerned. There should just be Giants and Brooklyn Dodgers. If God had been right in his heaven that day, there wouldn't be any Mets. There'd be those two clubs, and Seals and Oaks and all those good things. That day Al Weis hit that home run off of Ferguson Jenkins. Opposite field home run. This guy hit like eight home runs in his life. He's hitting this off a Hall of Fame pitcher. Come on. We've got everything upside down. Rod Gaspar, whose son is going to be a first- or second-round pick, he's got a ninety-five-mile-per-hour fastball. I saw that name. I said, "By God, that's that damn Rod Gaspar."

I guess it's kind of childish in a way. I used to think that, you know, when you're in your late thirties, early forties, you're just getting up the career ladder, "Oh, this is really kind of childish, to be involved in this kid's game." Then there comes a point in your life when you say, "Hey, maybe it's really not. It's been there all along, just going along with you. Why don't you just sit back and enjoy it?"

· · · · ·

SNOOKIE, DOTTIE, AND THE SQUIRT

SUSAN JOHNSON, FIFTY-FOUR,
IS A RESEARCH SOCIOLOGIST IN
ANCHORAGE, ALASKA.

I had my favorite players. Snookie Doyle was one of my favorites. She was a shortstop. I think I liked her name and I liked her position. I remember Dottie Kamenshek. She was a first baseman and very, very dependable. She always hit in the high .290s, low .300s, and was an impeccable fielder. I remember the left fielder was Eleanor "Squirt" Callow, because she had a sense of humor. I can remember her coming in and laughing about whatever had just happened. And she was their cleanup hitter, too, which probably didn't escape me.

. . . . .

I grew up in Rockford, Illinois. It's eighty miles directly west of Chicago. Although the area around it is rural, Rockford itself is an industrial town. It was famous for furniture early in its lifetime. During the war it was famous for its machined tools and therefore was a major war industry town. And the All-American Girls Baseball League teams were all placed in towns like that, because the idea was that this was going to be good, clean, wholesome entertainment for war-weary workers – go to the ballpark for the evening and see a ball game for an hour and a half.

My parents discovered the league for me in 1950 when I was ten years old. They must have seen an ad for it in the paper, and we all went off to the ballpark, which was maybe a ten-mile drive from where we lived. What I remember is just being stunned at how wonderful it was to see women playing baseball.

I played baseball as a kid. Pickup games at school recess. Baseball. I went to a country school. There were only three kids in my first-grade class. Everybody of all ages played together. Now, I was pretty good. I can remember eating my lunch really, really fast so I could get out and be first at bat.

We played work-up. Work-up is where you get to bat until you make an out. There are three or four people up to bat. And when one of them was out, then the pitcher came to bat. And then the catcher and first base, and you'd work up through the defensive positions. We'd play on a farm field. We didn't have a baseball diamond or anything. I don't know what we'd use for bases – a hunk of wood or something. The first five years I played school ball, we played in a field that was owned by my parents, because we lived right across the street from the school.

My dad played catch with me a lot. After work he'd come home, and we'd go out in the front yard. I can remember that real clearly. We'd play baseball catch when it was baseball season; we'd play football catch when it was football season. I can remember listening to games on the radio. I'm assuming they must have been White Sox and/or Cubs games. I wouldn't say my dad was a rabid fan. But he kind of had a little tomboy on his hands – this firstborn girl. I was really happy doing that stuff, so he encouraged it and did it with me. I can remember throwing a baseball against a garage door and catching it to practice fielding.

All this was before I went to my first game. I went for five years. I suppose we saw maybe a dozen games a season. It was called Beyer Stadium. And, of course, since my team was the Rockford Peaches, it was called the Peach Orchard. I can remember parking and walking to it. It would be one of those hot, humid, muggy midwestern nights. These were almost all night games. They played daytime doubleheaders on Sundays, but otherwise they were all night games. And you'd sit there in the lights, and the bugs kind of flew around the lights. It was an intimate stadium. It was a high school stadium, in fact. And it maybe sat four or five thousand people. Typically at a game, you'd have a couple thousand people. So you could get real close. I can remember sitting two, three rows behind the dugout. And there would be the women, not more than thirty feet in front of you.

What was important to me was it just wasn't baseball, but it was women playing baseball. Because I could identify with that. They were doing something that I respected since I was a tomboy, and they were playing so well. They had all those fans cheering for them. And, of course, their games were reported in the paper every day. And there were feature articles about them. So they got a lot of attention in town. I just thought it was wonderful. I was in heaven.

I cut out every single account of the game as well as the league standings every day and pasted them in a scrapbook. The beginning of the season, I typed up my own list of the rosters for however many teams there were in the league. I guess the miracle is that I kept those scrapbooks all of these years. It was so important to me. I couldn't bear to throw them away. They were my first source when I started to do my book about the league.* When I decided which players I was going to interview, I started right with my own rosters, which I typed up when I was ten years old.

Lots of times it was just my dad and I who went to the games. Sometimes the whole family went – it would have been my parents, me, my younger brother, and my younger yet sister. I don't remember trying to talk to the players at the games. I think there was something too impressive about them when they were there in their uniforms. But the Peaches Fan Club would have picnics, and I can remember going to those. There the players would be in street clothes, and somehow they would seem more approachable. I would get their autographs on glossy black-and-white pictures. When they were in uniforms, they were really impressive to me. It's like they radiated power. The uniforms were skirts, maybe three or four inches above the knee. And they wore baseball shoes with spikes and long socks. The home uniforms were black and white, and the road uniforms were peach colored.

The Peaches and the whole All-American Girls Baseball League lasted through the 1954 season. And then it folded. I don't remember when I found out, but I'm sure it must have been devastating. The only reason I can imagine why I don't remember is that it was so awful. I was in denial. You know how you can block things that are just too awful to conceive of? I do know that when I sat down in the movie theater to see *A League of Their Own,* the music started to play and the movie started, I just burst into tears. I think it was because I'd been missing it so much. What it felt like was Opening Day again. I had been missing it since 1954.

I kept being a fan. I watched the guys. I went to college outside of Philadelphia, so I went to a couple of Phillies games. I've been in a lot of different major league ballparks. I

When Women Played Hardball (Seattle: Seal, 1994).

usually get to a major league game maybe once a year. Ever since cable TV, I've been watching the Atlanta Braves. I was watching them when Dale Murphy was playing for them and they weren't any good. So I feel like I've earned all their achievements now.

In Anchorage there's a lot of softball. I go out and watch a couple of the women's teams. Because of my baseball book, I got to throw out the first ball last year for the Anchorage Glacier Pilots, which is a men's college summer league. But it's a completely different thing. The Peaches were a heart thing. I was in love with them. I remember last year seeing a game and I was sitting there in the stands and there was this little girl, I'll bet she was maybe ten years old. And there she was, she had her baseball glove. She was a little too little to fight with the boys to retrieve a ball. She was standing there at the fence and she was kind of looking wistfully out at the field, and I just thought it was the saddest thing. There wasn't anybody there she could identify with. She was obviously aching to do that. You could just feel the kind of confusion or frustration or sadness, or at least I could project it onto her. She was trying to find a place for her there. And there wasn't any place. She'll give up soon because she won't be able to figure out how to fit into baseball.

THE MAGNOLIA THAT STOOD
IN CENTER FIELD

LARRY TAYLOR, FIFTY-FOUR,
IS A MAJOR GENERAL IN THE MARINE CORPS
RESERVE AND A CAPTAIN WITH NORTHWEST
AIRLINES. HE LIVES IN ATLANTA.

I remember being very upset and writing possibly my first letter to the editor of the newspaper when I was a kid. They stopped printing the box scores of all the big league games and started printing line scores only. That just infuriated me.

I used to peruse those box scores. I remember very well when the Nashville Volunteers had a second baseman named Larry Taylor. I remember checking what he did every day, because he had the same name I did. I read box scores the way some people read the Bible.

· · · · ·

I remember when I was a kid, the Atlanta Crackers of Double-A baseball used to draw more people than the old St. Louis Browns. I didn't go to a lot of the games because we didn't have a lot of money. But we lived in the neighborhood and I remember driving by Ponce de León Park. I just used to be so fascinated. We'd drive by and I'd ache for that glimpse looking down the tunnel into the ballpark. Just that glimpse

146

of the green and the brown. It just intrigued me. It was just so symmetrical and brightly colored. I still get that same feeling when I walk into a ballpark. I guess that's one of the reasons I hate artificial turf so much.

When we actually went to a game, I remember being able to hear everything that's going on. You could hear the coaches and the managers holler, the players hollering at each other. And the players could hear everything we were saying. Even when I was a little kid, I had a fairly strong voice. I tried to make myself heard and I usually did.

One of my lasting memories was that there were a lot of intense rivalries in the minor leagues in those days. I remember the biggest rivalry in Atlanta was the Atlanta Crackers and the Chattanooga Lookouts. That was like the Yankees and Dodgers or the Giants and the Dodgers. If I was going to get to go to a half-dozen games a year, I wanted it to be Atlanta-Chattanooga. I remember seeing a humongous brawl one day in a Sunday doubleheader. I'll never forget Whitlow Wyatt, who was a coach for the Crackers, was in the middle of it. It was one of those things that was imbedded in a young guy's brain.

I remember being confused as a kid over the fact that black people had to sit in a separate part of the ballpark. There wasn't a black ballplayer in Atlanta in the minor leagues until Johnny Joe Lewis, who played a little bit with the Mets later, broke the color barrier around 1960. Another game that really, really registers on my brain – this had to be within a year after we moved to Atlanta. Jackie Robinson had been in the league a year. And the Dodgers came barnstorming back up from Vero Beach, heading back toward Brooklyn. They played an exhibition game in Atlanta.

There was such a demand for tickets, especially from the black community, that they put in a rope twenty feet in front of the fence in the outfield and they sold standing-room tickets to the black citizens of Atlanta. It was just a sea of black out there behind that rope. I think there was somewhere in the neighborhood of twenty-one thousand people in a park that was only supposed to hold fourteen thousand. I was there. I remember seeing Jackie Robinson attempt to steal home. I can't remember if he made it or not. All I know is that it was the loudest roar you ever heard in your life when he broke from third. It was what everybody had come to see.

The magnolia tree that stood in center field at Ponce de León Park was sort of the symbol of baseball in Atlanta. Not only was it standing on an embankment, on a kudzu embankment, in center field, there was no fence in front of it. So if a ball got by the center fielder and rolled up into that kudzu where the magnolia tree was, it was almost a guaranteed inside-the-park home run. All ballparks are special to me, but this was sort of where I matriculated as a fan. The tree is still there. The rest of the area where the park was is a failing shopping center. So that empty parking lot is sort of a forlorn place. But out there where center field was, there's still that magnolia tree. I run a lot. I'll occasionally run by there just to see if it's being kept up.

The Crackers. There was a guy named Bob Montag. He never made it to the big leagues. There was an outfielder named Ralph "Country" Brown, who was a local hero. He was very much a local celebrity, too, because he never made it to the big leagues. He was a guy who stayed with the Crackers year after year after year. Eddie Mathews. The first kid, the first young guy who I focused on who obviously was going to become a star in the big leagues was Eddie Mathews. He was here when he was nineteen years old. I remember seeing him hit three home runs one day. He hit thirty or thirty-two home runs that season and committed two errors for every home run. I loved watching him. And I remember how hard he worked, and he developed into a pretty good third baseman.

· · · · ·

Every now and then, I'd go watch the Black Crackers. There was sort of a mirror-image league in those days. I remember the Black Crackers used to play the Birmingham Black Barons. There were big rivalries in that league, too. I was just going to watch a baseball game. I never really gave a lot of thought as a young man as to why there were these separate facilities and leagues. It didn't seem right, but it certainly seemed out of my league to do anything about it at age ten or twelve. The days that the segregation barriers were breaking down were when I was in high school. I remember thinking, "Yeah, this just doesn't make sense. It's just not right. That's as true for the ballpark as it is for the schools."

I went to college and went into the service. In '66 I was stationed at Camp Lejeune, North Carolina. I came back home for the very first game they had here in Atlanta. Willie Stargell hit a home run in the top of the eleventh, I think it was. I remember Tony Cloninger, who was supposed to be the big horse of our pitching staff, he went the whole eleven innings and it was a chilly night. He was never the same after that.

One of the things that always bothered me was that I spent the entire year of 1967 in Southeast Asia. That was probably the greatest pennant race that had happened in the American League until that point. That was the year the Red Sox barely beat out three other teams. I was working for a company called Air America. I was flying helicopters in Laos. I didn't really get the news on a daily basis. That great baseball season and I didn't really find out about it until after it happened.

I was at that game when Hank Aaron broke Ruth's record. Of course, two million people claim they were there. I was in fact there when he hit that home run. I remember taking my mother, may she rest in peace, and my son, who was only twelve. I remember we sat there freezing our buns off, and Hank Aaron hit it in his second at bat. There were fifty-two thousand people there, and forty-eight thousand got up and left after the cheering stopped. That was pretty damn exciting. I remember my son saying, "I can't believe we're really here." Hank Aaron, in my youth, was playing in the minor leagues in Jacksonville, Florida, in the old Sally League. That was several years before any black player was allowed to play in Atlanta. Ironic.

I attached myself to the Braves and have remained attached, although I have to admit it's really hard to root for the same team that Jane Fonda roots for. It began to dawn on me as I got older that the thing that attracted me the most to baseball was that it was the most quantified human activity on the planet. I guess it is the ultimate meritocracy. Kind of like the military, in a way. Except even the military is more subjective than baseball. Everything that you do or fail to do on a baseball field is recorded in some fashion.

A story I like to tell. I go to spring training every year. I show up at the ballpark as soon as they open the gates. I wander around. Most of the other folks would be old folks. Retirees. They wander around and talk to their friends and talk to the players. Then finally they settle into their seats sometime before the game. Then they doze off. They sit there and doze for most of the afternoon, then comes the last out, the crowd cheers, and they wake up. It always occurred to me that that's the way to spend your declining years. Sitting there, drinking a beer, and dozing at the ballpark after having spent the first hour or two talking baseball with your friends.

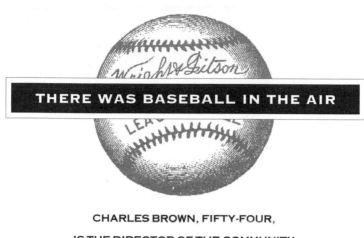

THERE WAS BASEBALL IN THE AIR

CHARLES BROWN, FIFTY-FOUR,

IS THE DIRECTOR OF THE COMMUNITY

LIAISON PROGRAM FOR THE TEXAS

DEPARTMENT OF CRIMINAL JUSTICE. HE LIVES IN

HUNTSVILLE, TEXAS.

Everybody played ball in Key West. It was like a ritual. The weather was so good that we had baseball year-round. Baseball was the in thing. Of course, we're talking way back in the '50s.

We played morning and afternoon. Our only concern was playing baseball and, after playing ball, jumping into the Atlantic Ocean to take a swim.

. . . . .

We had a lot of teams coming down to Key West because the weather was so ideal. We even had teams coming from Cuba. You had the Grapefruit League. We had semipro teams like the Kansas City Monarchs. The Miami Marlins were pretty big. They would play at the high school. We also played on the naval base. We had a naval base and a marine base in Key West. They enjoyed playing local boys. That was big. On Sundays, oh, man, that was the thing. You would go to the ballpark and everybody was rooting like this was the major leagues.

The Kansas City Monarchs. Those guys, man, they looked like giants. They could really hit the ball. It was kind of amazing to see that. Back then, radio was the thing. You'd listen to the radio and then to actually see somebody throwing the sliders and knocking a few over the fence. It was just like, man, this is great. The Cuban teams, those guys could play. They had guys throwing those big breakers. They had some guys who could really drill that ball. Some of those guys could go in the hole and get 'em and turn the double play. The crowd would just roar. Those guys, I think they would rather play ball than eat. On Key West there's not a whole lot to do. But baseball is something that seemed to attract people. If they got word that the Cuban team was coming, they didn't have to put it in the paper. It went by word of mouth.

If your parents would take you up to Miami, you could see the big boys. The Yankees, the Dodgers, the Sox, and all those teams that would come up there. You would see these guys prior to the game and how they would bat, hitting those balls over the fence. That was like a child's dream come true. We used to go every year. Sometimes we would spend the night, catch the Saturday game and then the Sunday. Sometimes we caught a twin bill. It was jam packed. You would have fun. Have popcorn, yell, try to catch foul balls. It's a pretty good drive from Miami to Key West – 158 miles. That was the thing: "You've got to be a good boy to go to watch the Dodgers and the Yankees."

I saw superstars, man. These guys were just good. We would get to the park early. Every now and then, we got autographs. I kind of liked Roy Campanella. It was amazing to watch him play. It was like he was made for baseball. You couldn't wait till you got back and then got to school the next day. "Hey man, I went over and saw the Yankees. I saw the Dodgers."

The Dodgers just seemed like they were the premier team. We would go up to Miami and watch them play in the Grapefruit League, then we'd come back and try to emulate what we'd seen them do in spring training. We'd get together and have different teams. "I'm playing third base. I'm Billy Cox." I remember so vividly how some guys would try to get into a crouch like Stan the Man. Baseball cards were a big thing on the island. Everybody tried to swap out and get the top players, like Gil Hodges, Carl Furillo, Duke Snider, Mickey Mantle, Hank Bauer, Steady Eddie Lopat.

When we'd listen to games on the radio, we listened real attentively. And when we played, we tried to emulate people who we thought were good, whether they were black or white. We just enjoyed the game of baseball. I don't think we were hung up on the race thing. There was so many ethnic groups in Key West. Puerto Ricans, Cubans, blacks, whites, Filipinos, you name it. And they played a lot together. In the pickup games sometimes we would have blacks mixed with Cubans; sometimes the Cubans played with the whites. Sometimes we had all-Cuban teams; sometimes we had an all-white team. If you were good, I don't care if it was a white team or a Cuban team, they wanted you playing with them. It was somewhat similar to the Jackie Robinson deal. I mean, who wouldn't want Jackie Robinson on their team?

We were so involved in the baseball thing. We would go by this little place. The guy's name was Johnson, I think. But everyone called him "Treinta-tres." For thirty-three. That was his nickname. See, everybody in Key West had a nickname. Anyway, he had a little place we couldn't go in because they had drinking in there. But we could sit on the outside. They would play dominoes, and they had this baseball pool. This guy had the names of all the teams painted on a large blackboard. They had this ticker tape. As the information would come in by ticker tape, he would keep the innings updated and he would write who hit the home runs.

We would sit outside on the stairs, looking through a window. We would sit there for hours at a time. We would wait till he changed the scores. If we were pulling for the Dodgers and they were behind, we would get a feeling if they were scoring some runs in their at bat. It seemed like it took the longest time for that ticker tape to come in. Then we'd see that they scored seven runs.

We played ball two and three times a day. I mean, we played, we played, we played. Do you remember George Mira? He played quarterback for the Forty-niners. I went to school with Georgie Mira. Mira was probably one of the best ballplayers to leave the island. And Boog Powell. Boog played with Key West High School. He used to drill them out of the stadium all the time. I remember Boog because he was so big. We used to play the schools out of Miami. We had a guy by the name of Paul Higgs. He was from Key West. but his parents moved to Miami. Man, he was a nemesis to Key West. He was real good. He and Mira used to hook up all the time in pitchers' duels. It was just a lot of fun. I wish every kid could have an experience like that growing up.

I left in '60. It was never quite the same. When you were there, you ate and slept baseball. When you woke up, man, you got your glove ready. There could be a little pickup game on the way to school. It was baseball in the air.

OFF THE PORCH AND INTO THE TREES

MARSHALL FOGEL, FIFTY-FOUR,

IS AN ATTORNEY IN DENVER.

This is kind of a Field of Dreams *story. I used to beg my father to play ball. He never played catch with me. He was born in Europe. So finally one day I got him to do it. Finally I got him out and put a mitt on him.*

He threw the ball to me and I threw the ball to him. One time. Broke his thumb. That was the end of it. He never played ball with me again. He was a good guy, but I broke his thumb.

· · · · ·

I grew up in Denver. At that time it was a pretty sleepy town. As a child, we had what was called the Old-Timers League. We were sponsored by different small businesses. My team was the Tick-Tock Lounge. In later years I found out that was a gay bar. You'd put on your Converse tennis shoes – we didn't have cleats – jeans, and they'd give you a T-shirt. And then you'd go to the park, and you just played and turned in your score. No umpires, no coaches. And after that you'd hang out. Talk baseball.

You put neat's-foot oil on your glove, tied a rubber band

around it. That was kind of a big event during the week, to get your mitt ready. If you wanted to wear a uniform, you could wear the pants. But they were wool. A lot of us used to put pajama bottoms underneath because that wool would scratch the heck out of you. It was everything. If you played baseball, you were kind of a little hero.

My father used to take me to Merchants Park, where the Denver Bears played. At that time it was the Western League, A-ball. We'd go to games from time to time. My dad used to tell me that Gehrig and Ruth would come through here barnstorming. It was a park that was covered along the grandstand side, all the way around from right field to left. I remember it was pretty dilapidated. It always leaked when it rained, and we had to move around to avoid the leaks. But, gosh, I thought that was pretty exciting to go to a ball game. Especially when my father would take me, because he worked quite a bit. It was a chance for he and I to get together, which was not often.

I remember, later on, we were a Yankee farm club. Don Larsen played here. Tony Kubek, Bobby Richardson. Those are the players I remember. I remember as a Yankee fan, everything seemed to rhyme: Tony, Bobby, Casey, Mickey, Whitey, Yogi, Yankee, Jerry, who was Jerry Coleman. It was kind of a mystical thing to me as a kid. It just seemed to be all-American. I was a catcher. My idols were Yogi Berra, Mickey Mantle, and the Yankees. They were the perennial winners. Year after year the same players were always there. I can't think of a kid who didn't like the Yankees or the Dodgers.

I don't know if anybody else did this. We all used to get together in our neighborhood, which had a lot of trees. We'd turn the radio on. We'd listen to the Yankees play. So if I wanted to be Mickey Mantle, I would be the person who would be up at the plate, which was the porch. So when

. . . . .

Mantle got a hit, I'd run to the first tree. If he got a double, I'd run to the second tree. So we used to use the trees in the neighborhood and turn the radio on and pretend we were part of that team. We'd play nine innings, or till whenever we got tired. That was kind of a big thing in our neighborhood.

We had a place called Candyland. That's where you'd buy your baseball cards. In 1953 – that was the first year I remember Topps were sold here in Denver. They only sold the last series. I used to get Willie Mays after Willie Mays and Satchel Paige after Satchel Paige. I remember I had tons of those. I remember that Mantle was an idol. Nobody could get that card. Everybody wanted it. Finally a couple of guys got one. They were pretty much the heroes of the neighborhood. I always kept my baseball cards. My mother never threw them away. She couldn't find where I hid them. I always got there before she did.

The Bears had a guy named Andy Cohen. He was our hero. I'm Jewish. Our book of sports heroes is pretty thin. Hank Greenberg was kind of a hero. Sandy Koufax. I remember when he didn't play on Yom Kippur in the World Series. In fact, I met him and I said to him, "God, my parents thought you were a real hero. You didn't play." He said, "I'll bet I made a lot of kids unhappy." I said, "Uh-uh. You made a lot of us proud." Andy Cohen was going to be the Giants' Jewish ballplayer. That was in the '30s. Then he came to Denver and became an incredibly successful manager. He used to have a little thing, a little superstition. In those days a manager would coach third base. He'd get right on the end of the little ground they were supposed to stand in, and he'd curtsy. Every inning. He'd bend his right knee, like he was curtsying to a queen.

I remember the Opening Day when they moved to Mile High. It was called Bears Stadium then. There were so many people there, they let you sit on the warning track. If you hit a ball on the warning track, it was an automatic double. I went to see the Yankees when they played here. I was in a daze. I didn't even know what the score was. I just couldn't believe they were real. My father told me years later that someone like Mickey Mantle, he should never die. He'd live forever. I still remember him telling me that. When I thought of Yankee Stadium, I thought it was around the world somewhere. It was a dream. Who wouldn't want to be like Mickey Mantle? Who wouldn't want to play for the Yankees? God, I used to play ball in the winter. I used to go out with my friends in the snow and play ball. Because we were going to play in the majors.

But I went to college during the early '60s. You could see the change taking place. People were interested in civil rights. I think baseball kind of faded from everybody's mind during those years. I lost interest, like a lot of people did, because there was such political upheaval in this country. Castro was in Cuba. Kennedy was president. This was during Vietnam. A lot of people who would have watched baseball were interested in the war. A lot of them went to war. I think it was just a bad time for baseball. Nobody cared. The players got traded. I remember Mantle saying he'd take a salary cut to stay with the Yankees. Mantle was gone. All that dynasty was gone. I only paid attention peripherally to the game.

It came back. In 1989. Boy, did it ever. Somehow, I can't explain why, it was always with me. That's how much I love the game. I started enjoying the history of it all. I started buying baseball cards. And memorabilia.

The game has been a glue to the history of this country. You say to yourself, "Why is it that baseball attracts so many people, as opposed to other sports?" The reason's simple, if you've ever watched *High Noon* with Gary Cooper. Here he is, standing alone in the street. The odds are against him, and he comes out to be a hero. There's a similarity in baseball. It's

. . . . .

the only game where it's only you that can win. You're up there alone. And there are nine other gunmen out in the field to get you. And you're Gary Cooper.

In 1988 I took my son to Boston. I bought some tickets from a scalper. Told me they were great seats and they were the worst thing in the world. But I saw Fenway Park and I took my son. All the things that you dream of. Just being with my kid at the ball game. I flashed back to all those times when I was a kid. Now we've got the Rockies. Can you imagine? Opening game, Mile High Stadium. Over eighty thousand people there. Bottom of the first inning. The first-ever Rockie is up to the plate. He hits a home run. Do you think that noise has ever stopped? This is great. Coors Field? It's just like Ebbets Field. Just like it. Boy, is it neat.

I play catch. I've got all the gear. I go out and play with the kids. My arm's killing me at the end, because I abused it as a kid. I do it because I enjoy it, because my father never did it very much. It brings my son and me together. He listens to absolutely nothing I tell him. He's fourteen. It's kind of disappointing, because I know Mickey Mantle's father really was an influence on him. Well, I'm no influence at all on my kid, except to play catch and keep my mouth shut. But I get a kick out of it. You know, time doesn't change what baseball does for you. The equipment's different, lots more sophisticated, and the game's more demanding. But the same results come from it. What I got out of it in the '40s, my son's getting out of it in the '90s. It's just the same thing. It's always good.

One bit of advice. If you have a radio, you ought to try that thing with the trees. As a matter of fact, I'm thinking about doing it again myself.

· · · · ·

Off the Porch and into the Trees   159

ME AND THE MICK

**CESAR PELLERANO, FORTY-FOUR, IS A
CARDIOLOGIST LIVING IN MIAMI LAKES, FLORIDA.**

*I had put together a Mickey Mantle scrapbook. I had four of them. In
'68, just before he retired, I went at two in the afternoon for an eight
o'clock game. I waited at the gate until the Yankee bus came in. I was
the only kid there. But I wasn't a kid anymore. I was seventeen.*

*When Mantle came, I showed him the scrapbooks. He signed them
for me. I think I literally skipped out of the ballpark. I was seventeen
years old and I was going out with girls and I drove myself to the
ballpark. And I must have felt like I was nine years old.*

*Years later, 1985 or '86, I got to know Mickey pretty well. I said,
"You know, the first time I wanted to meet you, I had these scrapbooks
and I waited from two o'clock on for the bus to come in from the
hotel."*

And he goes, "Did I sign them?"

I said, "Yeah, you signed them."

*He goes, "Boy, thank God. You'd be surprised how many guys tell
me they waited for hours and I brushed them off."*

I still have the scrapbooks, even though he misspelled my name.

. . . . .

When I was about five years old in Cuba, my grandfather was an incredible baseball fan. He would listen to the games. I didn't know all the players, but I knew who Mickey Mantle was. My grandfather gave me a bat for my birthday. A Mickey Mantle model bat. And a black glove. I started playing. I can't remember not playing baseball.

Cuba had four teams in the winter league. Willie Mays played there one year. A lot of major leaguers would play there. Those teams were very popular. Of course, the Yankees were popular. I think that's where I became a Yankee fan. We're talking about the 1950s. They obviously dominated baseball. They had all the marquee players. They were in the World Series almost every year. I believe the World Series used to be broadcast down there, although I don't remember listening to it. I do remember my grandfather talking about it.

We came to the States in '61. We immediately moved to Tennessee. East Tennessee, in the mountains. We didn't have a whole lot of money. My cousin, who is only two years younger than I am, came to live with us. For the first time, I had a brother. He loved baseball, too. Between the two of us, we started following the Yankees. Of course, the '61 season was the Mantle-Maris race. We only got two channels on television. So I remember following that mostly on the radio, hearsay at school, and some in the newspapers. But I remember the race and I remember rooting for Mickey Mantle.

We moved to Johnson City, which was only thirty miles away. It was still pretty distant from major league baseball, but the Johnson City Yankees used to play there. They were a minor league team in the Appalachian League, which in those years was very active. If I'm not mistaken, Roy White was there. And Bobby Murcer. The stadium that they played in was directly behind the tennis courts, and if they hit a home run, the ball would land on the tennis courts. It was a great way to get baseballs to play with. We would play all the time. We didn't play organized Little League in those years. We played a lot of sandlot baseball. I taught myself how to switch-hit playing Wiffle ball in my backyard with my cousin. The people in Tennessee were wonderful. I never felt uncomfortable. I think being able to play ball helped us merge into the mainstream quicker.

The first organized baseball game I ever went to was there. I was just thirteen. All the seats were bleachers and in the very front they had folding chairs, and those were your box seats. I remember sitting there and watching and being on top of the field, which had very poor lighting, but to me it was terrific. I remember wishing that I would be able to play someday. It was just exciting to say, "Wow, some of these guys that I'm watching now are going to be New York Yankees."

It's funny, when I think about the years that we did things, I think about baseball. I remember which house I watched the World Series in and because of that, I can remember which year we moved. I remember seeing the '63 and '64 World Series in Johnson City. I remember distinctly watching the '63 World Series and crying. That's when Koufax struck out fifteen guys, and in the last game Frank Howard hit a two-run homer off Whitey Ford and the Dodgers beat them, 2–1.

We moved to Baltimore in the summer of '65. I became even more immersed in baseball. At the end of the '65 season, I saw my very first major league baseball game. I saw the Orioles and Steve Barber pitching against the Indians and Sam McDowell. That I remember as being very captivating. I think almost everyone who loves baseball describes their first experience in a major league stadium the same way. I'm walking up the ramp to our seats in the upper deck, and looking through the ramps, and seeing that green grass and the bright lights. It's a hell of a feeling. You think like you're in heaven or something. "God, I'm actually in a major league stadium. And the grass is greener than any green grass I've seen. The lights are brighter." You actually see your baseball cards come to life. I remember Jackie Brandt playing for the Orioles that day, and Brooks Robinson, Russ Snyder.

From that point on, I was very taken. In fact, I became a regular at the Orioles games after that. Especially when the Yankees came to town, I would ride the bus three or four hours before game time so I could watch the Yankees take batting practice. I still have the scorecard from '66, when I went to see the Yankees play. Mantle, Maris, Howard, Richardson. I went to the stadium and for the first time, I bought box seats. In those days you could walk up and buy a box seat relatively close. I was sitting between home and the first-base dugout, which is where the visitors would be at Memorial Stadium. The first time I saw Mickey Mantle out there – that sharp number seven – it was just a huge thrill. I'd watch him in batting practice just hit bombs. It was exhilarating. When Mickey Mantle retired, I was devastated. I was like a fish out of water. For the first time in my life, I remember looking at the box scores and not seeing Mantle there.

I played high school ball. I played the outfield – I always played center because of Mickey. The one talent I had in baseball was the ability to pick up the ball off the bat. I would strike out a lot, but when I hit it, I would hit pretty well. I entertained thoughts, but I was never a prospect. I'll tell you a story. There was a guy in Baltimore named Greg Arnold. Greg was very fast. In fact, years later, I read that the pitcher in *Bull Durham*, Nuke LaLoosh, was patterned after him. This kid was so fast it was unbelievable. One time in high school, he struck me out four times on twelve pitches. I just didn't come close. That told me something. If I can't hit this bozo, how am I going to hit Denny McLain and Bob Gibson? By my sophomore year of college, I started to get serious about studying.

In '71 or '72 we were living in Florida and I had come home for Easter. We were at Miami–Dade North and we were just practicing. Charlie Hough, who had just come up with the Dodgers in September, was on the field adjacent to us. A guy comes over and says, "Hey, Charlie Hough's over there and he wants to throw to some live hitters. You guys want to hit?" So we all went over there and I faced Charlie Hough. He threw a knuckleball. I'll tell you, I took twenty swings and never got a foul ball. When you're on the field with those guys, you realize you're a mere mortal.

I went to medical school and graduated from the University of Miami in 1978. During that time I always played baseball. We would get a bunch of guys, usually on Saturdays or Sundays. Once I became a resident and a physician and everything, I became more and more immersed in baseball. Let's put it this way. Except for personal relationships, it is probably the number-one love affair in my life. It's as much a part of my life as my career. It's more than a passion. It's something that you try to be close to. I'm not a particularly romantic guy, but I've read about how people are in love with a woman and they can't have her, so they do whatever they can to stay close to her. That's the only way I can look at baseball.

In 1985 I went to my first fantasy baseball camp. It was the Mickey Mantle–Whitey Ford camp in those days. Talk about a thrill. I'll never forget Mickey Mantle walking in the very first night, wearing a white polo shirt, saying hi to everybody. How many people grow up idolizing somebody and actually get to meet him? I've been to most of the camps since. I had a game once where some guy hit a ball in the gap in center field. I went out and I caught it. When I caught it, I fell to the ground and everybody cheered. I was coming in and Mickey Mantle turns to me and he goes, "You make it look so easy."

I STOLE DAD'S CAR FOR THE BRAVES

STEVEN BUDNIK, FORTY-SEVEN,

IS A REAL ESTATE TRAINING OFFICER FOR THE

STATE OF WISCONSIN. HE LIVES IN MADISON.

I remember around my ninth or tenth birthday, I got a transistor radio from my parents so I could listen to the games upstairs in my room instead of downstairs in the kitchen on the big radio. I had my own room with my brother. There were various pictures and pennants on the wall. I would twist the radio every which way trying to get the signal in. Earl Gillespie and Blaine Walsh, the Braves' announcers, were people I listened to almost nightly. Those two voices were second only to my parents' as far as being recognizable to me. I'm sure I had to replace a lot of batteries before their time, because I fell asleep and had the radio on all night.

· · · · ·

The Milwaukee Braves. I went to my very first game at County Stadium in August of 1956. I was eight years old. It was a Sunday afternoon, Braves against the Brooklyn Dodgers. Bob Buhl against Johnny Podres, and the Dodgers won. Braves tickets were a little hard to come by. My dad worked in a foundry. His dad was kind of the boss and had gotten these tickets. He must have got them about a week in advance. Several days, at least. I'm absolutely convinced that from Wednesday till Sunday, I didn't sleep. The anticipation. And finally going to County Stadium that first time. It's just something I'll never forget.

The interstate wasn't there, so we had to go through a couple of little towns to get from Manitowoc to Milwaukee. I remember getting there and it just looked to me like the biggest parking lot I'd ever seen in my life. And there in the distance was the stadium. Just walking in through the gate and up the ramp and seeing that field for the first time. I don't think I'd ever seen anything that green in my life. It was a beautiful, sunny day. From there, I'm sure I was just hovering off the ground the rest of the afternoon. I lived and died Milwaukee Braves baseball from that point on.

It meant everything. Not only that you were an eight-, nine-, ten-year-old kid getting into the game, you were smack dab in the middle of the Milwaukee Braves' glory years. In October of '57, when the Braves won the World Series, in Manitowoc, eighty miles away, everyone was outside. It was a Christmas Eve type of feeling. I remember calling one of my friends. We probably didn't make much sense. We were just so utterly happy. My dad, who wasn't a big drinker by any means, went across the street and had a couple of beers. Whooped it up a little bit. It was just incredibly joyous.

I don't have a lot of real vivid memories of when the Braves lost the World Series in '58. The next year, when they ended up tied with the Dodgers in '59, I have a real vivid memory of listening to that play-off, where they lost. I remember how they basically kicked the Dodgers up and down the field and should have won the game, but didn't. How could they possibly have lost that game?

From the earliest years on, I've always been a scoreboard watcher. You almost can't start the next day without knowing

· · · · ·

the updated standings. I can remember the feel of who was in the pennant race, or whoever the Braves were chasing, or whoever was right behind the Braves. I would look at those scores and comment to whoever I was with, "It's the seventh inning and Chicago is taking a long time."

One of the things I remember is the incredible loudness of the crowd cheering. A ten thousand or twelve thousand crowd in Milwaukee would be considerably louder than a twenty thousand crowd somewhere else. One of the finest foods still today is salted, in-the-shell peanuts. That smell, the hot dog smell. Those are the things I remember most.

It was a special place. Whether you sat lower deck or upper deck, box seat or bleachers, I guess I came to regard it as, "Mom, you're in church. You're talking when you shouldn't be talking." There was kind of a reverence of being there. I know between innings and before the game and after the game, I always liked to walk around or just look around. Just take in the entire picture of the stadium.

They were a very big part of my life. I can remember saying more than once, baseball has always been 365 days a year. Some days they're playing games, and some days they're not. In the winter the Braves had caravans and they came up to Manitowoc. I remember at least two or three times insisting that my parents and I go downtown to the hardware store where I remember meeting Birdie Tebbetts and Andy Pafko and a couple other players in January. This was in the early '60s; I was twelve or thirteen. I wasn't old enough yet to realize they were human beings who sometimes did bad things. There was a reverence. That feeling of awe. It was a special thing. Christmas was over and you wanted spring training to get there. This kind of thing in January helped it along. Just perpetuated the idea that baseball is 365 days a year.

You always thought about baseball, almost every day. I can

. . . . .

remember Clark Oil Company was one of the sponsors of the Braves. There was a Clark station in Manitowoc. I remember I told my dad, "You really ought to get gas at this place, because they sponsor the Milwaukee Braves." Even the sponsors had to be good companies, from my standpoint, because they were associated with the Braves.

We ate, slept, and talked baseball. It was a constant topic of conversation. Around '61 or '62, I remember being in a drugstore on Manitowoc with my mom and for the first time laying eyes on a *Sporting News*. This was like Indiana Jones finding the Covenant. From that time on, there was a trip to the drugstore every week to buy the *Sporting News*. It was that important.

During the '64 season, I definitely remember strong rumblings. I know I remember Lou Perini, he owned the team at the time, stating he wanted to sell. I remember thinking, "How could this possibly happen?" The people who were buying the team were essentially from Chicago. I remember thinking, "A big city like Milwaukee, there's got to be somebody rich enough to buy the team. Why does it have to be sold to somebody from Chicago?"

At the end of the '64 season, they did attempt to move, and the county got some sort of injunction and forced them to play one more season in Milwaukee as a lame-duck team in 1965. I remember just an incredible sadness. This team's not going to be here anymore. The thing I remember most is September 22, 1965. I basically stole the family car and went to Milwaukee that night.

I said, "Dad, this is it. We've got to go." I don't know if it was a last-respects thing or a fear that maybe major league baseball would never, ever come back to Milwaukee. It was just a feeling – "If I have to walk eighty miles, I'm going to Milwaukee." My dad wasn't a real serious fan. He worked in a foundry and he worked real hard physically. He didn't want

* * * * *

to go. He usually never put his car keys out on the kitchen table. But this time he put his keys out there, almost like he wanted me to go. I got home from school and he'd just gotten home from work and I took the keys. I'd only had my driver's license for a year. And I'd definitely never driven to Milwaukee before. Somehow I got there, without getting into an accident.

Even after thirty years, that night is so vivid. In a way, it's a little hard to talk about it. Again it was the Dodgers, and the Braves lost. And there were only about fourteen thousand or fifteen thousand people there. But the thing I remember most about it was the game was over, and nobody left. I was four weeks short of my eighteenth birthday, and I remember the game was over, and I basically sat down and cried for a while. Not misty-eyed. Just cried. It seemed like nobody left. I don't remember talking to anybody. I remember sitting there and thinking and crying a little bit and looking up at the scoreboard. I remember how powerful a feeling that was. That these people realize it's over. I don't think I've ever seen that before other than, I was in Tennessee a few weeks after Elvis died. I saw the same sort of look in people's eyes.

Somehow, I made it back home. I remember my mother basically grounding me until I was twenty-one. And my dad not approving, but saying, "No, no, Mom. It's OK." He had to put on a discipline front, but he understood. I guess he was happy I got the car back.

As far as I was concerned, I was always going to be a Braves fan. There was never any doubt that I was going to be a Braves fan. For two or three years there, there weren't any games at all. WSB-Atlanta. You could get them at night. You couldn't listen during the day. And at night, if the weather was bad or the wind was wrong, it always seemed like it would cut out when the bases were loaded. Through a number of those college years, that was the way I listened to the Braves.

The first year I went to Atlanta was 1970. I went with a couple of college roommates. We drove to Atlanta. We saw three games, I think. I've been there thirteen or fourteen times. The Brewers arrived in 1970. As much as I was a Braves fan, I was also a city of Milwaukee baseball fan. And the Brewers were going to be my favorite American League team. But if it ever happened that the Braves met the Brewers in October, I was a Braves fan.

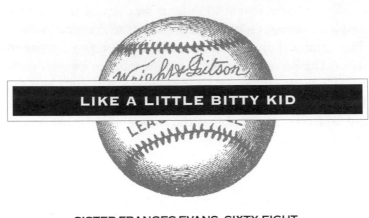

LIKE A LITTLE BITTY KID

**SISTER FRANCES EVANS, SIXTY-EIGHT,
IS A MEDICAL SOCIAL WORKER LIVING IN
FORT WORTH, TEXAS.**

*We played baseball in the convent. It was at our mother house in San
Antonio. We had the long habits on, too. Black, and it was hot as the
dickens.*

*The way our habits were, there were hooks on them and you
hooked up the skirt. You pinned up the sleeves as much as you could.
We just got out there and played ball. A bat and a ball. We had no
gloves. Just simple. Just like when I was a kid. Some of those gals
were big country gals and they were darn good. They could hit the
ball. We didn't exactly look like penguins out on a field. It was fun.
Just plain old fun.*

$$\cdot\ \cdot\ \cdot\ \cdot\ \cdot$$

I grew up in Temple, Texas, which is in central Texas. It's a
small town. My mother owned and operated a boardinghouse.
We were right on Main Street. Everybody knew our house.
I'm an only child. And I'm very much of a tomboy. My
mother really wanted a little girl with lace and frills and she
didn't get one. I was climbing trees and playing baseball.

Just out in a vacant lot with the fellas, with a bat and a ball. Nobody had a glove. Just had a bat and a ball. We started out rough and ready. In grade school, during recess, we always played ball. I played catcher and shortstop.

We moved from Temple when I was a freshman in high school and my baseball days kind of quit. I moved to another little town called Corsicana, which is about fifty miles south of Dallas. In high school, girls were dating and dancing and those kind of things. I do love to dance. I guess I kind of forgot all about baseball. We had no big teams or anything around. In high school, football was the thing.

I went into the convent in 1950. I was twenty-four when I entered. We were not allowed to go to games. Sisters didn't do those things. When I came to Fort Worth, there was the Spurs. I didn't get to go to games of any kind. When the Senators moved to Texas and became the Texas Rangers, I was determined that I was going to see that opener. I had a friend working at the university in Arlington. I had a little money and I had him buy me two tickets. I wanted something behind home plate.

Sister Magdalen and I went. I was really looking forward to it. I was so excited, I was like a little bitty kid. I was forty-six. I remember the crowd, the makeup of the crowd. Baseball is a real family sport. We saw little kids. Teenagers. People in wheelchairs. The crowd at a baseball game is so different from a crowd at a football game. It's beautiful to watch them. I remember Frank Howard hit a home run. I thought I'd come unglued. I was screaming and yelling. We were in habit then, too.

We had a little bit of money. So we had the peanuts and the popcorn. The hot dogs. I'd never been to a big league game. And Maggie had never seen anything like this. So I was determined she was going to get the whole nine yards in case we never got back to another baseball game.

· · · · ·

I was so elated and excited by the game, I was determined to get back there some way or another. And we did that year. We sat all over that stadium. Whatever we had the money for — bleacher seats, whatever. We'd get a ticket and go. Sometimes people would give us tickets. Those would be good seats. It was just, oh, it was just nice to sit out there in the open air and talk to the people and watch the game.

A friend of ours found out we liked the baseball. This was in '73. He started buying our season tickets. And a parking ticket. Angelo bought them. He has a barbecue place. Best barbecue you'd ever eat. Everybody knew us at the park. We went out in our short skirts and our veils on. I was always sad when the season was over, because we were never even close to a pennant. The last game, you'd kind of hang around and visit with all your buddies. When the season would open and you'd be there for the opener, it was like a homecoming. You could hardly wait to get out there.

I like the competition. When I'm at the game, I'm at the game. I've got my radio. We have glasses. I'm there to watch baseball. I'm not visiting. I'm just into the game. I was very sad at the last game at Arlington Stadium. We had a lot of memories there. We sat there until security said, "Y'all have to go." We watched them take up home plate and move it to the new ballpark. It was sad. It was just an old stadium. But it was like home. I spent a lot of time out there. I sat out there in the rain until one o'clock in the morning. We have some yellow ponchos. We were like two old hens out there.

We've been praying for the Rangers ever since 1972. Some of those guys, like Fergie, Bibby, and Mike Hargrove, Toby Harrah, Jim Sundberg, we got to know them. You were almost like a family. I am very loud. I have a certain little call I do at the game. It's loud. At one time we had a cowbell we used to take out there. Someday we're going to be in a pennant race and we're going to win that pennant. Before I get too old to get to the ballpark.

We have baseball memorabilia all over our convent here. We've got baseballs coming out our ears. I have a bat that Billy Martin gave me. I have George Brett's bat that was cracked. Baseball has come alive here. At the hospital, that's all the doctors talk about when they see Maggie and me. We talk baseball. When the oncologist started practicing at our hospital, he treated children as well as the adults. With kids, they're scared and they don't talk too much. I'd use baseball to establish a relationship with them. And with their parents, too. And many of the older people. They all like baseball. We talk baseball all the time. Around hospitals you're not gloom and doom constantly. You've got to have something that's upbeat. Baseball is one of those things. They talk baseball much more than football. Even when the Cowboys are playing.

Baseball is part of my heritage. I just love the game. You know, when you work in a hospital all day, and the kind of work I was in, you saw sadness and you saw death. You were there to support the families and help the individual dying. By the time the day was over, you were done in. You needed to gas up again. To go out to the park . . . you just left all that behind you. It was like the wind would just blow it out of your head. You felt revitalized. I know it sounds crazy, but it's the truth.

✦

I've got a baseball mitt now that Bobby Bragan bought for me at a pawnshop. We took that to fantasy camp with us. The first year we went was in '91. First we were outfitted for our uniforms. Then we were on our way to the Rangers' new spring training place at Port Charlotte. We were out at the airport early. We had the time of our lives. All the campers had a game. One of the campers, he was an ob-gyn man, was pitching and he was wilder than a March hare. I was up to bat. He conked me right on my thumb. Broke it right open. I spent that day at the emergency room. The next day I was suited up. I was third-base coach. It was the first time I'd played since I was in the convent, when I was a novice. We were like little kids again.

We went to spring training a lot. We used to go to Pompano Beach. The first year they were at Port Charlotte, the Rangers took us. That's another exciting thing, to go to spring training. You really get to rub elbows with the guys. Chew the fat. Spit sunflower seeds. I learned how to spit 'em, too. Just like the fellas.

BROKEN WINDOWS IN SUMMER

BARBARA GREGORICH, FIFTY,

IS AN AUTHOR LIVING IN CHICAGO.

I never encountered anybody, I don't recall a single incident of anyone ever saying I shouldn't be playing and that girls can't play. I don't ever recall anyone saying, "Oh, you throw like a girl; you run like a girl." I think that when you grow up on a farm, when you slop hogs and shovel manure, all of which I did as a kid, it never occurred to you or a boy working alongside you that you can't play baseball because you're a girl.

. . . . .

I grew up in a small town in Ohio, Masury. It's south of Youngstown and right across the state line from Sharon, Pennsylvania. There were a lot of empty lots around, and my brother and cousins and I would always play baseball. I can't remember not playing baseball.

We would play on the empty lots around the various houses. There was one lot that was kind of in a swampy area. It had the fewest houses around it, so it was best for playing baseball, in that you didn't break any windows. It was the least good for playing baseball because if the weather were at all wet and the creek were high, you would have to move up to high ground, where it was quite possible to break windows. And we did. Probably broke two or three a summer.

We'd play two or three games a day, I suppose from early spring to late October. I can remember even then thinking with regret, as the days got colder and people turned to football, that we wouldn't have baseball for another four or five months. I would become annoyed when people turned to football. I just saw no need for that.

I was three years older than my brother and two years older than my cousin John. When they were old enough to play in Little League, my uncle who lived on a farm plowed up a regulation Little League field for them. That was fun because then my cousin Kathy and I got to play what we thought amounted to Little League baseball, because all kinds of kids from Little League would come over to play and we were always on the team.

This was, of course, when girls weren't permitted in Little League. I remember being very disappointed. In those days there was no trying out and testing the waters, to challenge it. In those days no one would have ever thought of that. You were just told that you can't, because Little League is only for boys. It didn't spoil my enjoyment of the game. I would go to every single game that my cousin and brother were in.

Masury was a small town. It was in those days racially segregated in the sense that most of the black families lived on certain streets. But they would be right next to the streets that the white families lived on. The kids in the '50s, we would always play with the black kids. It just never crossed your mind not to. It was almost always an integrated game. There were very few girls. My cousin Kathy and I were the only ones I can think of who would play ball. Later, when I was in eighth grade, a new girl moved into town, Janet, and she enjoyed playing for a couple of years. But then she became

. . . . .

a cheerleader. She stopped playing baseball and began cheering for the football team.

Most of us had bats and balls. I would say about half of us had gloves. When we were real young, I'd say five, six, seven, we used to play with a rubber ball that was painted white with the red stitching on the outside. We'd go down to Murphy's five- and ten-cent store and buy them. It seems to me that in about three weeks all the paint was peeled off of them. You were down to the basic red rubber. By the time I was nine or ten, we were playing with a regulation baseball.

My dad was not a baseball fan. My dad was born in what was then Yugoslavia. He came to this country when he was fourteen years old. He was much more interested in soccer and football. I think you have to grow up here to be a baseball fan. But he knew that my brother and I really liked it, so he said, "Do you want a glove?" I said yes. I got one before my brother did because I was older. I remember he took me down and I picked one out. I don't remember what model it was, although I had it for years and years and years.

The Pennsylvania state line was about a quarter of a mile from our house. Right near the line, I can't remember if it was on the Ohio side or not, there was a community ball field with bleachers and everything. I remember going there several times when I was maybe seven, eight, or nine, which would have probably been '51, '52, '53, to see Negro League teams. I'm not positive that I saw the Homestead Grays, but I'm pretty sure I did, because I distinctly remember a game in which everyone was all excited because one of the best Negro Leagues teams around was coming to town to play a local semipro team. I remember that the black team won. I remember just being thrilled at what good baseball I was seeing.

Around the time I was ten or so, I became a fan of the Brooklyn Dodgers. Don't ask me how. I think, when I look back on it, I was very aware that they were the team that had

Jackie Robinson and he was the first black man to play in the majors. I found that very exciting and somehow fair. Maybe *fair* is the wrong word. Correction of an injustice is better. My brother and I began to follow the Dodgers on the radio. We began following them in the paper. In those years, in the early '50s, the Dodgers were almost always in the World Series.

When I was in third grade, I went to my first big league game, at Municipal Stadium in Cleveland. I was on safety patrol in school, and we got to go to three games a year on a safety patrol bus. I would have been eight years old. I remember sitting there and how vast the field looked to me. Just gigantic. And so green. I was just thrilled at the excitement. Everything about it – the sale of the hot dogs, the sound of the public address system. I don't remember who they were playing the first time I went. But let's say I went to ten games as a safety patrol member – the Indians lost every single game. By the time I was in fifth grade, I was no longer a Cleveland Indians fan.

I would just always hope whenever we went to a game that we would get to see the Red Sox, because I thought Ted Williams was just phenomenal. I was always interested in hitting. I loved hitting. I loved to look at hitting, I appreciated hitting, and I just thought Williams was absolutely wonderful. Although I must say, I also enjoyed seeing Jimmy Piersall in the field.

I played until I was maybe fifteen. That was about the time sandlot baseball in the area where I grew up was phasing out. It was harder and harder to get kids together for games. The schools offered more things for kids. I did attend high school baseball games all the time. There might have been seven people in the stands. I went to Kent State University, '61 through '64. I also went to see the baseball team then.

There was a period of six or seven years when I didn't

· · · · ·

follow baseball very much – probably from '63 to '70. That was about the only time in my life that I didn't. It was during the antiwar movement and the civil rights movement and the women's liberation movement. I was very active in all those things, and they just take a tremendous amount of time, day and night.

My husband and I moved to Boston. I had always liked the Red Sox because of Ted Williams, and Phil and I went to as many games as we could. We moved to Chicago in '73. We have season tickets to both the Cubs and the White Sox. Partial season tickets.

One of the things about baseball that always appealed to me, as an infielder – I usually played short, sometimes second – is that the possibilities always seemed endless. What if he hits it here? What if he hits it there? You have all these things thought out. Sometimes, even now while I'm watching a White Sox game, I think of all the possibilities. I find that infinitely appealing.

There are parks and sandlots around here. Very close. But everyone appears to be playing organized ball. I can't say I see anyone playing the way we used to play.

The swamp where I used to play is now a house. There are two houses built on the lot. The ball field my uncle had on the farm is all overgrown with weeds. You'd need a machete to hack through to find where home plate was.

I still play. Phil and I, every spring, we go out and toss the ball around. We even hit fungoes if we can.

· · · · ·

HORNSBY HIT ONE OVER MY HEAD

JON DANIELS, FORTY-SEVEN,

IS A CERTIFIED PUBLIC ACCOUNTANT

IN CHICAGO.

After Musial retired, Gibson became the player I followed the closest. So I made a point of going to watch him pitch. The whole summer of '68, I was in Chicago, and it was that summer when Gibson had his almost invincible season. I was still in my MBA program at the time. I never missed class – I missed only two days as an undergrad because of illness and I didn't miss any as a graduate – until the day I skipped a class to watch Gibson pitch that last game in the World Series.

. . . . .

When I was six or seven years old, I had a cousin who collected baseball cards. One day he happened to be visiting and he said, "Why don't we go to the store?" And when we were in the store, he bought baseball cards. And I thought what the heck, and bought some, too. The thing that made me buy more cards was that Musial was my favorite player. And I wanted to get his baseball card. The only problem was, there was no Musial card put out between 1954 and 1958. I just kept buying the cards. But he never was there.

I got an allowance for doing farm chores. When we would go to the grocery store, I would buy cards. At one grocery store, I could buy Topps. There was another grocery store where I could buy Bowmans. The Bowmans were a penny for one card and one piece of gum. The Topps came with five cards and the gum. I was always more interested in the back of the card than the front. The ones in those days came with a lot of verbiage about the player rather than a lot of stats. I kept my ball cards by team in a shoebox in my dresser drawer.

My father, who had a strong interest in baseball, kind of got me started in following the Cardinals. This was in 1954. We lived thirty miles outside of St. Louis on a farm. So I went to only one game a year for four years. Going to the ball game was a real event. The first time I went, the Cardinals were playing Cincinnati. My father, who had his own company, got tickets right behind the dugout. I could rest my soda right on the dugout. It was the best seat I ever got.

I remember Musial, the first time he came up, getting a hit, but the people I remember most are Brooks Lawrence and Tom Alston. They were the only black players the Cardinals had at the time. I also remember my father always liked to get the hot dogs outside the ballpark. He said it was thirty cents inside the ballpark, twenty cents outside the ballpark.

My father wanted me to get more interested in playing baseball. So I was on a Little League team and very quickly realized I didn't get much enjoyment out of playing. My father didn't push me a lot. But rather than going to summer camp, in 1957, when I was eleven years old, I went to Rogers Hornsby's baseball camp. It was located outside of Hannibal in a place called Honeywell, Missouri. I was there for three weeks.

Hornsby was only going to be there a few days. But they had one ballplayer who had retired from the Texas League a couple of years before by the name of Vern Kennedy. He was a pitcher for the White Sox who won twenty games one year and actually pitched a no-hitter against the Cleveland Indians in the '30s. He was responsible for the barracks. Everything this guy told us to do, I did three times. I just followed everything he said. I bunked right beside him and listened to him talk about baseball. I asked him to relate his no-hitter, the different batters that he had to pitch against. I was like this guy's shadow. I followed him everywhere during the whole three weeks.

I remember Hornsby coming up for three days and he was real ornery. He was born in 1896, but he could still hit fairly well. Being a little kid watching this guy hit was just overwhelming. He had this habit of liking to hit to all fields. I was playing in right field. He hit the first ball to left field. So I knew the third ball he was going to hit was going to me. I just started running back as fast as I could, and he still hit it over my head.

We were way behind in one game that Hornsby came to watch us play. In the last inning, we made this tremendous comeback and scored enough runs to win the game. But he still gave us a hard time about the fact that we were so far behind. He told us we were going to have to practice extra hard the next day. Since I was real close to Kennedy, I would listen to him and Kennedy talk. Hornsby, toward the latter part of his career, became a manager for the St. Louis Browns, and he put himself in as a pinch hitter and hit a home run to beat Kennedy one time. And Hornsby just wouldn't let up on him about it.

We moved back to St. Louis County in 1960. In the mid-1960s, when there was talk about a new ballpark, every Sunday after church, when I would go with my little brother, we would go down and look and see how much further they had progressed. We'd just take this trip downtown and take a look. I felt so relieved, because I had this tremendous fear of

· · · · ·

being located behind a pole. It always bothered me to no end. I was always worried about it, that I wasn't going to be able to see the game. There weren't going to be any obstructions in this new ballpark. To me, that's all that was important.

In 1963, in the latter part of August, Musial announced he was going to retire at the end of the season. I went to Musial's last ball game. Jim Maloney was pitching. When he was on, he was as fast as anybody. Musial got two hits. They weren't what you'd call very hard. They went between the second baseman and the first baseman. In fact, they were just beyond the outstretched reach of Pete Rose. He was playing second base at the time. It was kind of sad. When your first hero retires, it's just an end of an era.

In Vietnam the first thing I did was have my mom send a lot of my stuff over, including that year's baseball cards. They always had little premiums they put in with the cards, and the premium that year was pictures on thin paper you could unravel. I put my ball cards up on the wall and I put these pictures up there. I tried to have my little shrine in these barracks. They would have a game of the week on radio. They would sometimes do a delay. I would listen to the games live. I'd be listening at maybe two o'clock in the morning.

I got to Vietnam in September of '69, and I kind of got caught up watching all the Chicago guys ragging on the New York guys and the New York guys ragging on the Chicago guys about the Mets and the Cubs. They were constantly giving each other grief. Of course, the New York guys were mostly gloating.

In Vietnam, the enemy could be anywhere out there. I was in this unit that had a bunch of helicopters, and so at night we'd have to go out and pull guard duty. You'd be out on the berm, the outer perimeter. When I pulled duty, it was against the rules, but I took my radio out and listened to one of those World Series games. I just wanted to be close to it. I always had a way of fitting baseball into wherever I was. Even when I was in Vietnam.

I got married in 1974. She was a so-so baseball fan. I took her to a ball game in September '73, and she saw Catfish Hunter shut out the White Sox. We got married in St. Louis. To demonstrate what I call true love, I got married in St. Louis the day the Cardinals were playing the Phillies in a doubleheader. I should have been at the ballpark. That day the best man's job was to keep track of the games. This was in early August, and the Cardinals were within a game of being on top. At the reception, my best man's toast was: "John is a CPA, that takes care of the money and the wealth. Marge is a nurse, and that takes care of the health. And the Cardinals just won the first game of a doubleheader and are in first place. And that takes care of happiness."

WE NEVER TALKED,
EXCEPT AT BASEBALL GAMES

KATHRYN CUNNINGHAM, FIFTY-SEVEN,

IS A REGISTERED NURSE LIVING IN

ST. PAUL, MINNESOTA.

Most of us played pretty much at Newell Park. It was the dads who took turns taking us. But my dad was pretty much there all the time, teaching us how to play ball. We lived three or four blocks away. We used to ride our bikes down there and played ball with all the neighborhood kids. We all just kind of ended up there.

When I could hit a ball, it was very, very exciting. My brothers would always say, "Easy out. Easy out." And then the infield would come in. Then I'd hit one.

· · · · ·

I'm from St. Paul and my dad used to play baseball in the Classic League. When he and my mom got married, he always said he was going to have a baseball team. I came first, but that didn't slow him down at all. He was the one who always took us to play ball. There was a park nearby, and he taught my brothers and the neighbors how to play ball. Because I couldn't run – I had short, stocky legs – he taught me how to hit. I could outhit the boys for years and years and years. Dad didn't play in the league anymore after he got married. But he used to take us to his old team one night a week and introduce us to the pitcher and the catcher. We really enjoyed that the most. Baseball players at that time were really popular people. It was exciting. My dad was always so busy, I guess it was mostly the relationship with him. It was something that everyone could do together.

When I was in grade school, on the girls' baseball teams we had to play with kitten balls. They're quite big. Bigger than a softball. You could barely hit those at all. I preferred baseball. With my brothers, I was one of the boys. I didn't care for girls' teams like that. Pretty boring.

We had the St. Paul Saints at that time. It was very expensive, and Daddy always made like it was a big deal to be able to go to games. That's how he bribed us during the week. If we were really, really good, we could go. St. Paul and the Minneapolis Millers were very competitive. There were a lot of fights. It was very exciting. They played in Lexington ballpark. Popcorn. It was an outdoor stadium, of course. I guess I remember the dads would wear suits. My dad would wear a suit. No moms at all. Pretty much just dads and some kids. I remember the hot dogs and the good things that go along with baseball.

I think it was a special thing between my dad and us. He was a mechanic. He worked days and in the evening. We didn't see him a lot. He was very quiet. We never talked, except at baseball games. He knew all the players and he knew all the stats. The most verbalization he really did was in the middle of the game.

◆

In '61 my husband and I we were married and having children. We used to take the kids to Metropolitan Stadium – Lexington Stadium had been torn down. I didn't drive in those days.

· · · · ·

We would just hop on the bus. In fact, I used to write a note for the opening game and say that the children had dental appointments. Then they all came back to school with sunburns the next day, so I just started writing notes saying I was taking them to the opening game.

We had four children, kind of right in a row. When my children were little, I worked part-time. I wasn't really much of a housekeeper. The first thing I did was spend a lot of time outside and taught the kids right away to play ball. We lived on a three-sided block and there were forty-eight kids. They all pretty much played right on the street. The dads kind of moved their cars and respected where the kids were playing. Windows got broken. But they got fixed.

We liked the Twins right from the beginning. It was a family thing that we could all do together. Sometimes we'd take children from the neighborhood with us. We'd load up the old station wagon and take them with us. Harmon Killebrew, he was one of the ones I really liked. My kids told me not to say this, but I check out the buns. I just thought he had great buns. He got so big that he couldn't run, so he had to hit. I thought, "Kind of funny. Just like me." That's the same reason, too, why I like Kirby Puckett, because I think he's got great buns. But the best buns in baseball were Bert Blyleven.

In '65 my dad went to the World Series and he wouldn't take me. I was very pregnant at the time. My daughter was due in December. He was just very nervous about me. I was really disappointed. I wanted to go. When they went to the Series in '87, it was like a lottery to be able to get tickets. We got tickets for all the play-offs and World Series. I stood in line for five or six hours just to get tickets to the play-offs.

During that season our son had died. He took his life in July of '87. It was very traumatic. It was the night of the All-Star Game that he died. I didn't really know how we were

· · · · ·

going to make it through. The Twins starting doing very well. Kirby Puckett was hitting in almost every game in July. That's what really kept me going was to follow them. That kind of took our minds away from Mike a little bit. It was kind of what kept the whole family sane. You could holler and scream, get rid of all your anger and hostility and hurt and anguish. It was really a turning point for us.

Baseball is part of life. I think it relates back to being a special thing with my dad. Sometimes I still think he's sitting next to me when I go to the games. After the children came and I was an adult, we pretty much didn't go to a lot of the games together. I really missed that.

We see baseball now even more than we used to. We have season tickets for the Saints. It's absolutely wonderful. They started three years ago. It's the Northern League. It's kind of an independent, off-the-wall league. It's filled almost every night. It holds about sixty-three hundred. It's called Midway Stadium. It's off a really busy street next to a train station. The trains go by. The Twins absolutely hate them because they're attracting so many people. They have a pig who has saddlebags and he takes balls to the umpires. They have a haircut place and a nun who gives a massage. It's outside and you can bring the kids.

The last time I played . . . my brother lives in a small town and they had a fire department league. We played with the children. I got up to bat and the kids all hollered, "Easy out! Easy out!" My brother, who was pitching, just kind of smiled at me. I smacked a ball right out to center field. I could still hit. Unfortunately, my son caught it.

COOL PAPA BELL WAS MY HERO

LARRY LESTER, FORTY-FOUR,

IS A TELECOMMUNICATIONS ANALYST

IN RAYTOWN, MISSOURI. HE IS ALSO RESEARCH

DIRECTOR FOR THE NEGRO LEAGUES MUSEUM

IN KANSAS CITY.

I'd be throwing the ball up in the air in the front yard. Or throwing the ball against the bottom step so it would bounce back to me. The steps were made out of wood, except for the bottom step, which was concrete. I would throw the ball against the concrete. I would practice fielding grounders that way. You know how it is. You don't always hit that bottom step. My father was a carpenter, so he wouldn't have any problem fixing it, but I'd say, "I don't know why that second step from the bottom is always broke. Rotten wood or something."

· · · · ·

My earliest memories of baseball were of the Kansas City Athletics in the late '50s. I grew up five blocks from Municipal Stadium, on 27th and Brooklyn. That was the main thorough-fare leading to the stadium, so I used to watch car after car going to the game. It was just fascinating. I was curious as to why we had all this traffic. My father said, "There's a ball-park down the street." I wanted to go and see what it was all about.

You'd walk up to the ballpark and there'd be this mass of people. So many people, you were just bumping into every-body. You'd walk in and everybody seemed to be friendly, having a good time. I always remember the smell of the hot dogs and the popcorn. I eventually made my way to those green seats. I remember pushing down the wooden green seats and sitting there, usually by myself, just me and my scorecard. I would just sit there and enjoy the game. De-pending on how much money I had, I would sit in the better seats, where most of the whites would sit. Or I would sit in general admission, where everybody would sit. There was a common bond. We were all there for the same purpose. I didn't really see any difference. They cheered when I cheered. They booed when I booed.

I remember Connie Johnson of the Baltimore Orioles beating the Kansas City A's quite convincingly. At the time I wanted to know who Connie Johnson was. There were very few black pitchers in the league. As it turned out, he had played with the Kansas City Monarchs in the '40s. The connection was starting to form at that time with the Negro Leagues. I followed all the other black stars in the league.

Basically the ballpark was located in a black neighborhood. And so I was always curious as to why there were so many white ballplayers. Where in my small world – which was my neighborhood, my church, my grocery store – the majority of people were black. So I was always amazed. "Where did all these white men come from?" The older gentlemen in the neighborhood said, "Well, there was a time when the teams were all black and all white." "Well, what do you mean?" "Well, we had the Kansas City Monarchs and the Indianapolis Clowns and they played right there in that stadium. Right down the street, Larry. And they were outstanding ballplayers in their own right." And they would proceed to tell me these fantastic stories. The base-stealing feats of Cool Papa Bell, the pitching exploits of Satchel Paige. The batting feats of Josh Gibson. All these great names, like Mule Suttles and Turkey Stearns. Bullet Rogan. We would sit on our front porch. They would sit back, like older people do. They would just tell me these great stories, and they could see my eyes were big. They knew they had somebody hooked.

I proceeded to start following the National League. Because it had more black players. By that time, I knew about Jackie Robinson. I started to follow the National League closer because they had Joe Black, Jackie Robinson, Roy Campanella, Willie Mays, Hank Aaron, Roberto Clemente. People that I could identify with. I was still loyal to the Kansas City A's. Until All-Star time came. Then I would root for the National League.

I don't remember when I first heard about Jackie. All I knew was he was the first black in modern-day baseball. When I heard he was coming to Kansas City, I begged my father to take me down there to see him speak. I wanted to actually see the man, the legend himself. I thought this was an opportunity to actually reach out and touch him. President Eisenhower was running for office and he was campaigning for him. It was at what we call the Music Hall, Convention Center. I remember the speeches being pretty dry, somewhat boring. But when Robinson came to the podium, I got to the edge of my seat. I hung on every word. I remember my dad never saying anything during his entire speech. I just thought it was so great of my dad to do that for me, to take me, knowing I wasn't going to get a whole lot out of it. I just wanted to see the man. I can see him as he walks to the podium, with that little high-pitched voice. He was very professional.

✦

We had what we called neighborhood teams. I played on the Wabash team. That was where my mother lived. My parents were separated when I was in the fourth grade. We had our little three-team league. Park, Olive, and Wabash. Our next-door neighbor had between eighteen and twenty-two kids. We were able to get four or five boys from them to form the nucleus of our team.

We would play every day. I still remember who always pulled the ball, who to back up on. We did everything except steal, for the simple reason we didn't have catching gear. There was a park right there on Linwood and Brooklyn. We played there. It was a converted tennis court. The right field kind of went up on a hill, similar to Municipal Stadium. The right-field fence was short, just like it was in Municipal Stadium. Left field on our field did not have a fence, so once you got it past the left fielder, you could run all day long. It was one of the best times of my life. It was stress-free. All I had to do was play baseball. In the evening I could go to a game if they were in town. I couldn't ask for a better life.

The retired men in the neighborhood showed me how to play. I would be playing catch with myself. They'd walk up to me and say, "You want to play catch?" They would stoop down in the catcher's position. They'd call the balls and strikes, and I could never seem to throw three strikes in a row. I'd catch the corner and they would call it a ball. They would just infuriate me to get better. I never had good stuff, but when I got to the Little League, I was one of the better pitchers, because I could throw a strike.

I liked Little League. It was more competitive. I got to see other people. Plus, I got to wear a uniform, which made me proud. It was quite an experience to put on that little flannel uniform. It was blue pinstriped on beige. We were the Satellites, whatever that meant. You'd put your cap on and you got that feeling you could play with anybody. You'd put the spikes on and that really blew your mind. You felt a little taller.

I tried to emulate Cool Papa Bell when I played Little League baseball. That was my style of play. I knew from the stories the men in the neighborhood used to tell me. These were men who had seen him play. They said, "If you hit the ball to right field, Larry, you take your wide turn at first, and the man throws behind you, Cool Papa Bell would go to second." That was the way I played Little League baseball. He was kind of my idol. He was who I tried to pattern my play after. All this little tricky baseball. They would show me, "If you're on third base, Larry, and the catcher throws the ball back to the pitcher, you can steal home easily." I stole home two times like that in one game.

When the A's moved, I was pretty bitter. When the Royals came, the excitement was not there. They were new players. My team was in Oakland. The Kansas City Royals played in Municipal Stadium one or two years. They moved to the new Royals Stadium and tore down Municipal Stadium. At the time I really didn't care. I didn't want to even witness the pain. I just ignored it. I knew I couldn't walk to the ballpark anymore. But it was there. I could still see it there. To me, it was never gone. I could see it right there. Even though it was flat and leveled.

Robert Peterson came out with the book *Only the Ball Was White*. All the stories I had heard from the neighborhood came to life. I was thirsty for more knowledge. I eventually realized old newspapers were on microfilm. I could go back and relive those moments by looking at the *Kansas City Call*, which was the local black newspaper here, and learn about some of these great men. Every now and then there would be this "Where are they now?" type of article. You would see, "Here's Frank Duncan, who used to be a catcher for the Monarchs, living right here in Kansas City." Wow. I just went over to his house and knocked on his door and said, "I'm here to talk to you."

In 1984 I got in the car and traveled to St. Louis. Knocked on Cool Papa Bell's door and he let me in and we talked. I remember the difficult time I had finding his home. It was on Dixon Street. I eventually found it. At the time it was named James Cool Papa Bell Avenue. I went up there and knocked on his door. A red-brick duplex. I remember him taking those three locks off his door. It wasn't a real safe neighborhood.

It seemed like people didn't visit him very often. There was nothing but baseballs on top of the fireplace. There must have been twenty or thirty baseballs signed by some of the greatest ballplayers I'd ever read about. Trophies were all over the room. He had more trophies than he had furniture. I sat there watching this man. He was more excited than I was, that he actually had a visitor. He had an old sheet across the couch that we sat on to cover up its condition. This man had on a tie and suit. He wanted to impress me. When I got to St. Louis, I called him. By the time I got there, he had on a suit.

I asked him the questions any fan would ask. He said, "Do you want me to autograph something?" I said, "Why sure." I ran out to my car and got a baseball. Of course, he had to unlock the three locks again. The sad part is, I'm sitting there and I'm thinking, "If this man had been a white ballplayer, would he be living in this type of condition?" As I left the house, I looked up at the street sign. It said James Cool Papa Bell Avenue. This little kid walks by and I asked, "Do you know who that is?" The kid said no. I thought it was sad that this young black kid never heard of one of the greatest ballplayers who ever lived.

· · · · ·

MAGIC

GALE CAREY, FORTY-TWO,

IS AN ASSISTANT PROFESSOR OF ANIMAL

AND NUTRITIONAL SCIENCES AT THE

UNIVERSITY OF NEW HAMPSHIRE. SHE LIVES

IN BARRINGTON, NEW HAMPSHIRE.

With these two buddies, we would go to lots and lots of games that season. I was prayerful, constantly. I would go to church. And when they would lose a game, particularly when I had prayed really hard, I remember going to confession and asking Father Sweeney, "How come when I pray really hard for something, it doesn't turn out? Why? Why did that happen?" He said, "The Lord works in mysterious ways."

· · · · ·

I grew up in Natick, Massachusetts. When I was I guess eleven or twelve, I vividly remember my father took me to my first baseball game at Fenway Park. It was wonderful. It's so clear in my mind. Growing up with five of us in the family, it was rare to have a one-on-one with a parent, particularly my dad, who was working full-time. To have a night, just the two of us, was pretty special just to begin with. The thing that I remember the most is getting to the ballpark and – this was a night game – walking in the gate and smelling the cigar smoke. I hate cigarette smoke, but cigar smoke I love because it reminds me of the ballpark. Then the thing I remember is walking up the ramp and bright, bright lights. We walked into the brightness, and there was this great big place with green everywhere and bright white uniforms. It made such an impression on me. Holding hands, walking up the ramp, and it was like walking into a beautiful church. That's what it felt like.

My dad bought me a scorecard and gave me a pencil and taught me in the course of the night how to keep score. I was just so taken. I didn't know professional baseball. I didn't know any of the players, the names or anything. But that night I memorized everything. How to even spell Yastrzemski. Conigliaro. George Scott, I think, was playing. Bill Monboquette was pitching. Joe Foy. Dick Stuart was playing. The catcher was Bob Tillman, I think. But I wrote all of this down and committed it to memory. It was a magical night. You know, I loved to play, also. And when I was watching them play, I said, "I'm going to play for them someday." So then began the plot of how I was going to someday play for the Red Sox.

My plot was that I would become a really solid player. And I would disguise myself so they wouldn't know I was a girl. I would disguise myself by wrapping Ace bandages around my middle and build it all the way up to here so it was just straight. And I'd have some friends. Tony Conigliaro and Carl Yastrzemski would know, and they'd protect me. So when it came time to take showers, I'd always have an excuse not to go into the shower. I was going to play right field and Tony was going to move to center. That was the plan. I think it disappeared with puberty.

In '66 we came in last, or next to last. It was just heart-breaking. I grew up Catholic. I really liked going to church. And I started praying that they would do better. That winter, to walk to the junior high, I went by the church. Often on my way home from school – this was when the churches were still left open – I would stop in the church and in the quiet and pray that they would do better next year. I did this all through the winter and spring.

In '67 I had two partners in crime, two other young girls who were also baseball fans, and we became fast friends. In '67 we skipped school on Opening Day to go to the game, and wouldn't you know, our picture was in the paper. They had a big panoramic shot of all the people waiting to get into the game. It turned out Opening Day that day was rained out. So we had skipped school, gone and waited in the rain, had our picture in the paper, and the game was never played.

There was a lot of magic going on. Once, the Red Sox were behind and they scored nine runs to come back. I was listening to this game and could feel it coming on. I just knew in my heart they were going to win. It was as if I had a very spiritual connection. I had this quiet confidence. When they would score runs, I would just sort of smile. "Yes, I know. This is how it was meant to be." So when they would win, I would be terribly excited, but it was as if it was divinely inspired.

That was the season Tony Conigliaro got hit in the head. That was really devastating. But there was this magic that wouldn't die. My two girlfriends and I, usually on Opening Day we would stop at the ticket office and buy tickets for the last day of the season. Because we wanted to be at the beginning and the end. So that year, when we came in for the rain-out, we bought tickets for the last game. Box seats. Little did we know that game would be the deciding game for the pennant.

That was the culmination of it all. We had box seats for

the final game of the season. It was another very magical game, where they were behind. Lonborg was pitching. They were behind until the sixth or seventh inning and they came on to win. It was as if that was the way it was supposed to happen. I knew all along. I never would tell people about that. But that was why I believed there's a God. It sounds so silly as an adult, to say that, but that season, the way I felt in my heart and the connection that I had, this spiritual connection, it was as if this was God's way of showing me that he could shape events. It was magical.

The World Series was a little bit of a downer. That was hard to swallow. Father Sweeney really didn't have any magical words for me on that one. It did go right down to the seventh game. It was almost like we were in over our heads. I remember I had injured my leg playing field hockey. I had a chance to go to one of the World Series games. But I was on crutches and I couldn't. I was crushed. From that, I knew something wasn't quite right. So when they lost, I didn't feel like God let me down. I thought, "Well, you know, I really only did pray for the pennant."

We got to high school, and the three of us sort of went our separate ways. Boys came into the picture. By the time I graduated, baseball was still there. But it wasn't the magic of '67. I still would go to games. And then each year I sort of drifted and drifted away. I sort of lost that fever.

I moved to Baltimore. And the year that I moved there, in '83, the Orioles were in the World Series. And it was almost like an instant reconnection. The town was on fire, and I was sort of thrown in the middle of that. The magic returned. The next season I went to games like I used to in '67. I would go by myself and sit in the bleachers. And also from my lab at Johns Hopkins, I could see the stadium. I could see the lights. I'd listen to the game and see the lights. I knew when the game was over and the crew was finished cleaning up because I'd see the lights go off.

The Orioles took over top billing. The Red Sox, in all honesty, they have never regained that feeling in my heart. I was an Orioles fan. I was excited in '86. I watched it all. And when the ball went through Buckner's legs, I remember very vividly what I was doing. I had just gotten married that summer. My husband was due home any minute. This was late on a Saturday night. And sitting there watching and thinking they had the game. They had the Series and I was thinking, "They're going to do this. This is so unprecedented." It was like double-dating with a former boyfriend. You can enjoy their company, but there wasn't that connection. I was a little surprised to see them within inches of winning it all. George walked in the door just before the ball went through Buckner's legs. It hurt, but I could face the music.

My dear friend, closest friend in the world, Corena, is from Baltimore. And she and I went to lots of games together when I lived there. I told her about my love of new ballparks. I said, "Why don't we have a ladies' baseball adventure every year and go to a new ballpark?" She liked that idea. We've been to Camden Yards, SkyDome, Cleveland. Everybody has their own thing that is magical to them. For me, there's magic in it because of 1967. There's God in it because of 1967. The picture I painted of that very first time I walked in with my dad? That happens the very first time I walk into a new ballpark. Even if it's Seattle. It all comes back.

THE ELEGANCE OF FLANNEL

**JERRY COHEN, THIRTY-SIX,
LIVES IN SEATTLE, WHERE HE IS OWNER
OF EBBETS FIELD FLANNELS, A COMPANY
HE FOUNDED IN 1987 TO REPRODUCE
OLD-TIME BASEBALL UNIFORMS.**

The first big league game we went to was a rain-out. It was also the year of the New York World's Fair. My dad took me and a friend of mine from the street. A kid named Sean, who was the super's son. It rained. I remember being incredibly crushed. Until we went across to Flushing Meadow and there was this World's Fair. Soon after that we went to another game. I remember being dwarfed by the grandeur of it. The immensity of it. The spectacle. The public address announcer. Shea Stadium was brand, spanking new. It seemed incredible to a five-, six-year-old kid. The crowds. The idea that you could yell. I remember practicing yelling.

. . . . .

My earliest baseball memory, and this is very clear, comes from when I was three or four years old. My dad always had baseball on TV, in the background, whenever he was home. I remember being annoyed because I couldn't get his attention. I remember him sitting me down and telling me what he was watching. It was the expansion Mets. And then it changed. It became something that my dad and I did together.

I grew up in Brooklyn, in Crown Heights. It was an urban, multiracial neighborhood. Middle class, lower middle class. Most of my friends were black. There were a lot of Puerto Rican kids. Black kids. Jewish kids like myself. Baseball was the common denominator. It was such a wonderful, innocent age. You were just kids playing ball.

I remember playing in an alley at the side of our apartment building. A very narrow alley. And sort of making up the rules because there wasn't enough room for conventional baseball. I remember the alley was uphill. So you'd have to run uphill and tag the wall. We could play with any amount of kids. You didn't need nine men on a side. I remember coming out of my house, my apartment, and teaching the other kids how to play baseball.

I played catch with my dad. We had a couple of parks near us. Occasionally, on a weekend, my dad would take me to a park. He used to play Police Athletic League baseball. They actually had these concrete fields with painted baselines and they'd play hardball on them. It was insane. Later, when we moved to the suburbs, I got involved in more conventional pickup games. I would just show up at the park – just a suburban park in New Jersey, in Bergen County. There was a group of kids who would meet, semiregularly. If there were enough guys together, we'd choose up sides. If there weren't, we'd hit ground balls, or play stickball, or play some variation. I remember spending a lot of times with friends just pitching. Then when I was nine, I joined Little League for the first time. It almost ruined it for me. It took the fun out of it. It was more competitive and the adults were involved. There was so much pressure. I remember thinking at nine that this isn't how it's supposed to be.

I remember the spontaneous games better. Because you could always fantasize that you were your favorite Yankee or Met or whatever. The kids would have all their favorite players and would try to bat in that stance. I really remember Mantle, Carl Yastrzemski, Willie Mays, McCovey, the Alou brothers, Orlando Cepeda – that was really my period. When I started to pitch in Little League, I remember I emulated Sandy Koufax. Because my dad, being a Brooklyn Dodger fan, knew about Sandy Koufax from before. He would always say, "Jerry, come here and watch him pitch. Watch what he does."

I became a big Met fan right away. It was in the blood. Because of my dad. My dad had that Brooklyn Dodger blood. I got some stories from him. The story he always told me was about going to see the Dodgers at Ebbets Field. His mom would give him a nickel for the subway. But he would keep the nickel and walk so he could buy a hot dog. I don't know what he must have gone through those four years there wasn't any National League baseball in New York. He used to talk about it a lot. It would have never occurred to him to go see a Yankee game to get his baseball fix. It just wasn't done. It didn't matter if there wasn't anything else. I remember dragging my dad to Yankee Stadium as a kid because I wanted to see Yankee Stadium. I remember him seeming very uncomfortable.

I remember in '69 I was just living and dying with the Mets every day. I was eleven or twelve. That was the most exciting couple of months in my entire life. The World Series was still being played during the day. I remember running home from school to see the World Series. I remember working out a

· · · · ·

series of hand signals in school with somebody who had a radio in another class across the hall. And our teachers were sort of winking at it. It was such an exciting time. It was like Christmas, when during the school year the rules are sort of suspended for a while. It was that magical time, what people say it was like in Brooklyn during the '55 Series. There was so much excitement, you couldn't deny these kids, who were so excited they couldn't think about what they were being taught.

It didn't change for me until roughly junior high school, when I went through adolescence. I became really interested in rock-and-roll music. At that age, you're sort of all or nothing. I remember being surprised by the Mets' second pennant in '73. I wasn't following every day, like I used to. In '73 they might have already won it when I found out about it. I was pleased. But it was like hearing about an old friend who'd got a new job. That was probably the first year I didn't look at the standings every day. It made me feel like this was something I was past. I think it's important to mention this: during that difficult period of time when I was a teenager and rebelling a little bit, and maybe doing things my dad didn't understand, baseball was the one thing we could talk about.

In the early 1980s, baseball sort of gradually reentered my consciousness. I was in my early twenties. I remembered how much I'd loved it. I got a bunch of my rock-and-roll musician friends and people who had never even touched a baseball and managed to talk them into going out semiregularly where I lived in Arizona. I started pitching again and we got a little casual team together. It felt great. It felt fantastic. It was just like an old friend. I do remember what prompted it, too. For Father's Day, for some reason I decided to get my dad a Brooklyn Dodgers cap. This was before anybody made one. I had one made. I bought a blue cap and found a woman who hand-embroidered that Brooklyn *B* from a baseball card. I gave that to my dad for Father's Day. And that was the sort of spark that got me back into thinking about baseball.

Even as a kid, I was interested in baseball beyond playing the game. I used to watch every old baseball movie that came on TV. And I had a real romantic attachment to the past, to baseball history and the ballparks. The movie *Angels in the Outfield* had a huge effect on me. I remember seeing old Forbes Field – those old girders and the wonderful silhouettes of those stands – and being really captivated by it. I became a student of the uniforms, too. I would buy baseball card sets to see the uniforms, not to get the players. There was something about those old flannels. Something about the way they looked. I remember drawing on T-shirts. I would draw these old logos and these old designs. I'm sort of living that out now.

I started with the very basic supposition that baseball alone among sports is ingrained in the fabric of our culture. When I look at a film of Babe Ruth or of Satchel Paige, I get a feeling, I get a buzz, from that look. Just how they look. And the uniform is the biggest visual part of it. And there's a timelessness about it. A classicism about it, if you will, that I think was thrown out in the '70s when they first went to the double knits and started all the pullovers and wild color combinations. I thought that was sort of like if you're a Catholic, you go to church and see your priest come in wearing gym shorts. There is an elegance to the sight of Lou Gehrig wearing his Yankee pinstripes, his flannels. I took it upon myself, I had this mission from God, I guess, to bring that elegance back. There's just a beauty about them. When I started the business, I thought, "Either I'm totally nuts, or this is something that other people feel also." To my delight, I found out other people felt the same.

I almost believe in genetic memory. Baseball has been around since the second half of the 1800s. Fathers have been

· · · · ·

playing catch with sons since then. And it's more than a game. It's a shared cultural or familial activity. It also has a history that's poetic. That has a lot to do with the type of game it is. It's hard to get misty-eyed about basketball players from 1940. I mean, who cares? But baseball's different. I don't think basketball could have produced a *Field of Dreams.*

It's hard for me to enjoy a major league baseball game now. I'm in Seattle and we have the Kingdome. I'm looking out my window now. It's about seventy-five degrees. The sun is out. I can see Puget Sound. I'm looking at the water. And I have to drive across town and go sit in the Kingdome, an air-conditioned, concrete building. I can't do that. Baseball's made to ponder, absorb, and contemplate. Between the innings, you think about the situation. I find that whole dimension of it difficult when they're playing rock videos between innings and commercials. It's almost like they're apologizing for the fact that it's baseball being presented. I go to minor league ball. I go to Tacoma, where you can still sit back and have an honest beer for a couple of bucks and actually look at these guys and hear the ball hit the mitt.

I went to Cuba last November, and the thing that struck me is that you saw kids everywhere playing baseball. In every nook and cranny, in every open space. We're not living in a society where kids congregate at a park and choose up sides on a bat anymore. I saw that in Cuba, and it brought tears to my eyes. I got to my hotel the first day, and I went out for a walk. I got to this big traffic circle. And in this plaza there were three separate groups of kids – one with really young kids, like six, seven, eight years old; one with a little older; and one with like seventeen, eighteen years old. And I was shagging flies for the kids for a while. And then the older kids asked me to play. It was just like going back thirty years and getting in a pickup game. It was great.

I think that's something that's sort of disappeared from our

· · · · ·

culture. It's sort of been corrupted by Little League and organization. And now other sports compete for our attention. And video games and television. There's too much competition. Do you know what I think? I think I grew up in the last generation of kids whose first love was the game of baseball.

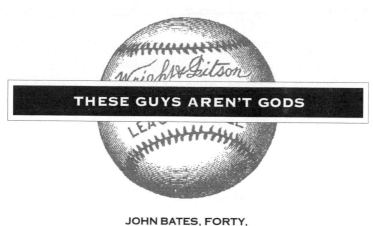

THESE GUYS AREN'T GODS

JOHN BATES, FORTY,

IS AN ADMINISTRATOR WITH THE SEATTLE

PARKS AND RECREATION DEPARTMENT.

*My son Cory's baseball team went to a batting cage and got an hour
of free instruction from an ex–big leaguer. I didn't catch his name. He
told the kids where he grew up, he lived on a beach, and he'd go down
and hit rocks into the water. Cory turned to me and smiled. I'd recited
the same story to him often. Where I grew up, they were putting the
freeway in. There were a lot of rocks. Every night after dinner, I
went out and hit those rocks. Developed my batting eye. Cory could
relate to it, but most of the other kids, it went right over their heads.
It's not the same as when we were kids. I don't see too many kids
with their metal bats, hitting rocks.*

· · · · ·

I was born and raised in Seattle. My first real involvement
with baseball was probably when I was six or seven. A friend
was collecting baseball cards and I got hooked that way.
Seeing the pictures of Willie Mays, Mickey Mantle, some of
the stars you heard about and saw on Saturday afternoons on
television. To have those in your hand was pretty appealing.

209

One of the first packs I ever bought, there was Willie Mays, right at the top of the pack.

We had Triple-A ball here. The Seattle Rainiers. You could listen to them on the radio. Take the radio into bed with you at night. I can remember Ewell Baney was manager for a couple of years. Jay Johnstone spent some time here. Andy Messersmith spent some time here. Bubba Morton. Tom Burgmeier. Rico Petrocelli was here. There were a lot of stars that you could attach to for one year, then they were gone to the majors.

You had Sick's Stadium here, which was a great Triple-A ballpark. If you got there early enough, you could go down and sit on the dugout and get autographs and just chat with some of the ballplayers for a while. It was special. Mount Rainier was sitting out there in right center. You couldn't ask for a better thing.

The stadium was right on the corner of two main streets. The outfield abutted one of these streets. On the other side of the street, there was a hillside where the cheap seats were. People would just sit on that hillside and watch the game, because you could see over the left-field fence. Every time you went to a game, you could look out there, and there were fifty to a hundred people with chairs.

I can remember the very first time I went. To get into the seating areas at Sick's Stadium, you climbed up a lot of steps. Bam – all of a sudden there was this emerald green grass, very finely manicured. The smells of outdoor baseball. The grass, the cigar smoke. It's very, very vivid, even to this day. You just really got the feel of baseball with that stadium. If you were able to get there an hour before and they were warming up, you could go down there along the sidelines and talk to the players. If you were lucky, you'd get a ball. Pretty easy to get autographs.

. . . . .

One thing that really sticks out is 1966, when the Rainiers played Tulsa in the Pacific Coast League championship. They took it in seven games. I was able to sneak that radio into bed and listen to it every night. I tried to squelch the cheers and the moans because I was supposed to be in bed asleep. The excitement that the announcers put into it – I can remember that very vividly. And of course the excitement of the home crowd. You could hear it in the background. The Rainiers had a custom whenever they scored. At the end of the inning, they always rang a bell for the number of runs that were scored during the inning. If there were multiple runs, every time they'd ring it, the cheers would get louder and louder.

This was a real Seattle Rainiers town. They got a lot of support. Everybody loved them. It really didn't depend on how they were doing. It was kind of sad the last year, when you realized the Rainiers were no longer going to be here. I went to the last game the Rainiers ever played in Sick's Stadium. That was pretty touching.

When major league baseball – the Pilots – came along, it was a whole different arena. All of a sudden you've got spring training to look at. Spring training games. Players are coming from Boston, New York, Baltimore – all this history is all of a sudden going to come to your town and be playing your hometown team. I was fourteen. Oh, I was excited. You bet. Listening to the radio every night. Every day I clipped a box score and the article about the game out of the newspaper. I can remember one of the games I went to was in May. We were playing the Tigers. Joe Sparma was pitching for the Tigers. And he had a no-hitter going through the eighth. That was as exciting as all get-out. I can remember another game when we were playing the Senators and Frank Howard was playing for the Senators. The first time I ever saw that guy, he was like a giant. One swing of the bat, he just hit a

· · · · ·

These Guys Aren't Gods   211

line drive that never seemed to elevate. It was on a line the whole way. Smacked the center-field wall behind the seating area. Finally landed in a seat that they eventually painted red.

I think at the beginning of the season, the town and the fans were pretty excited about finally getting major league baseball. As the season progressed, the team went through a thirteen-game losing streak. Fans kind of went south. By the end of the season, they were drawing seven, eight thousand per game. I was still rooting for them and listening to them every night. Tommy Harper became a big star that year. I enjoyed Tommy. Kind of the sentimental favorite of everyone was Ray Oyler. Once Oyler was drafted by the Pilots, a famous disc jockey on one of the radio stations in Seattle created what was called the Sock-It-to-Me Fan Club. Jim Pagliaroni was a catcher. I can remember being down early for a game, down at the fence, talking to some of the guys, and Pagliaroni was down there. He was just a clown. I can remember going to one game and Luis Tiant was warming up with some players over by the Pilots' dugout. When he was ready to go in, he tossed me the ball.

Steve Barber was on the Pilots. I remember very early in the season going to one of the first games of the home stand. Barber – you tried to talk to the man and he just totally ignored you. Since that was one of the first games I went to, I compared it to the access I had when the Rainiers were here, where the guys would talk to you pretty easily. And here you are at your first game at the major league level, and the guy couldn't care less if you were there.

I don't remember a heck of a lot about when they left. I must have blocked that out. They were coming home from spring training, and they went east instead of west. I can remember that summer, though, that all of a sudden there's no baseball in town. All of a sudden your major league baseball fix was in the newspapers, not on the radio. It was really depressing. I was a Cardinal fan, so I followed them. I followed Milwaukee a little bit that first year but really didn't get turned on by them.

I think it was a year after it came out that I was able to get a copy of Jim Bouton's book, *Ball Four*, and read it. I was sixteen or seventeen. That was an eye-opener. We had always been shielded from a lot of stuff that he wrote in that book. What the players are doing on the road after the game, what they're doing out in the bullpen with the binoculars, looking up in the stands. I don't know. Maybe I was raised in a sheltered life, but I never, ever considered that stuff going on. These guys were supposed to be ballplayers thinking about ball all the time. They get to play this game. You really looked up to them. You idolized them. They were everything that you dreamed about. That book kind of knocked them down a level or two. Unfortunately, I probably kept that in the back of my mind for a while. You grow up and you realize these guys aren't gods after all. They are human.

I'm still a baseball fan. I've got twin boys, one of them very interested in baseball. They're almost ten. I'm trying to encourage him to enjoy baseball for the game and not to get too involved with the superstars he sees on television. To me, that's not baseball. One of them got interested in Rickey Henderson. I tried to temper his enthusiasm for Rickey by showing the other side of Rickey. The kind of person Rickey was, as opposed to the ballplayer. Trying to instill in him that who you might see on the field might be totally different from who he is outside of the field.

You've got these guys with guaranteed contracts and all of a sudden they see Joe Blow is making more than them, so they say they're not going to live up to that guaranteed contract. That just flies in the face of what baseball is all about. I'm trying to show Cory that baseball has changed. It's a business now, not necessarily a sport. It used to be a simple game. That's the thing I've tried to warn him about, the difference between then and now.

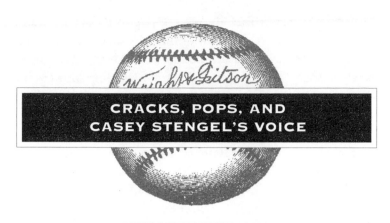

CRACKS, POPS, AND
CASEY STENGEL'S VOICE

GREG ORTIZ, FORTY-ONE,

IS AN AUDIO TECHNICIAN LIVING IN

ELIZABETH, NEW JERSEY.

Whoever took me to the game, I would always ask them, "Can we sit in the box seats so I can hear them play?" We didn't always have enough money for that, but once in a while we would get to sit either behind the plate or third or first base, where I could hear the sounds. When we went to a ballpark, I could almost tell where we were sitting by listening to batting practice.

When I went out to Yankee Stadium later on when I was in my teens, we would sit in the bleachers because they were cheaper seats. You didn't hear as much, but you were out even more in the open. There were just people all around. If you sat near the bullpen, you could hear the pitchers warming up. That was fun. It's sunny; the breeze would be blowing. Sometimes I used to go by myself. I'd bring my radio and hang out at the ballpark all day. The best thing about it is being at the ballpark. Sitting in the seats, the sun is in your face, the crowd is all around you, you're all rooting for the same team.

· · · · ·

I was born in New York City and grew up there. I really didn't become interested in baseball until I was nine years old. I'd broken my wrist, so I was home a lot. The Mets had just been newly formed the year before. I started listening to them on the radio. One day it just happened that I listened and I liked what I heard.

I have no vision whatsoever. I never have. Any kid who has normal vision who likes baseball will tell you his heroes are the ballplayers. The ones I really enjoyed were the announcers. Bob Murphy, Lindsey Nelson, and Ralph Kiner. My favorite announcer was Bob Murphy and he still is. He makes you feel like you're right at the ballpark. Of course, if you don't see, your imagination runs pretty wild. You just sort of picture yourself as the batter facing the pitcher or the pitcher facing the batter.

My first experience I remember was going to the Polo Grounds. We were there to see the Mets against the Reds. My stepfather had taken me with a couple of friends. He realized that I'd started liking baseball. "How would you like to go to a game and be in the crowd? You can hear the crack of the bat or the pop of the mitt behind the plate." I was very excited. And when we went, I had so much fun.

The bigness of the ballpark. Just going through the tunnels up to the seats. Hearing the crowd. You know, you hear the crowd on the radio and you know they're there, but when you're in the ballpark, it sounds so much more real and live. It's all around you. Just taking in the smell of the hot dogs, the soda, and the beer. Just the total ambience of the surroundings. It had sort of a festive-type atmosphere that made you feel happy. I brought my radio, and that helped tremendously. You're hearing the crowd swell when somebody hits a base hit or hits a home run. Just people all around you have the same thing in common, that they're having fun watching the game. You can hear it, but you can also feel it. Just the excitement of the crowd. The crowd will tell you everything.

I didn't want the game to end. I didn't want to leave the park, even though it was a very cold day. It just stayed with me for a long time. I was, "When could we go again?" In those days they had a lot of Sunday doubleheaders, so we would try to get out there to watch two games for the price of one. Just be out there all day. It was like being in a candy store. You just didn't want to go.

I also listen to them on TV and I'm able to follow them as well. A lot of blind people have trouble with that. But I've been able to form a pretty good mental image of baseball. I've been on a baseball field. A diamond. Once in a while in Central Park, a sighted person with me would say, "Let's walk around the bases and see how it goes." Somebody had showed me by hand on a piece of paper what a diamond looked like. It was easy to form the mental picture of where the outfielders were. At the beginning of each game, the announcers will tell you what the dimensions are, down the lines and in the power alleys and in straightaway center. I was pretty much able to form a mental picture of how the ballpark was shaped. They'd always tell you if the ball bounced off something or landed. That would also help tell you how a ballpark was built.

An uncle of mine had played ball just for fun when he was much younger. He would show me his bat and show me his outfielder's glove. He didn't have a baseball. He showed me what the glove looked like. He had his shoes. I never knew what spikes were like before that. We were at a ball game from school and somebody caught a foul ball at batting practice. They passed it around. It was the first time I'd ever felt a baseball. All the seams around it and stuff like that. The thing I really noticed was how hard the ball was. That sort of connected in my mind why it sounded the way it did when the bat hit the ball. It almost sounded like hitting a rock. I was feeling the baseball and I squeezed it to see how hard it was.

As I grew older, I just followed the Mets, even though they were such a losing team. Because they were new and the team was so young. It was like watching a plant grow or watching your favorite pet grow up. You were just totally emotionally involved in the game. When they'd lose, you felt sad. When they'd win, you felt very happy. I would listen to every game I could.

I went to school at the New York Institute for the Blind. We boarded there during the week. A few of the teachers at the school were Met fans. They arranged every year to take us out to Shea Stadium. We brought our radios with us. The first year we went was to the Polo Grounds in '63. We were sitting behind home plate. They arranged for us to meet Casey Stengel and a couple of other Met players. Duke Snider might have been one of them. Casey Stengel, his voice – since he was old, it was kind of gravelly. You know he was long-winded. He was just a very, very nice man.

They would tell us the score of the Met game every morning in school. And maybe some highlights. During the World Series, they would stop school in the afternoon and let us listen in the classroom to the teacher's radio. Before the game would come on, you just couldn't wait.

It was quite a summer. This was in '69. At the beginning no one thought the Mets would end up the way they were. They started winning, and it was like a snowball. They kept rolling and couldn't stop. I was in high school. I think the pinnacle of it was when the Mets were playing the Cubs in September. There was a three-game series at Shea Stadium. They were pretty much even. Listening on the radio, you could just hear the intensity of the game. After that the fever was so high. Then when the Mets went into first place for the first time, I was just beside myself, jumping up and down. When they won the World Series, I was in school. They let us listen. I was outside on the school grounds. When the last out was made, I just yelled as loud as I could for as long as I could. A bunch of us yelled, "We're Number One! We're Number One!" for about five minutes.

After high school I went to college for one semester, but it didn't work out, so I dropped out. I had a lot of time on my hands, because I couldn't find work that easily. There were times when I was unemployed and had very little money. Things were very hard, so baseball sort of took your mind off things like that. Mostly I would listen on the radio. I couldn't afford to go to too many games. I would try to pick up the other games at night. The Red Sox on TIC in Hartford. Sometimes I could get KMOX in St. Louis if I was in the right spot. Baseball always was and always will be a part of my life.

We had our own brand of baseball. Of course, it was adjusted for blind people. In the high school, they had their own baseball field. The baselines were dug into the dirt. They were indented, so the blind person could follow the dirt. We played with a basketball or soccer ball. The pitcher would bounce the ball over home plate. After the first bounce, you would hit it. We devised our own way of playing. We'd put the totally blind fielders around the infield. The kids who could see would be in the outfield. Some of them could catch the ball on the fly. The rules we made up were, if the ball hit a blind person in the field, if he made contact with it, the batter was automatically out. We would play a lot of times in gym class. Lots of times we would also play after class. After breakfast in the morning, we would just play pickup games. "I'll take this guy; I'll take that guy." It was a lot of fun. You did what the players did. You ran the bases. You hit the ball. As long as there was light out there, we would play.

· · · · ·

POETRY

JOHN W. HART III, THIRTY-SIX,
IS AN INSURANCE BROKER IN
BEVERLY HILLS, CALIFORNIA.

I wanted to learn how to throw a sinker ball. I'd practice the motion while I was in my office, talking on the phone. And I'd go home and throw a ball against a garage door for a half hour. I get to the point where I feel pretty confident with it. And we go to Greg's birthday party. It's at Greg's mom's house. It's the old gang, but now we've got wives and kids. And beer. And I brought along the Wiffle ball and bat. We organized a ball game.

The first inning I was doing real well. I was able to snap off some real good sinkers. Then people started catching on to it. I was telegraphing it. Then, all of a sudden, James just laid back and was waiting on my fastball. I gave him the heater on the low, outside corner. He crushed it into the neighbor's yard. And the neighbor's dog stole the ball. Then Greg's mom yells out, "Dinnertime!" And we collect our jackets and our gloves and we're, "Oh, Mommmm, do we really have to?" It's just like when you're eleven years old. Except we were thirty.

. . . . .

I grew up pretty much all over Los Angeles. My first baseball team was the Generals. It was sponsored by General Tire. We moved to Beverly Hills and I played in Little League there. I was terrible. I was like this giant of a kid. And absolutely clumsy. My first year my coach asked me what I wanted to be. I said I wanted to be a substitute right fielder.

When we moved to Beverly Hills, that was really an interesting scene. I played with Sammy Davis Jr.'s son. Monty Hall's son was my Little League coach. Mel Tormé's son played on an opposite team. This was '72 or something like that. I had a really good Little League experience because the parents were all so supportive. Sammy Davis Jr. would be there in the stands. Instead of pulling the star act, he was a father. He was rooting for his son. He would come to every game. Same thing with Mel Tormé. They were just parents with kids.

I can't tell you some player's batting average. That just doesn't interest me. I've always been interested in the characters. The poetry. Also, I've considered myself lucky because I've grown up with Vin Scully. At nine, ten, eleven years old, I'd have to play the game at very low volume. Bedtime was nine o'clock. I'd stay up to 10:30 to hear the game. Sneaking Vin Scully. I just liked the games. The usual clichés. It's not over till it's over. Anything can happen. After a while you really start believing that.

I have this vivid image. Was it '65? We decided to go get a hot dog at this hot dog stand up the street. It was during the World Series. I was amazed because, wherever I went, it was on the radio. We're here getting hot dogs, and there were these old men with transistor radios. With little earplugs. And everyone was listening to the game. I still see that.

In 1984 I had a girlfriend who lived two blocks from Dodger Stadium. Our date very often was to go to Dodger Stadium. My girlfriend was a baseball fan, but she was a casual fan. Whenever she got bored, we'd take a walk around the stadium. And just see the different parts of the stadium. When I got another girlfriend – who became my wife – I noticed when she got bored and I'd say, "Let's take a walk." Then it sort of became a thing between us. She was getting more and more interested in the game. The first game she brought a book. More and more she got interested in the team and the characters; 88 was Mickey Hatcher and Orel Hershiser and Steve Sax and Bill Madlock.

The courtship with my wife made it more special. We had something in common. It was fun for me to see her genesis. From showing up with a book to when we were there for the World Series. We were there for Kirk Gibson's home run. That was incredible. Here we are. It's the World Series. I'm with my wife-to-be. Summa cum laude. She's got her master's degree in special education. And she punches the bottom out of a soda cup and starts yelling, "Go Dodgers Go! Go Dodgers Go!" I couldn't believe it. When Gibson hit the home run, it was like historic. Everyone knew it was historic. No one left the stadium for forty-five minutes. We cheered for forty-five minutes. And on the way home – we had a convertible at that time – we had the top down. Everyone's shaking our hands. It was great.

I started working really hard. Working late at night. Insurance is just a lot of paperwork. I'm just doing my paperwork and listening to the game. Vin Scully was keeping me company. Along that same time, I started writing poetry. I'd always been a closet poet, growing up. The idea of being a poet is you write a poem a day. That's what makes you a poet. After about two years, right in the middle of the '88 season, I got the idea I should be writing a poem a day about baseball. Then I just started listening to the game and started thinking of the poetry in each game. I went through the '89 season, which was a letdown. I assembled a book and was able to get it published.

What I was trying to do was, I was trying to find that one snapshot which was relevant beyond baseball. Something that could be a symbol of something else, outside of baseball. I was spending more time looking at the subtleties. I remember one game where this rookie came up, Mike Huff. His first time up, he hit a single. And I just thought about it. How long did it take for this kid to get to this point? Like, playing catch in the backyard with Dad and working up to that point. I remember later on Eric Young, one of his first games, the way he rounded third and headed home. He was running for more than just the team. I could almost see like a Roadrunner cloud behind him.

We're at the park and the ball is fouled off. There's a little kid and an older man. The ball comes screaming back and it ricochets off the kid's leg. You could hear it. That sick kind of sound. And the older guy picked up the ball. And maybe he's been going to baseball games for fifty years. And maybe for these fifty years, every time he goes to a ball game, he's been wanting a ball. Maybe this was his redemption. But the people in the crowd started to yell, "The ball! The ball!" The guy would just look forward, very stone-faced. He wouldn't budge. People are saying, "Ball! Ball! Give the kid the ball!" He just looked forward and held the ball. He wasn't going to give it up.

I wrote the book of poetry; I got it published. Now I want to meet Vin Scully. The publisher had a publicist for me. She got me interviews. At the end of the 1990 season, she got me on the Dodger postgame show. I wasn't going to let this moment pass without at least making a play. I'm a salesman, right? I said, "Why don't we do it at the ballpark?" So I got to go to the ballpark. I got to go there before the game and see batting practice. Got to go on the field. It was like a dream come true. You grew up looking at it. You don't know what the grass feels like. It's spongy. It's a different kind of grass. It's like grass I've never walked on before.

Then we go into the locker room. I tried to play it cool, but I'm sure my eyes were popping out. So we walk in and there's Gibson. And he looks at me and says, "Who the fuck are you?" I go, "Uh, um, I'm a poet." He says, "Get the fuck out of my face." I'm sure he was thinking, "A poet?" I was absolutely amazed. I thought it was going to be a more supportive atmosphere. I got to sit in the press box, which is really weird, because it's like a mausoleum. Really uptight. Then Vin Scully walks by. I had a book for him. I gave him a book and I got to shake his hand. I got to meet God. I got to shake hands with God.

I'm listening to a game right now. It's just part of my routine, part of my soul now. I just look forward to the day when the four of us can go to a ball game. Me and my dad and my two sons. I got the season's seats again this year, but it was tough to come up with the money. I look at it as real estate. These are great seats. Maybe in 2010 or something, my boys will be poking the bottom out of soda cups and yelling, "Go Dodgers Go!"

You watch the game and you watch the watchers. I'm still looking for that snapshot. I have a friend who's a Mets fan. He calls me and we go to the game. He's a scorecard guy. I'm not into scorecards. But they're great to have around, because they can tell me things that I've forgotten. It's like the eighth inning. It's a typical Los Angeles crowd. The place is emptying out. He got some seats way, way out in left field. We were able to walk down and saw some seats behind home plate open. We decided we wanted to get a foul ball.

He looked at his scorecard and saw we had three Mets batters coming up. They're all left-handed. We knew that the

· · · · ·

pitcher was a fastball pitcher. Very scientifically we figured out, "OK, we need to be on the loge level, because that's going to be above the screen. And we need to be somewhere around aisle 105, 107, because the ball's going to be coming off toward the third-base side." We get in our minds that we're going to get a ball. That's the object of going to the game. You've seen the hallelujah hands. The ball's hit and all the arms go up in the sky, waving their arms, praying for the ball to come down and bless them.

We take our seats. The first batter comes up. He fouls maybe one ball off, two balls off. They're coming in our direction, so we figure this is the right place to be. The next batter comes up and he fouls one off. It's getting closer. Finally the moment hit. Fastball. Fouled off. Right off the bat, the ball comes screaming at me. This is my moment!

And I duck. It was moving too fast. I wasn't going to catch that. It was going to hurt. How's that for a life lesson for you?

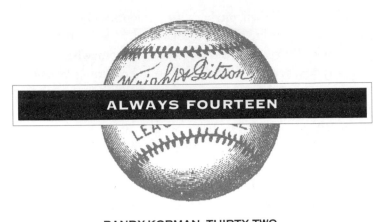

RANDY KOBMAN, THIRTY-TWO,

IS A TRANSPORTATION BROKER LIVING IN

CINCINNATI.

I'm around twelve. Everybody had Cincinnati hats. You know those little hard hats that they wore? You wore them to school. You couldn't wear them to class, but you couldn't wait to put them back on. You'd take your glove to school and put it in your little table that lifted up. You'd wear your jersey where you could, just to be proud of your hometown team. You are the Reds. That's a great team and you want to be part of that. I still have my helmet. Why, I don't know. It was just something that you treasure.

$$\cdots\cdots$$

The person I idolized right off the bat was Pete Rose. He was down at River Downs, at the racetrack, on a Saturday afternoon. It was the Fourth of July or something like that. I think it was 1969. My dad said, "There's Pete Rose." I'm like, "Where? Where?" I went over there and said, "How are you doing, Mr. Rose?" He said, "Fine. Can I get you a Coke, kid? A Coke and a dog?" So he bought me a Coke and a dog. I ran back to my dad. "Dad, Dad, you're not going to believe this.

Pete Rose bought me a Coke and a hot dog." That was a thrill for me. That stuck so clearly in my mind. He had the burr haircut. I still remember it. I can see him standing there, just ordering a Coke and hot dog and saying, "Here you go, kid."

Later that fall, that's when my Little League team got to go down to the field. I think I was seven or eight when I remember going down to Riverfront Stadium. Just walking into a stadium, the whole awe. The atmosphere and the seats. That little bitty diamond down there. It was just an overwhelming experience, coming from the diamonds with a few little bleachers. Going to a real game was a very exciting thing.

My dad got us down on the field. We got to see the players. I'm looking for Pete Rose. I'm not looking at anything else except for Pete Rose. Sure enough, he remembered. He said, "How are you doing, kid?" That was a thrill. That was a hero of mine. My dad always said, "Now you watch. You watch the way Pete Rose does this. Fields the ball, runs the bases." I think just the overall intensity of the way he played the game attracted me to him. Pete Rose was the guy I concentrated on the most to be like. I always wore number fourteen. It's funny how you do those things as a kid.

Being a hometown kid, you don't pay any attention to the Yankees and the Red Sox. Growing up, all I knew was the Cincinnati Reds. I didn't even notice who they were playing. All I was thinking about was the Reds. Everybody had their own player on the Reds. There weren't any other players on any other team. Everybody was Cesar Geronimo or Jack Billingham or Bench, Morgan. Joe Morgan – everybody flapping their arm. As a kid, you imitate who you see. Getting down in a crouch position like Pete Rose when he gets in the batter's box. Geronimo holding the bat up. Tony Perez with the wing out there. Back then it was just the Reds.

When I got to the age of ten or twelve, I started to go to

more games. When they went to the '75 World Series, I was able to go. I just remember the fans. I remember the noise. I remember when, of course, Pete Rose got up to the plate, people just went bananas. And you got caught up in it. You were yelling and like, "Wow. What am I yelling about?"

I was sitting home with my dad and my brother and my mother watching the sixth game. I remember it in my mind so clearly. The Reds had it wrapped up. Then the Red Sox got that home run to move it to seven games. Then the Reds turn around and they win it. What a thrill that was in '75 to go and wear that hat. To wear that hat back out on that street. To be a kid and be part of that is so much different from being an adult. That's the golden time, when you're a kid.

When Pete Rose left in '79, I was starting high school. Because I'm a Rose fanatic, I followed him. When Philly came into Cincinnati, I was at those games. The whole series. Just to see Rose. No one else. I think Cincinnati lost something when Rose left. Something was missing. He was the anchor of that team. When he left, you couldn't believe it. Why did he leave? Why did he want to leave? You still wear 14. He's still your man. I had a Phillies hat. And a Phillies jersey with his number. Fourteen doesn't change. It still has Rose on the back of it. You miss going down to the ball game and not seeing the person you idolized. I really enjoyed seeing Pete Rose. I think it all stemmed from him buying me that Coke when I was five, six years old.

◆

In '81 we went down to Riverfront on a businessman's special. I was a senior in high school. George Foster was still there. He didn't replace Rose, but I started to watch Foster more and more as a home-run hitter. About the eighth inning, he was up. He hits a foul ball. I'm sitting in the first row behind home plate, in the green section. Green section is the middle deck. Foul balls look pretty big. When they're coming back at you, they look like a softball. I watched it and turned my back to the field, thinking to myself, "I want to get this ball. George Foster hit it."

I lose my perception of where the field is and where I'm sitting. And I flipped over the railing, grabbed the ball, tapped it to the guy in front of me, and somehow reached over and grabbed the railing, pulled myself back up and got up back into the stands, sat down, and everybody gave me a standing ovation. Have you seen the video? You've never seen anything like this before. I fell over. I flipped entirely over. I've slowed that video down – it looks like I did a cartwheel. It's been on *Wide World of Sports*. It was on *This Week in Baseball*. Even today, fifteen years later, people remember that.

I got a phone call two days later from George Foster's agent. He said, "He wants to meet with you." I got off the phone and said, "How often does anybody get to do this?" My brother and I went down to the Playboy Club and had lunch with George Foster. He gave me an autographed ball. He gave me posters and books. And free clubhouse passes. A week later they go on strike. The '81 strike. After that, George Foster gets traded. I don't get to go to the clubhouse. And that was devastating for me. I never got to use those passes.

◆

Starting around when I was four years old, my dad put us into organized baseball. He was the coach. I started in T-ball. We started young. That was my dad's priority, to make ballplayers out of my brother and me. I think he lived his life through us. He played in the Boston Red Sox organization. That's where I think the love of baseball started, with my father, but, more importantly, with getting into organized baseball, with coaches and scoring and running around the bases. You always play in your backyard, Wiffle ball and all those good things,

Always Fourteen   229

but from day one, they had organized baseball in Cincinnati. I jumped right into it. I didn't have to play stickball.

I played all the way through high school. You thought about possibly moving in that direction, somehow. That's what you want to be in life – a baseball player. I think most kids do. I think you grow out of wanting to be a fireman somewhere in life and you want to become a ballplayer. I was a pitcher. I wanted to throw against the Pete Roses. When you're twelve and thirteen, you want to be like them. You want to do what they do. I went out to Indiana University and played one year of baseball with the reserve. I opted to play football. I started lifting weights. In the spring I got pressured to play football and I kind of stuck with it. I wish that I had stuck with baseball.

When the Rose scandal hit, it was like when the O.J. Simpson scandal hit. You're like, "What? Pete? Pete? Nah, he didn't." I felt as though he didn't do it. Pete Rose wasn't a player anymore. He was the manager. You denied it. It was a tough thing to see. At the same time, if he did it or if he didn't do it wasn't a big concern of mine. He was Pete Rose in my eyes. And he will always be Pete Rose. He'll always slide headfirst into third. That's the only thing I remember about Pete.

When he was banned for life, that's the part that disappointed me. I feel like they took something away from baseball, and they took something away from this kid in Cincinnati. I also think nobody can take away what Pete Rose did. Whether or not he ever makes the Hall of Fame, he's made the Hall of Fame in my life.

✦

I play in the thirty-and-over league on Sunday afternoons. There isn't a lot of competition, but it's fun to get out there and throw and hit again. To get that childhood feeling again,

. . . . .

somehow. I started thinking about that when the strike started in August of '94. I started thinking about it again when they definitely were not going to play any more baseball, in October. The thought kind of left me until December, around Christmastime. Then somebody told me about these tryouts for replacement players they were having down in Plant City. So I started throwing some tennis balls at a sports club I belong to. I started throwing tennis balls – those big shopping carts of them. Then I started picking up the hardball.

Coming around January I was feeling pretty good. I started throwing to a catcher. I got a friend, I bought a catcher's glove and some equipment, and I said, "Let's throw." We started throwing and throwing, and I finally came home one night and said, "Deb, should we go or not?" She said, "Randy, I think you ought to just go. Get it out of your system." I had the rental car all ready outside. She didn't know that. My bags were packed and we left. Got down there, got checked into a hotel, a little nervousness set in. Did my running; we stretched out and started working out in the bullpen. My first pitch went over the backstop. I threw and I thought that I made it. I thought I made it. I threw hard. I got clocked at ninety-two. And I'll tell you something, my heart sank when they didn't call my number to stick around.

My time is past. The thrill to be down there, to throw off the mound, to take some batting practice, just to be part of that for that one moment in time, brought back years of memories. Reliving those experiences you had as a kid, coming back to you as you're out there on the mound. Going to those games. Hitting the T-ball when you're four years old. I remember thinking of this as I'm throwing, as I'm warming up in the bullpen. I'm thinking of all these thoughts. And when I thought I'd made it? For that one moment, I had a feeling I haven't felt for a long time.

· · · · ·

When I left down there, I was devastated. I was a little mad. But I was more emotionally hurt. Then reality set in, that, hey, you weren't supposed to make it. You were just down there to remember what happened when you were young. The games, the World Series, Pete Rose. Apply those to your life – his determination, his will, hustle. Get out there, don't give up. I got a gray shirt. You know, one of those things you buy and you iron on the numbers? I put 14 on the back of it.

MOM, APPLE PIE,
AND TOWER OF POWER

BETH HAMON, THIRTY-ONE,

IS A MUSIC TEACHER IN PORTLAND, OREGON.

I have to tell you, there is nothing like the plop of leather into leather, when the ball goes into the mitt. That is one of the most beautiful sounds in the history of aural perception. There's just nothing like it. And if you can hear it and feel it in your own hand at the same time, it's even better. It's a comfort thing. It's like Ovaltine on a cold winter's night, when you have hot Ovaltine and you snuggle up with your teddy bear. If they ever introduce aluminum bats into the major leagues, I'm going to have a cow.

. . . . .

I was born in Brooklyn, New York, and lived in Queens. My parents were jazz musicians who met in Greenwich Village in the late '50s, early '60s. I did not have a middle-America upbringing. I was born on the edge. It was really weird. One of our first baby-sitters was Mama Cass. We had another baby-sitter who was a drag queen at the Jewel Box Revue. Baseball was probably as close to Mom, hot dogs, and Chevrolet as I was going to get.

When I was five, we moved to Philadelphia. During the

summer days, my mom and I would lie on the couch and watch baseball games on TV. She would explain to me what was going on. Slowly I started to understand the game. The big turning point for me was probably when I was in second grade. It was the fall of 1969. I came down with a really scary case of bronchitis. They had to take me to the hospital and put tubes down my throat for a couple of hours. I was so sick, I couldn't even get out of bed.

So Mom set me up on the couch with my Barbies and a heat vaporizer, under mountains of blankets. I was really too tired to do anything except watch TV. We were flipping the channels and the cartoons were over and then they showed the World Series. I said, "Momma, let's watch that." She said, "OK." And at this point she started telling me stories about the Brooklyn Dodgers.

She'd watch Ron Swoboda make some great catch and she'd go, "Ahhph, but you know, this is nothing like when I was a kid." She told me all about growing up near Ebbets Field and going to the games. She told me stories about her favorite players, Roy Campanella and Jackie Robinson and Gil Hodges. She taught me little things to look for.

It was just one of those neat, beautiful things. My mom and I have had some estrangements over the years. This is the one thing that has kept us from completely breaking apart. I think baseball has been the continuity, the line that runs through my relationship with my mother. She doesn't share this with anyone else in my family. My sister could care less about baseball. My parents have been divorced for many years. My dad watches football occasionally. He thinks baseball is just the most boring thing in the universe. It was this thing between my mother and I.

We watched the World Series. She missed the last game. She had to go out and run some errands. And I watched the game by myself. By this time I had decided that I was going to root for the Mets, because the Dodgers weren't in Brooklyn anymore. I was doing it just to make my mom happy. I remember the last game was such a dramatic game. It was this edge-of-your-seat, biting-your-fingernails, bad B-movie thing. When they won, I jumped off the sofa and I jumped up and down and whooped and hollered. And then I just sat down kind of dejected because there was nobody there! There was nobody to tell that the Mets won the Series!

While we were living in Philadelphia – we lived there until I was nine – my best friend in the world was a little boy in the next cul-de-sac over. His name was Jeffrey Blackman. He was my age. Jeffrey was a cute little blond, blue-eyed boy with a divorced mother and a guilty father. He had all the best toys. He was cool about coming over and trading baseball cards. We did a lot of trading. I would give him all my Phillies cards, and he would give me all his Mets cards.

It was difficult being a girl who loved baseball. I was not a big, strong person as a kid. When I was a kid, I was tiny. From the time I was about seven or eight, I played a lot by myself. I was never a very good athlete, because I didn't have anyone there teaching me how to play catch. So I had to make it up all by myself as I went along. When I was nine, we moved to the Bay area. We found a cheap little apartment in Walnut Creek, which at that time was a cheap little community. At night, in the evenings after school and in the summer, I'd eat my dinner early and I'd go watch the Little League games. Sometimes they would let me be their batgirl. That was a nice way of getting involved in it. It was very exciting for me.

Sometimes I'd wait until the game was over. I'd wait until everyone had left and the lights had been dimmed and the moon had come up. I'd have to make sure nobody was looking, because I was so afraid people would watch how clumsy I really was and make fun of me. And I could pretend. I

· · · · ·

never pretended I was one of the major league stars. I always pretended that I was a grown-up woman playing major league baseball with these guys. I usually liked to play either catcher or short. I didn't have a baseball, so I'd find a good-size rock. I found a baseball bat with tape all around it at a yard sale. I'd toss the rock up in the air and I'd hit it with the bat and I'd start running. I'd say, "OK, I think I'll practice sliding into second."

I loved to slide and I loved to get my clothes dirty. And I'd come in from these sessions just exhilarated and kind of high and kind of giddy. But it was a very private thing. I never told anybody I did this. My mom would go, "Where have you been, getting dirty?" And I'd go, "Oh, the boys were playing baseball and they let me play with them." It kind of made her feel good because she'd feel like, "Oh, good, Beth's got some friends. That's good." I really grew up very lonely. I was a very, very solitary person. I did all this alone, and I never told anybody about it because they'd think I was nuts. "God, how schizophrenic, you play baseball all by yourself."

But it was beautiful to get baseball dirt on my knees. And it was beautiful to get it on my elbows. I had a very active imagination, and I could transport myself from this tiny Little League field with rocks in it to Shea Stadium or Veterans Stadium, and I would be the shortstop for the Mets and we'd be playing the Phillies and Jeffrey Blackman would be playing for the Phillies and we'd be all grown up with these other great players. It didn't occur to me that they would age and they wouldn't wait for us. I could see the bright lights and I could hear the mobs just screaming and cheering.

I was this tiny little wisp of a thing. I think in the fourth grade I weighed fifty-five pounds, dripping wet. The kids in school called me names. The worst was "Toothpick." Or they called me "Hambone," which I hated. If I could get into baseball, in my own little world, I could escape from a lot of that ridicule. It didn't do much for my socialization as a child. But baseball was always there for me. Mom would ask me when I was a little kid, "What do you want to be when you grow up?" I said, "I want to be a fireman and I want to be a shortstop for the Mets." The fireman thing died kind of quickly. Then in sixth grade it was "I want to play drums for Tower of Power. And I want to be a shortstop for the Mets."

In the spring of 1973, I was in fourth grade. My dad was working at the Palace Hotel, and he got comped with little gifts, like a bottle of Rothschild '57 or tickets to a concert or tickets to the opera. And a lot of times this one repeat customer would keep giving him ball tickets. We'd go to the games, and we'd come back to the hotel and wait for Dad to get off work.

In March there was an exhibition game between the Giants and the L.A. Dodgers. Anybody who played the Giants stayed at the Palace Hotel. My mom and I were in the lobby waiting for my dad, and these guys started walking in and we recognized them from the game. "Momma. Those are the Dodgers." We walked up and introduced ourselves. I met Manny Mota. I went up to Don Sutton and I said, "Excuse me, Mr. Sutton? I just want to tell you I think you pitched a great game tonight." And he smiled and said, "Why, thank you, young lady. What's your name? How old are you? What school do you go to?" And he's starting to go into this nice little schoolgirl thing, which I'm sure he's done a zillion times. And I just wouldn't have any of it. I said, "I read the Green Pages every day before I go to school. And I want to know what you think of . . ." And I just started reeling off stats.

His eyebrows went up and his jaw went down a little bit. And his lips stayed closed and pursed. And he kind of broke into this little bemused smile. He was very tall and I was very short, so he kind of knelt down to talk to me. And we start talking stats. We started talking about different players on the

Dodgers. Then he realizes that my mother is standing there and that I am just such a Philistine. I haven't even introduced my mother. They shake hands and they smile and then Don Sutton goes, "I'm having a really charming time with your daughter. Would you mind if I took her into the little snack bar over there and bought her a Coke cola?"

So we went into the Minute Chef and talked. I introduced him to the waitress there named Ruth. She was a friend of the family and a Dodger fan. Diehard. So we sat there and drank our Cokes and talked, and Ruth took a break and came over and talked with us. We were in there for, gosh, almost half an hour. Ruth goes, "Isn't your daddy getting off soon?" I said, "Oh, yeah. I bet they're waiting for us."

Don Sutton looked at my mitt and he goes, "Why is your mitt empty?" "I didn't catch anything." He was wearing this leather coat. This dark brown leather coat. He was fishing around in his pocket. And he pulled out a baseball. He walked me back into the lobby. He said, "Go back. Go back. Further. Further." Now I was standing next to the glass display case that the hotel's gold service is displayed in. My father realized what was about to happen and muttered, "I hope she can catch a baseball, Gloria, I really do. I like working here." And Don Sutton tossed me this baseball. And he said, "Catch."

So the ball plopped into my mitt and I stared down at it. It said OFFICIAL BALL, NATIONAL LEAGUE. It was kind of scuffed a little bit. And I went, "Where did this come from?" He said it was the last ball that was used in the game. Traditionally that goes to the winning pitcher. I said, "Wow. So you're going to give me this ball?" He said, "Beth, I get them all the time." I thought I had died and gone to heaven. I slept with the thing under or near my pillow every night for a week. Then I put it away on a bookshelf.

Shortly before Easter vacation, which is what they used to call spring break in California, my dad got a phone call at the

. . . . .

hotel from someone in the Dodgers office. Somehow, Mr. Sutton was raving when he got back to L.A., "I met the weirdest kid when I was in San Francisco. She's a total baseball nut. I've never met anyone who was so into it, being a girl and being so young." He was talking to everybody in the Dodgers office about this baseball nut. And that's what he started calling me, his Baseball Nut.

Apparently some of his teammates decided to throw him a surprise party during the last weekend of exhibition season. His birthday was on the day of the last exhibition game and the season opened the next day. His friends thought it would be a really neat little joke to fly me down for the couple of days to surprise him at this little birthday dinner. They said, "We'd like to fly your daughter and her sister and a chaperone down to Los Angeles for two days. We will hide them out during the day when they get here. We'll send them to Disneyland for a few hours."

I had never been away from home before. I had never been on a plane before. We flew down, my sister, Sari, and I, and Ruth, the waitress from the Minute Chef, was our chaperone. Ruth put my hair up in a nice little bun. I took my glasses off and put them in a case in my purse. I had this white dress, white gloves, white Mary Janes, the whole bit. I was very dressed up. The cab took us to this hotel, and we were escorted to this room. I was seated next to where Don was sitting. He looks at me and he says, "Do I know you?" He's just staring at me. I stood up. I put my glasses on and said, "Happy Birthday, Mr. Sutton." and I gave him a card I'd made for him. He went, "You're the Baseball Nut from San Francisco!" I went, "Yeah." It was wonderful. I had shrimp cocktail and 7Up and felt bubbly and giddy.

The next day there was a doubleheader exhibition game between the Dodgers and the Angels, and it was at the Angels' park in Anaheim. At the park, about seven rows

• • • • •

behind us, this very large, fat lady is yelling at her kids. She's just making it miserable for everybody sitting around her. She was having a bad hair day, a bad dress day – just having a bad day. She caught this ball. The women caught it barehanded and didn't flinch. Puts it in her lap. She's rooting for the Angels. The Angels have this drive in the eighth inning and they start batting in these runs. This woman stands up and cheers and she's bawling, like this operatic thing in a tin hat with horns. And the ball falls out of her lap. And she doesn't notice it. And it goes plop, plop, plop, plop, down the stairs. And I see where it's going and I dive for it. I grab it and I stick it in my lap and throw my mitt over it. And Sari goes, "Aren't you going to give it back to her?" I said, "Uh-uh. Serves her right for rooting for the wrong team."

We got back to our hotel after the doubleheader; there were two wrapped packages waiting at the front desk for us. One for Sari, one for me. Sari opens hers and it was this baseball they sold at Dodger Stadium that had machine-imprinted in black printer's ink signatures of the stars of the team. It was in a little plastic case with a blue platform that said DODGERS. It was a really neat thing. My package was the same size, so I assumed that was what we both got. But Mr. Sutton had taken a real baseball and passed it around to all his friends on the team and asked them to sign it with a ballpoint pen.

Over the many years, because we were still moving and being nomadic, the ball that I caught in the hotel was stolen. The Anaheim ball, I gave to my sister, and it was lost in our next move. The baseball that Don Sutton gave me that he got all his friends to sign, I still have. I have sat on this thing for twenty years. I know exactly where the ball is. It's in a box. I think about it and I can see it and I'm ten again. And I smile. That ball stayed on my nightstand for years. I slept next to it or it stayed on my bookshelf over my bed. I took it to college with me. All the guys at college wanted to see it. It was this instant respect thing.

I recently took it to a friend who owns a baseball card shop on the Oregon coast. He said, "Do you have this thing insured?" I said, "No, why?" He said, "You should." And I imagined it was worth maybe one or two hundred dollars. He wrote a number on a piece of paper and pushed it across the counter and it was considerably higher.

I said, "I really didn't want to know what this ball was worth. You've sullied it for me." He said, "Then tear the piece of paper up and take the ball home. Love it and keep it forever. And forget about what I just told you." I took his advice and the ball is magic for me again. I don't have children and I won't have children. If neither of my nieces develops an interest in baseball, then I will not leave the ball to either of them. When I am in my eighties, I will sell it and throw myself a wonderful party. We will have a big-screen TV and refreshments and baseball. And it will be a wonderful time for all.

✦

I've lived in Waldport for the last seven months. It's about fifteen miles south of the Newport–Lincoln City area on the central Oregon coast. It's nowhere. It's a little timber town. I got so hard up for live baseball that I would go and watch the high school games, I would watch T-ball, I would watch the Babe Ruth games. We'd drive to Newport and catch a Legion game. It was really poor. I befriended the lady who owned the drive-through espresso stand and she said, "My nephew. He's going to play T-ball. Want to go?" I said, "Yeah."

It was really beautiful, having grown up with major league baseball, to step into this other world of small-town baseball. Major league baseball, when I was a kid and I'd go to games at Veterans Stadium to see the Phillies, there was still this

· · · · ·

community, this camaraderie. Strangers would talk to one another and share their beers. You don't have that as much now in the ballpark in the major leagues. Everybody has paid their zillion dollars per cheap seat ticket and they're sitting there, penciling in the score in the program and talking on the cellular phone.

Minor league ball is still kind of real. It's still kind of down-to-earth. It's still baseball. It still has some of the romanticism and the innocence that the major league game has sacrificed. So I will go and I will cheer the Portland Rockies. I will go to high school games. It took me growing up to realize what baseball had to offer for me. That was the innocence, the romanticism. Growing up on the edge, the child of weird jazz musicians, I'm nostalgic for things I never had. I envy my friends who grew up in one place, because they had a sense of stability I never had. Baseball gave me some of that stability. It still does.

A TREMENDOUS SLICE OF AMERICA

ROB MAYNARD, THIRTY-SEVEN,

IS AN ACCOUNTANT, AND BEATRICE MAYNARD,

FORTY-SEVEN, IS A SYSTEMS ANALYST.

THEY ARE MARRIED AND LIVE IN

NOTTINGHAM, NEW HAMPSHIRE.

Beatrice: My father came to visit me one year from Paris.
Of course, I took him to a baseball game.
I don't think he was very impressed.
Rob: Well, he's not too interested in sports. And he's French.
Beatrice: He's not too impressed with anything.

· · · · ·

BEATRICE: I was born and raised in Paris. I didn't know anything about baseball. Just basically, it was an American sport, but I had no idea. I moved to New York when I was nineteen, in 1966. I was in New York for twelve years until I got involved in baseball. I learned the rules of baseball in a bar. Guys I used to work with taught me the rules with nickels, dimes, and quarters. I think the quarters were the base, the nickel and dimes were each team. They moved the dimes and nickels around.

Then I went to a game in the midseason. The first game was a night game. I was between home and first base. It was hot. The stadium was so incredible. So big. And the noise. And the grass was really green. There were so many lights. It was overwhelming. So magnificent in a way. It had its own beauty.

I went with a guy who I was dating at that time. It was a business thing and he was taking another couple. I was asking a lot of questions. Things like, "Why would they bunt?" I couldn't figure that out. To this day I still don't understand bunting. I understand it – I disagree with bunting. He made me smuggle a bottle of champagne, because he figured no one would search me. So we had champagne with hot dogs. I loved it from that moment on.

The Yankees were fourteen games behind, and they kept on catching up, catching up. And then there was a tie with the Red Sox, and they had to play a Monday afternoon in Boston. I was at work, but I got a call from my boyfriend. He was down at a bar on Second Avenue. I left work and watched the game at the bar. That famous home run by Bucky Dent. Second Avenue was going totally nuts. It was like a New Year's Eve. Everyone was honking their horn. Everyone was laughing and talking to people in the street. It was just baseball fever.

I couldn't wait until the Opening Day. The following year, I went to about twenty games. I'd take the subway. The subways were pretty packed with people going up to the Yankee Stadium. I used to go with just girlfriends. I always had in my wallet a schedule of the games. If they were televised, I made sure I stayed home and watched the game. I used to clean my house at the same time the game was on. One time I heard the Yankees were trailing. I didn't know what trailing meant. The next day, I had to ask at work. When I'd watch games, the next day I would ask guys if there

· · · · ·

was something I did not understand. My education in baseball went on for at least two or three seasons. I bought myself a helmet for the Boston games. There were always so many fights. I had a T-shirt: BOSTON SUCKS. It took me twelve years, but once I got started, I was nuts. I was nuts about baseball.

ROB: Of course, baseball will always be special to us, because it's the way Beatrice and I met.

I grew up just outside of London, about thirty miles west of London. Right between London and Oxford was my part of the world. A little village called Little Missenden. About 250 people. I knew nothing about baseball. The reason I wanted to see a baseball game when I first came here was because of *Peanuts*. The *Peanuts* cartoons were always on the back of the newspaper I used to read. This image of Charlie Brown pitching to Lucy. This "Strike one! Strike two!" stuff. I had no comprehension of what it was about. It was obviously part of the culture. There were also a lot of American airbases in the area I came from. You'd go to the pubs in that area and hear the use of baseball terminology in common English – "Let's touch base on that."

I came to this country in 1980 to visit a friend. He said, "What do you want to do?" So I said, "One of the things I really want to do is go to a baseball game." He had no interest in baseball at all. He was an English guy. He was kind of a snob, I guess. He associated baseball stadiums with ruffians, heathens, low class, blue-collar, and he wouldn't be seen dead. Of course, that didn't concern me. He said, "I have no interest in the game, but I know somebody who's really into baseball and I'm sure would take you." That's how Beatrice and I met. We arranged to go to this game.

It was a night game. So here I am, this Englishman who arrived a week and a half, two weeks before, who hasn't done a lot of traveling, who's intimidated by everything that's going

· · · · ·

on, being led around the Bronx by this Frenchwoman. Culturally, I come from a very rural environment. And I'm dropped into this ultimate urban scene. You get off the subway in the Bronx on a hot August night. Just the fastness of the action. The shouting, the noise. I'm scared witless at this point. The vendors with the peanuts and the hats.

BEATRICE: And the guy selling the joints. "Yankee joints here! Yankee joints!"

ROB: I had never seen a pretzel before in my life. These things hanging on the wire racks. The program sellers. I'd been exposed to stadium environs before. I'd been to Wembley to see Cup finals and things like that, where a lot of vendors sell scarves and pennants. But it was different at Yankee Stadium because of the way they were selling them – much louder.

The thing I remember most is it's a hot night. Typical New York, sticky, late summer's night. And the lights being on. I do distinctly remember coming out of the tunnel into the seats and looking down. Especially at nighttime, I think it's exaggerated because of the bright lights – the green was just superb. It was a deep, deep green. Just an incredible color. The contrast between that and the running areas, the orange-red cinder, and the green, still sticks with me. And the Yankee uniform is kind of nice. Those guys looked pretty impressive out there. The pinstripes were pretty cool.

Initially my first attachment to baseball was the whole atmosphere. The whole environment. The whole thing of being in a crowd like that. I'd been to sporting events with crowds before, but there was something special about the crowd there.

BEATRICE: Its smell. Its light. Its noise.

ROB: There's that incredible camaraderie, especially in New York. The throwing of the peanuts and the passing of the dollars. The passing of the beers down the seat rows.

· · · · ·

Watered-down beer, covered with plastic wrap, sloshing around in there. Also, a lot of New York chitchat going on. A lot of rapping between people, the joking, pulling each other's legs.

You get that very gregarious nature of Americans. You get that spontaneous nature of Americans. At every baseball game you go to, you get a tremendous slice of America. The characters. You've got the basic low-down hoods. There's also the businessman in the business suit, entertaining guests. Then there's the family group. Everywhere you sit, there's a character. Somewhere there's either some loud, obnoxious person you'd just wish would shut up or some little boy scoring on his scorecard who's been to every damn game. That was the nice thing about being at the stadium. It was a wonderful experience. I wanted to do it again. It was a bug.

I started getting more into the game for its own sake when we started watching games on television. Beatrice had this little black-and-white thirteen-inch TV. She had a brownstone. No air-conditioning. You'd flop out on the bed in a pair of shorts, with fans on you, listening to Phil Rizzuto do his thing on the TV.

BEATRICE: I knew all their stats, I knew the players, the team they came from. I was able to fill Rob in on all those things.

ROB: Beatrice introduced me to a lot of American curse words that I didn't know. The first game we went to – and, again, I had not been in this country very long – I was sitting there, watching this game. And Beatrice came out with, "Boy, the pitcher is pissed." I'm like, "Wow, he's a professional sports player and he's drunk?" Because in England "pissed" means drunk. That's how I learned what "pissed" means in this country.

She was not exactly a French lady at the games. She was not your true Parisienne. Beatrice would get into it. She'd

· · · · ·

stand up and yell with the best of them. That rubbed off as well. Her affection for the game.

BEATRICE: We were married in 1981. The year we got married, there was a baseball strike. We flew to England to get married.

ROB: My family recognized that baseball was the way we came across each other. Of course, they were surprised Beatrice was taking me to baseball games. I discussed baseball and talked about it in the pubs while we were there. The typical English attitude toward America was "bloody stupid game." I said, "At least it's over in three hours, as opposed to cricket, which takes five days." I guess in a way I was defending American culture. I'd grown to like it. Those old boys in the pubs. "Bloody Americans. They wear these bloody stupid gloves." Defending baseball, I suppose was defending America.

NOTHING'S PRETTIER THAN AN EMPTY BALL FIELD

GINA SATRIANO, TWENTY-NINE,

IS A DEPUTY DISTRICT ATTORNEY FOR

LOS ANGELES COUNTY. SHE LIVES IN

MALIBU, CALIFORNIA.

I took so much crap for wearing a baseball cap in junior high school. The teachers would tell me, "You don't look like a young lady when you wear your baseball cap." They didn't understand.

Now, if I could wear one in court . . .

· · · · ·

I grew up in baseball. My dad played for the Angels and Red Sox. As a kid, I always remember running around with a ball in my hand. Baseball just always felt comfortable to me. A very vivid memory is running around stadiums – usually empty, during batting practice or during spring training. I would just run row to row to row along all the seats and up and down the stairs. Chasing foul balls in the stands. Chasing my sister.

Anaheim Stadium. I remember watching the players on the field and their uniforms being so clean. I always wanted to be in a uniform. When I dreamed of being a professional baseball player, I always dreamed of night games. I don't know why. A couple of times I remember being down on the field with my dad holding me, walking me around on the field. That was the best, to be down there with all the players.

There was a period of time when we went to a lot of Dodger games. And I loved it. I loved going to live games. As far as watching TV and keeping up with the stats, I was never real big about that. Going to the games, it's baseball right in front of you. My dad and I would talk about what pitches they were throwing and when. We'd talk about every aspect of the game. There's a smell, there's a sound to baseball. Nothing's prettier than an empty ball field. The grass is perfectly cut and green and the clay is just freshly raked. It's beautiful. I love the sound of the pop of the ball in the mitt. The snap of the bat.

Not only did I fall in love with baseball, it seemed natural to me. It just seemed like part of my life. When I go out on the field, especially during the off-season after a day's work, everything just disappears once I step between the lines. All my worries, all the stress, anything coming from my job, leftover cases that I have, everything just lifts and I feel free and I feel like a little kid. It's just so pure to me.

My mom was a primary encouraging force in getting me to play baseball. When I was seven years old, I showed up at the park for tryouts for Little League. And they told me it was a boys' Little League and because I was a girl, I couldn't play. This was in Canoga Park. My mom said she wanted me to play because I wanted to play. She ended up having to call the headquarters for the national Little League Association and threaten a lawsuit to get them to allow me to play. Then the parents gave us a hard time because they said I was taking up a spot on the team that one of their boys could take. Through the years I had players quit my team, teams quit the league, because they didn't want to play with a girl. Coaches refused to coach me.

We didn't play so much sandlot. We played a lot of pepper, pickle, and over-the-line. I played a lot of over-the-line with my dad. He really never pushed me to play baseball, but he was supportive when I did. Once I started pitching in Little League, he taught me a lot about strategy. As a catcher, there was a lot he could teach me about pitching. We'd do it anywhere. We'd play in the street; we'd play along the side of the house. We'd play in the driveway. Ballparks. Parking lots. He'd sit and catch me.

In high school the coaches said it was a boys' baseball team and the girls couldn't play. The girls could play softball. My mom gave me the choice. She said, "We will fight if you want to fight. I'll be behind you." And I said, "You know, I'm tired of fighting. I'll try softball." So I went and played softball in high school, but it was not a satisfactory substitute. I really missed baseball. I missed the vastness of the game. The game got so small in softball.

Then I went to college. I tried out for the men's baseball team in college. University of California–Davis. My mom called up ahead of time and said, "I have a player coming to college there and we want to come see the ball field and we want to play baseball and we want to talk to you about it." He said, "No problem, bring him up." She never corrected him. So we showed up and walked in and she introduced herself. He said, "So where's the ballplayer?" She said, "This is her." I said, "I want to play baseball. I'm not here to create controversy. I'm here just because I love baseball and I want to play and I want a fair tryout." So he said I could try out. I played three months and I got cut in the final cut. Looking back, I don't believe I got a fair shot.

I thought it was over. But I couldn't give up on it. So

during summer, I played men's semipro city league baseball in Los Angeles. Only woman in the league. The coach and my players loved it. I still got hassled by teams we played against. Rude comments and everything else, but as soon as I struck a few of them out, they usually shut up.

I got ill at one point. I developed a muscle disease and I stopped playing ball. I was completely focused on my academics. I went on to law school. I really thought baseball was behind me. I was done with it. I missed it. I'd see it or I'd go to games and I wanted to be out there.

It was one or one-thirty in the morning. I was out with some friends for a birthday party. I was talking with somebody I'd just met and she started talking softball, then I started talking baseball. And then she said, "Oh, really? I heard about this team. This guy's trying to start a women's professional league." I thought, "This is too good to be true." I ran out of the restaurant, ran down the street to the nearest pay phone, and called my mom. Woke her up in the middle of the night. She was the one who was with me all the years, through the fights and everything. I was crying and I said, "Mom, there might be a chance for me to play baseball again." I just cried to her. And she cried back.

Since there were no other teams to play, we practiced three to five days a week. At this point, I was a D.A. I had to drive fifty miles after work to go play. Sometimes there'd just be three of us out there. We didn't have lights, so we'd play by headlights. Anything just to take ground balls, hit. Even if we just hit into the fence. Anything to play.

When I'd come home from those practices at the very beginning – after a good twelve-hour day at work, play a couple of hours of baseball – and then work on a case for another couple hours, I'd be higher than a kite. I'd be bouncing off the walls. I really love this game. I just feel at home on a baseball field.

. . . . .

We got to play two tournaments that year. It was at the December tournament in Florida that a reporter came up to me and said, "Have you heard about the Silver Bullets?" He told me all about them and he told me how to get in touch with them. I flew back to L.A. from Florida Sunday night. Monday morning I called the Silver Bullets from work. By Thursday they had a ticket for me to come back to Orlando for a five-day tryout. Next thing I know, I get a letter inviting me to spring training. It is one of the most beautiful letters I've read. It took me about a half second to decide I was going to give up my job to play baseball. As it turns out, they've given me a leave of absence two years in a row. I'm taking a pay cut to play ball.

It's funny, I thought about it today. I feel like a little kid in this game. It just brings that out. And I love it. I'm so dedicated to it. I don't know what's so magical about it. We're not playing for the money. We're not playing for the fame. We're not playing for anything but for a dream we've had all our lives. A chance to play finally. Sixty- and seventy-year-old men come up and say they wish they could trade places with me.

We were at Shea Stadium, right? We got to go watch during batting practice. Just being down there. There's nothing like it. When we're playing in these big league parks, there's a different feel when your cleat hits the grass. I never thought I'd have the chance to be walking on the field like I belonged.

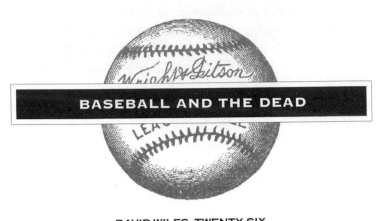

BASEBALL AND THE DEAD

DAVID WILES, TWENTY-SIX,

IS A RECENT COLLEGE GRADUATE LIVING IN

PEORIA, ILLINOIS.

I've always been a Cub fan. I think I got that from my dad and my grandfather. I guess the baseball in my family has come down from my great-grandfather. His name was Benjamin Caffyn. He played in the major leagues for a couple of years. His son, my dad's dad, was given up for adoption because my great-grandfather was always on the road.

My great-grandfather instilled the love of baseball into my grandfather, and my grandfather into my dad, and my dad always took us to the games. Even though I never met the guy, I really liked it when I found out that my great-grandfather was a baseball player. It's kind of neat to see how being a fan has come down through the generations.

· · · · ·

My first memories are me and my brother playing Wiffle ball in the side yard, pretty much every day until it got dark and then even after it got dark. We couldn't even see the ball and we were still playing. We played corkball at the school. We called it corkball, but we used a broomstick and a tennis ball. In the summertime it was all day, every day. If we weren't mowing lawns, we were playing baseball. We'd try to get something going every day until well after dark. Then we'd move to underneath the streetlights.

I remember everybody always used to ask the question in grade school. "Are you a Cub fan or a Cardinal fan?" It was pretty much divided fifty-fifty because we were halfway between St. Louis and Chicago. It was almost like if you were a Cub fan and it was a Cardinal fan asking you, they almost didn't want to associate with you.

I remember my dad used to take us to Wrigley Field at least once a year. The earliest time I can remember being there is when I was about seven. We went up there for a Cubs-Expos game. I think I remember having my first sip of beer. Going to Wrigley is almost kind of religious. Just walking in there, you kind of get goose bumps. It's so small. You get inside there and it's like you're at a little neighborhood ballpark. You just really feel good when you're in there. Much better than if I were to walk into Busch Stadium or any of the other big stadiums.

Eighty-four was a big year for us. I remember being really excited that they finally had a team that was winning. Everybody always said, "Wait until next year." I'm kind of wondering if the Cubs ever did win, if they'd lose some fans. Everybody is so into it, but some people are into being the underdog.

I travel a lot to go to Grateful Dead shows. Whenever we do that, we always try to work in a baseball game. I remember leaving a Dead show early one time because we had front-row seats at a Las Vegas Stars game. We heard the first couple bars of the encore and we were like, "Aw, we don't want to hear this song. Let's go watch some baseball." We didn't want to miss the first pitch.

· · · · ·

Years back we had tickets to see the White Sox play the Texas Rangers the night before the Dead were playing in Chicago. My VW van broke down. And Nolan Ryan pitched that night. We were really anxious to get to the game. We couldn't do it. We were in northern Indiana and still an hour outside of getting to the ballpark. We were sitting at an Amoco station getting an estimate and I was like, "Man, it's seven o'clock and Nolan Ryan is pitching." We were just like totally bummed out.

Another year we saw the Cubs and Cards at Wrigley Field. It was a noon start. Then we went and saw the Dead at Soldier Field at six o'clock. It was a long day, but a fun day because we got baseball and the Dead. I remember seeing guys standing outside at Dead shows with these tie-dyed T-shirts: CUB FAN, DEAD MAN." They had the skull with the Cub emblem inside. I saw the same guy selling them at Wrigley Field.

I don't know what it is, but the Dead have a couple of other connections to baseball, too. They have their own shirts that they have licensed. They say STEAL YOUR BASE instead of STEAL YOUR FACE, like their album. It's got a bunch of skeletons with baseball gloves and baseball bats. Even their tickets. Once in a while on the spring tour, they say SPRING TRAINING/SPRING TOUR. And they have skeletons as the catcher and the batter printed in glitter on the ticket. I've got another bootleg T-shirt that says WHEN HARRY MET JERRY. It's got those animated figures with the really big head and it's got Jerry Garcia shaking Harry Caray's hand. There are some similarities. Once you're into the Dead, you can't get out of it. You're probably always be longing to go back to another show. Just like if you miss going to a major league park one summer, the next summer you're just like really jonesing to get to that ballpark.

That feeling when you walk into Wrigley Field. There's no

other feeling like that in the world. I'm into the sport. I like the different aspects of the game where you have to use your head. That kind of thing gets me, like if I'm at a Dead show and I'm trying to pick out what song they're going to play next. It's like wondering what's going to go on. The bases are jammed. You need a run. Guessing what's going to happen.

A Dead show isn't like a concert, it's like a play. They'll play two and three nights in a city, and you've got to see them all. You can't just see one. It's almost like you'd miss the end or miss the beginning. It's the same way at a baseball game. A lot of people arrive late or leave early. You never know what's going to happen in the bottom of the ninth. It might be a terrible Dead show until the encore. There are some games that aren't that good, and there are Dead shows that don't get really good until the last three songs. They don't start jamming until the ninth.

I was at a show in St. Louis right toward the end of this summer's tour. And they played this song that I'd never heard live before. This was my ninth summer tour. It was just like magical. Kind of like seeing a grand slam.

I WAS A KID AND I WAS A CYNIC

TIM BOTTORFF, SEVENTEEN,
IS A STUDENT LIVING IN OLATHE, KANSAS.

I did see a lot of players as heroes, but I did understand that, yeah, a lot of those guys were out there for the paycheck. I understood that and I fully understood that baseball was big business. But I understand that it's also a game, too. The way I do it, I try to see major league baseball as two separate entities. The game and the business. I think the game on the field is still as beautiful and wonderful and awe inspiring as it ever was.

. . . . .

I think what influenced me more than anything else in my early years was probably the 1985 World Series. That was the so-called I-70 Series, between the St. Louis Cardinals and the Kansas City Royals. I was about eight years old and I watched the Royals make history. It was a big thing for me.

They lost the first two games at home, and after letting themselves get down three games to one, they came back to win the last three games. It seemed like they'd been coming back that whole year. They weren't supposed to win that year.

Nobody thought they could do it. They were the underdogs. So it wasn't only that I was at a young and impressionable age when my hometown team won the World Series. It was the way they won it. It was the magic of '85. Sometimes people say there was nothing magical about it, just luck and good ballplayers, but I know at least one kid who thought it was magic. And that's me.

I can't remember a whole lot of details of the Series. I just remember the whole thing was exciting to a kid. I was skeptical. I remember that, too. I said there was no way the Royals were going to do it. I said they were going to blow it. I was a kid and I was a cynic. I didn't think they could do it. They proved me wrong and maybe that's why I became hooked. I realized that a lot of things went into that victory. There was a lot of hard work and determination.

Up until that point, I hadn't really played a lot. I'd played soccer. I think it was shortly after that when I started playing Little League. I liked playing and all that. I mean, I really like baseball in this area. There's plenty of youth programs to play baseball and all that. It's always bothered me, though, that there's no sandlot baseball. There are no pickup games. I have never played a pickup or sandlot baseball game in my life. It's always been on an organized team. I've always thought that to play sandlot baseball would have been really neat. I just think it's more the way baseball should be played. It's more innocent. I think a lot of the innocence has been robbed out of baseball.

It was George Brett for me and has been ever since. Unfortunately, being as young as I am, I probably missed his best years. He's just a great player. But it was more than that with him. It was his attitude. It was his work ethic. I understood from the beginning that he did not have the natural talent that a lot of players had. He got there by guts and determination. The way he did it, the way the Royals did it, it really affected me. It has my whole life ever since. I've learned that you can do a lot just by guts and determination.

At one time, I know, baseball was the only game in town. Now it seems like kids, more often than not, don't like baseball at all. Baseball is no longer king with the youth anymore. I see it every day. People just aren't interested. You try to talk about it with them and they don't like baseball. They say it's too slow or this or that. I think part of it is the business of it. It's been too publicized with baseball. The strikes and everything are turning people off. Young kids don't have the faith or patience to wait out a long strike. Soccer's coming on big. There's a lot of soccer playing. Basketball is big. Football is very big. Strikes and labor disputes are very detrimental to baseball's future. When I was eight years old, I fell in love with baseball after seeing the Kansas City Royals win the World Series. But what did a kid who was eight years old in 1994 think of baseball? For the first time in ninety years, there was no World Series.

I remember things like Willie Wilson got into drug trouble for a while there. There's been other incidents like that. I understood what was happening and didn't like it, but I think I became a fan so much, I would just try to block a lot of that out. I think I was faithful to the point of being ridiculous. Some of the things now do bother me. I think players like George Brett and Nolan Ryan are disappearing. There are certainly some still out there like that. Blue-collar workers, the hustlers, the good guys. But a lot of them, the only thing they hustle for is to get their check to the bank. You can see it from the way they play. They don't care about the game and they do drugs and throw firecrackers. It's a bad image for kids.

But there's a quality about baseball that's very difficult to explain. It's our game. It's America's game. There's so much history. It has so many nuances. Baseball is so many different

· · · · ·

things. Baseball is the camaraderie of the dugout. It's the sights, sounds, and smells of the ballpark. It's the beautiful arc of the long-hit ball. It's the suspense of where it will land – fair or foul, in the fielder's glove or on the soft grass. Maybe off the wall or in the stands. It's the chalk kicking up on a barely fair ball. It's the graceful diving catch. The picture-perfect swing. The rally-killing double play or the flawless execution of the hit-and-run.

You can only explain it with imagery. The crack of the bat. The roar of the crowd. It's the sight of a little boy holding hands with his father, seeing his first baseball game. Or maybe it's the old man with a tear in his eye, seeing his last. It's Babe Ruth hitting a home run for a sick child. It's a father and son playing catch. It's all these beautiful stories and these beautiful emotions.

I get very sentimental about it. I'm probably overly romantic about it. You still go to the ballpark. The national anthem is sung. Old Glory waves in the wind. The sun shines above. The umpire calls, "Play ball!" The crowd roars. And all is once again good and pure.